THE FE EXAM

"HOW TO PASS ON YOUR FIRST TRY"!

CIVIL EXAM

By

Patrick J. Shepherd, P.E., PMP

This book is dedicated to Bob Lipp (Uncle Bob) – my engineering professor at the University of New Orleans.

Thank you for inspiring me to be the best engineer I can be.

Thank you for purchasing the FE EXAM "How to Pass on Your First Try!" book.

I know you could have picked any number of books for FE Exam prep, but you picked this one and for that I am extremely grateful.

The book was first published in 2013. I set out to write the book that I wish I had when I was preparing for this exam back in 2002- but never existed. Today, we are still going strong. We work hard to keep the book updated and relevant to the constant changes to the exam format published by NCEES.org.

I hope that this book adds value and quality to your exam preparation. If you enjoy this book and find some benefits in using it to study for this exam, I'd like to hear from you and hope that you could take time to post a review on Amazon. Your feedback and support will help this author to greatly improve his writing craft for future projects and make this book even better.

Please leave an HONEST review.

Also, if you purchased the paperback on Amazon and would like a FREE copy of the Ebook version, please visit and email us on our website: www.EITfasttrack.com and Email: EITFastTrack@gmail.com

We would love to hear from you!

Thank you.

Table of Contents

Acres of Diamonds:

I heard an old tape recording of Earl Nightingale talking about this Acres of Diamonds story. It's awesome. It's a story of a farmer who heard tales about other farmers who had made millions by discovering diamond mines. He couldn't wait to sell his farm and go prospecting for diamonds himself. So, he sold his farm and spent the rest of his life looking for diamonds. However, he never did find them. Sadly, he died of old age and a broken heart.

Meanwhile, the person who bought his farm accidently discovered a small somewhat shiny object near the creek on his new property. He brought it to a jeweler who explained that it was a very small diamond. It just didn't look like a typical diamond because it wasn't polished yet. Well, he was so excited that he started mining his new land and discovered it contained millions of diamonds. It became the largest diamond mine in the world!

The moral of the story is that if the first farmer <u>had only taken the time to study and prepare himself</u> to learn what diamonds looked like in their rough state, and explore his property before looking elsewhere, he would have discovered the diamonds and riches he was searching for his entire life were already in his own backyard.

We all have acres of diamonds already buried deep within ourselves, just waiting to be discovered. Before you run off exploring greener pastures, make sure that your own is not just as green or perhaps greener. We all have unique experiences and skills to share with the world.

My Hope is that you take the time to study and prepare for this exam. This is your first step to having a great career and becoming licensed in engineering. Don't just wing it. You already know the material; you just need to practice and follow some simple tips in order to bring out a passing score. And when you do pass, come find us again when you start preparing for the PE Exam. We got your back!

Best of Luck!

EITFastTrack.com

Welcome

Welcome Everyone!

Over the years, I developed a unique strategy to prepare for exams. As a student, I was always a great test taker. I developed a specific set of tips, strategies, and mindsets that help me perform well- not just on tests but also in life. I call this the Inner Game of Testing® and I would like to share it with you in this book.

Inner Game, in my opinion, is the most important thing you need. The Inner Game takes place within your mind and starts long before you even show up to take the test. It is played against such obstacles as fear, self-doubt, uncertainty, and limiting beliefs. The Inner Game is being played in your head before you ever go out into the world and take action. The game is being played whether you like it or not.

Having a strong Inner Game will allow you to achieve more, get better results, and will allow you to start playing the lead role in your own life – not just some supporting actor or victim role. It's my goal that you start being the cause, not the effect.

Inner Game of Testing:

In my experience, the concept of Inner Game was never taught in school. If it were, I missed it. I believe it allows you to use your thoughts and beliefs to assist you on obtaining your goals. There are two major games that we must play in life. The first one is called the "outer game" and the second one is called the "inner game".

The inner game is where it all begins – and it's the only area that you have 100% control over! It's so very important, because your inner world creates your outer world. Your physical world is just a printout of your inner world. Everything comes from thoughts. If your inner world is messed up and full of limiting beliefs, it can ruin your success in life because Results come from Thoughts. Behaviors are manifestations of your inner talk.

Lemon Exercise:

Please read the following paragraph and really try to imagine what it's saying. This might get a little weird, but follow me on this:

"Imagine, for a moment, holding a juicy lemon in your hand and looking at its yellow skin. Can you imagine how it might feel in your hand, the weight, the waxy texture of the skin and the size? If you can imagine this then perhaps you could imagine cutting the lemon in half, the resistance and pressure of the knife as it runs through the center of

the lemon and in doing so releasing the unmistakable smell which connects with nose. Finally imagine taking one half of the lemon and biting into it, the immediate bitterness explodes your taste buds and induces a screw faced grimace."

You can't tell me that you didn't taste the bitterness in your throat as if you were biting into a real lemon. Go back and read it and don't skim this time. This is an example of your imagination shaping your reality.

How is this possible?

Your subconsciousness mind cannot tell the difference between something that is actually happening versus something that is only being imagined. There are existing neutral pathways in your brain that associates a lemon with that bitterness taste. It doesn't matter that the lemon wasn't real, only imagined, your brain still made the connection. For every thought, there is a corresponding physical manifestation somewhere in your body.

In order to teach my own children the importance of positive self-talk/Inner Game and the dangers of negative self-talk, I like demonstrating the following experiment with them:

Tell them to hold their arms straight out in front of them – like they're sleep walking. Then tell them to say out loud several times, "I am hopeless, I am a failure". Repeat it many times. Now, see how easy it is to try to move their arms down to break their posture. It's very easy! They put up ZERO resistance. Their WILL is broken.

Now, tell them to hold their arms out again but this time say, "I am powerful, I am a champion!". Repeating it several times. Say it louder and with conviction. What happens when you try to break their posture this time? They don't let you! They fight back! They show a WILL to succeed. You cannot break them!

Look at the follow Equation:

$$T \longrightarrow F \longrightarrow A = R$$

<u>T</u>houghts create <u>F</u>eelings, which create <u>A</u>ctions, which create <u>R</u>esults.

In the negative sense, negative or disempowering thoughts create a feeling of being a victim, which most likely leads to not taking action, which doesn't get you any results. **Your thoughts have a direction relationship with the results you get.**

Look around at the results you've been getting in your own life. This shows you what your thoughts have been up until now and what you thought was possible for yourself. We don't attract what we want, we attract according to who we *already* are…

Now think about most of the bullsh$t we allow in our minds everyday – TV, social media, gossip, negativity, toxic relationships, politics, etc, and we wonder why most of the population has high blood pressure or is depressed, obese, and coping with substance abuse. I'm not discounting actual mental illness which is real. I'm referring to people who are like my coworkers. You know the type, the Debby Downers® - People who are so toxic they can't stop gossiping about the workplace or your friends/family who constantly try to hold you back. People who have no goals nor have a vision for their future. Why are you trying to get your PE license? You won't be promoted anyway.

Bla Bla Bla Bla.

At this point in my life, I stand guard at the entrance to my own mind. If you allow trash to enter, you'll probably get trash out. **Your own personal philosophy is the major contributor that determines the course of your life.** Your personal philosophy is like the set of the sail. How long do you think you have left? Nothing is guaranteed. I'm here to become the best version of myself each day and maximize my potential. Your personal philosophy determines if you will remain a victim or take action towards your goals. If you have free time, look up Jim Rohn on YouTube, his talks during the mid-80s will blow your mind.

All of us wake up every morning with the same pre-programmed thoughts already installed in our software/mind from the day before. The same thoughts will always lead to the same results. We are basically creating the same experience for ourselves every day. There's no reason to expect it to be any different. Your subconscious mind is dictating your every move.

There are ways to use this to your advantage- by using something called Creative Visualization in which I describe in the Self-Image section. The best part of this Inner Game is that it starts again every day! When we wake up every day, we can rewrite the script. You hold the power to change your life – you can do this by using positive and empowering thoughts. You are the one who holds the pen – the tool to create your new life each day. Every morning you decide what you want to create today. It's your life, you write the script, you have the right and power to design it anyway you choose. If you are interested, check out the work of Dr. Joe Dispenza. Or not, I don't care.

I don't need a double-blind study to tell me if it's "real" science or pseudo-science when it seems common sense to me. How your thoughts shape your reality makes perfect sense to me. Success isn't something to be pursued, it is to be attracted by the person you become. The Universe will send you more of the same energy that you put out. It sends it back to you.

Performance = Potential – Interference

Look at the above equation:

Rarely does your best performance come out when we need it

That's why sports teams play the game. If there were no chance of the weaker team winning, why even play? Doesn't the better team always win? No!

I want to show you how to minimize the "Interference" variable in the equation above. By doing so, it tips the odds in your favor so you can anchor yourself into a peak state of certainty, clarity, confidence, and courage during the test. It allows your best-self and performance to come through because you don't have to deal with all the bullsh$t (I mean interference). If you don't minimize the interference, it will affect your performance.

In life, interference can be things like hanging out with the wrong crowd, smoking, doing drugs, unhealthy eating habits, not setting goals, low level of standards, having a negative self-image, etc. It's anything that prevents you from being your best-self and accomplishing your goals.

But with taking the FE Exam, <u>Interference</u> can be:

- Not arriving 30 minutes early to the test center and all the parking spots are already filled up. You get frustrated and lose your focus.

- Not doing a drive-by of the testing center a few days before the exam to find out if your cell phone map is accurate or if there is any street construction that might delay you the morning of…. Why do that? Just leave it up to chance.

- Not doing your research and knowing that you need to pay for parking, and you don't have cash. You get really frustrated.

- Having study habits that suck. You think you can just wing it or that studying is a waste of time. You don't realize that this is all about developing problem recognition skills. You just need to put in the work upfront to be able to identify them. All you need to do is study a collection of solved problems in each category. That is what this book is about.

- Not reviewing the calculator policy on the NCEES website for the approved list and getting yours confiscated during the exam. Nice.

- Listening to a bunch of Debby Downers® right before the exam which affects your mood. Ignore the naysayers. No one has ever erected a statue for a critic. Going the extra mile is always lonely. Most people are stuck/conditioned to be at the bottom.

- Not watching your units!! Answering a fluids question in cubic feet per minute but the question wanted it in gallons per minute. We all been there.

- Not knowing there is a list of common conversions on page 3 and 4 (9 of 502) of the FE Handbook. Too bad, that would have saved you a lot of time!

- Not having any systems in place to help keep you on an effective study track. You just aimlessly work a problem or two a few times per week. You have no schedule set up, no dedicated study space and you leave it all up to chance. Let's see how that works out for you. How you do anything is how you do everything. You need to take this exam seriously and don't be lazy.

- Spending too much time on the harder problems and thinking that you must go in sequential order. You waste all your time. You don't realize there is low hanging fruit in the back of the exam, and you run out of time before you get to them.

- Not realizing that you can make up in numbers what you lack in skill. You don't have to be the smartest engineer; you just need to work more practice problems to learn to see the patterns and know where to find the equations. Success is always at the margins! The little extra things you do to prepare makes all the difference.

- Not trusting that the Law of Averages will work out in your favor. You allow small setbacks to rob you of opportunities because you quit when times get rough.

- Not disciplining your disappointments. You allow yourself to become frustrated during the exam because you feel like you're getting a lot wrong. You only need to get about 65% correct in order to pass. Progress > Perfection.

- You don't practice the Second Effort. You don't give 100% on every problem because you don't realize that it only comes down to a few questions that, if answered correctly, will make you pass. This separates the winners from the losers.

- Not being comfortable with getting 4 out of 10 questions wrong. You will probably still pass with just over 60% correct.

- Not preparing the recommended 8 weeks before the exam.

- Not playing the percentages nor choosing a good pitch to swing at. You spend 10 minutes trying to solve a very hard problem.

- Not becoming familiar with the layout of the FE Handbook. You wasted too much time trying to find the right equation during the exam. This is a big one.

- Not using the process of elimination. Just by eliminating 1 or 2 possible choices greatly improves your odds at guessing the correct one.

- Letting the test takers inside your head. Don't let the bastards get you down! They are purposely messing with you. It's like trash talking during a sporting event - good trash talkers- Athletes- can get their opponents so off their game because they get inside their head. Ever tried to shoot a free throw while someone at the line is trash talking you? It takes skill and confidence to either ignore it or tell them to look at the scoreboard.

- Flipping through the FE Handbook for the first time and becoming discouraged. It doesn't represent everything that you need to know, but only what could possibly show up on the exam. Just means that everything in it is *Fair Game* – just know where to find it. Don't have to be an expert at it.

- Posting your goals on social media -only for the validation. But you never had any real intentions on following through with it. Don't do it. Post after you pass. Under promise, over deliver. Posting goals is stupid and makes you less likely to follow through with it because you get the immediate dopamine spikes – good feelings- from everyone. But once it fades, most people don't follow through for the real reward.

- Not relaxing the day before the test. Don't get drunk either. Drink after you pass.

- Not having a Razor's Edge working for you. The line between winning and losing, passing or failing, is extremely thin. **Success is always at the margins.** My Razor's Edge when I took this exam was being able to flip to any topic area within seconds. I knew the layout by heart. That's how good I knew that FE Handbook. No one could do that on exam day. Only me. That's the Razor's Edge. I also worked more practice problems than anyone else. I could instantly notice what kind of question it was and where to find the answer. Find your Razor's Edge..or use mine!

- Not setting yourself up for success. Your personal philosophy and set of the sail sucks. Not having any goals you are working towards that pull you into the future. You're in the 97% group that aren't even trying. Join the 3%.

- Not realizing that opportunities are often disguised as work.

- Not eating healthy and regularly exercising.

- Not understanding that you must get in the proper "learning" mindset and realize that this test is an opportunity to develop new skills. No matter how hard it is at first, you'll be able to improve over time through hard work and practice.

- Not realizing your score will reflect the amount of work you put in - not just your raw intelligence.

- Not realizing that you must build speed, since you're battling the clock more than the complexity of the exam.

- Not understanding that you can create your own luck. When you take care of the little things, most things just tend to go your way. It's just the way it is. Cause and Effect. Luck is when opportunity meets with preparation.

- Not hanging up a blank certificate frame. Don't do it, I don't care. But it absolutely works and will motivate you. More on that to follow.

- Not knowing that you can mold your Self Image into anything you want. Great test taker, public speaker, inspired entrepreneur, fitness guru, etc.! It's time to upgrade your software by increasing the set point in your own mind. This is the greatest single concept I ever learned. Entire section on it.

- Not realizing that you already have Acres of Diamonds buried within yourself just waiting to be discovered and polished. It's not "out there", it's within you.

- Not setting up a finite schedule for studying. Something will take as much time as you allow for it- Parkinson's Law. Set a very specific time and ending for study. If it's an open block of time, you will fill it up with procrastination until that time is up. Read the section on *Why It's Important to Schedule the Exam First Before Studying.*

- Skipping batting practice. You need to practice at solving these problems. Why do you think the best baseball hitters of all time still had to take batting practice before every game? They're already good, why the need for practice? Because they need to warm up, there's a certain way to hit a fastball, curve ball, or a changeup. Batters are trained to look at the spin of the ball as it leaves the pitcher's hand, they are getting focused, working on their swing, working on their inner game, etc. Just like you should work all these different types of problems, be on the lookout for patterns, knowing how to find the equations for those patterns that keep coming up, etc. You need to take batting practice before the big game.

- Feeling frustrated during the exam from the feeling that there just wasn't enough time to finish the test. It is supposed to be that way. It's completely normal. The FE Exam is designed to be hard and not being able to finish. Care less. Get 4 out of 10 questions wrong and you will still pass. They purposely make some really hard questions to see if you're smart enough to skip them. You don't get any extra points for solving them.

- Not studying the format of the exam and knowing what to expect.

- Not studying the main topic areas on your exam and what types of question to expect. The greatest chess players of all-time study their opponent's opening repertoire, tendencies, habits, strengths and weaknesses, etc. They don't just show up and play chess. Same with pro sports.

- Not creating a Mission Control sheet as you study. Always write down what you learned on a separate sheet of paper. That's what I call my Control Sheet. Not the entire problem. But anything you should note" Like, "*Page 140 of the FE Handbook has common Beam loading diagrams with formulas for deflections and slopes already calculated for you! You **Do***

NOT need to solve this from scratch! Find the figure on the left which matches the problem that has a cantilevered support with a distributed load across it.". Simple things like that. Also things like "*If the problem didn't give you the E (Modulus of Elasticity), just look on page 138 for the E of common materials!)* etc.. "*When doing thermal deformation problems, if the coefficient of thermal expansion was not given in the problem, you can also look up the value on page 138 for various types of materials*" This is valuable information. That way, you can review these notes next time you study. By the end of your studying, you should probably have about 5-6 pages of notes front and back on your Control Sheet. It's like a journal.

- Not knowing ahead of time how many minutes per problem you have on average. That's sad. You need to have an internal gauge in your mind constantly monitoring it. Spending too much time? Skip.

- Not checking to see if your felt marker works when you sit at the testing table. Trust me on this one.

- Not realizing that this is only an exam and not representative of real life. Look in the front of any engineering textbook or test prep, it says "these equations are for study only – not to be used for design". Really? It's for theory purposes only. I could teach anyone how to pass this exam if they are decent at math. You don't even have to go to engineering school. That's sad but true. In life, you don't have to swing at every pitch, you get to choose which ones you want to swing at.

- Not realizing that your criteria for success should be if you are taking action each day. Not solving all the practice problems correctly.

We all need a vision for our future. Why are you doing this? What is your goal? Without a vision or goal, you're just drifting around and probably won't end up of anywhere. Rarely do people get successful by accident. It's a Result. A vision motivates and propels you into the future created by its imprint you review each day. After getting my PE license in Civil and Mechanical Engineering, my next goal was to write the best FE Exam prep book on the market. This book is 383 pages long, but I didn't write it in one sitting. I wrote about a ¼ - ½ page per day -which took me just about 3 years. Who can do that? ANYONE CAN! It might not be the best book but judging from the positive emails I receive every day; it made it worthwhile because it helps people. I may not be the smartest engineer, but no one can out-work me. In my book, hard work and cleverness beats "smarts" any day of the week.

There. I just summed up the entire book for you. If you can eliminate all the bullsh$t interference ahead of time, it will allow you to be in a flow state. None of these things take any skill to do- they're very easy to do.

Hang up a Blank Certificate Frame:

(The Vacuum Law of Prosperity)

I learned this from Bob Proctor. This might sound really silly, but the first thing you need to do is to go buy a blank certificate frame and hang it up on the wall where you can see it every day -perhaps on the mirror where you brush your teeth or as the homepage on your phone. I use this technique anytime I'm preparing for an exam or really any goal I'm striving to achieve. Write "Your Name, P.E.". To remind yourself why you are doing this. Or "Congratulations, Your Name, on passing the FE Exam!".

Imagine that you already passed this exam and are now looking at the passing certificate in its frame. How does it feel? What does passing mean to you? Perhaps it means ultimate success for all your hard work. A real sense of accomplishment. Feel how proud you are and what it took to achieve this goal. Look at it and visualize it every day. I used this technique many times in my life and it works. It sounds crazy but it's effective and motivating. Ask any Olympic athlete if they use visualization. They do.

The Vacuum Law of Prosperity says that the fastest way to manifest something in your life is to create a vacuum. By creating a vacuum and creating space, you allow your vision or goal to show up. But you must first create that space for it to manifest into reality. Visualization plays an important role. I use this all the time. If you can see it, it can happen. It's possible- because your inner world creates your outer world. Your physical world is just a printout of your inner world. Everything comes from thoughts. Once you decide to create space, nature has no choice but to adhere a vacuum. Like pulling a plunger out, it creates negative pressure - a vacuum. As the volume increases, air rushes in to fill the void. Basic engineering, right?

Do you want to create a successful business? The first step is to get a manilla folder and label it "New Business". There you go- it's a start. Want to pass a test? Hang up a blank certificate frame. Want a new wardrobe? Clean out the old clothes first. Want to write a book? Create a new document and name it "New Book". Want fresh and exciting new ideas? Let go of your old ones. That's the first step. Nature has no choice but to fill the empty space. Of course, you must follow it up with action. I know this sounds absurd and silly, but I'd rather be silly and successful/rich, then cool/hip & poor. Not bragging. Just Saying.

The Exam Format

The next thing you need to do is learn how the format of the test is set up. The transition to computer-based testing involved significant changes to the old format of the FE exam and to the procedures for administering them. Starting way back when in January 2014, the FE exam became a computer-based test (CBT). The test is now closed book, you can't use any of your own resources or notes, however, they do provide you with an electronic reference on test day. The reference is called the <u>FE Handbook</u>. This is what you will use during the test. It has all the equations and information that you will need.

You can download it from the NCESS.org website when you create an account and register for the FE Exam. If you know the layout of the handbook by heart, you are already in the 1% of all test takers. The odds are heavily in your favor -before you ever step foot in the testing center-because no one else will do this. I give the link below.

Go on the NCEES.org website (https://ncees.org/) and create an account in MyNCEES (https://account.ncees.org/login) and follow the onscreen instructions. Once there, you can review the FE exam specifications, fees, requirements, reference material, scoring, and pass rates.

Examinees will have a total of 6 hours to complete the exam, which will contain 110 multiple-choice questions. Please note, the 6-hour time also includes signing a non-disclosure agreement, a short tutorial, a 25-minute break, and a brief survey at the conclusion. So in reality, the actual test will be 5 hours and 20 minutes to answer the 110 questions. The exam will be divided into two sections but with a break in the middle and whatever time is left over from the first section will carry over to the second. The two sections will cover the same, discipline-specific material. Once you have finished the first section, you will not be able to go back. But you will be able to review your answers while in each section.

The biggest change for the computer-based FE exam is the discipline specific Exams.

You now have 7 different exam disciplines to choose from: Chemical, Civil, Electrical and Computer, Environmental, Industrial and Systems, Mechanical, and Other Disciplines.

This book specifically prepares you for the *Civil* **Exam**. A breakdown of the topics and percentage of types of questions for each Exam is included in this book on page 56 and is also available on NCEES website at https://ncees.org/engineering/fe/. As you can see, there are many overlaps and commonalities to the Exam topics, but each one is unique.

Register for the FE Exam

Go on the NCEES.org website (https://ncees.org/) and create an account in MyNCEES (https://account.ncees.org/login) and follow the onscreen instructions. Once there, you can review the FE exam specifications, fees, requirements, reference material, scoring, and pass rates.

FEE for the FE Exam

There's a $175 exam fee which is payable directly to NCEES. Please Note: Some licensing boards may require you to file a separate application and pay an application fee as part of the approval process to qualify you for a seat for an NCEES exam. Your licensing board may have additional requirements so please check with them.

Download the FE Handbook

A free download PDF of the FE Handbook is available on the NCEES website when you create a MyNCEES account to register for the exam. You need to download it before working any problem on this book. The entire purpose of this book is to teach you how to use the Handbook.

It is **highly recommended** to download your free copy now and use it in conjunction with this book. The solutions to the problems reference specific page numbers from the *FE Handbook* which allows you to become familiar with its layout and content prior to exam day. Please note, you will not be allowed to bring your copy of the *FE Handbook* into the testing center. The testing center will provide you with an electronic version on your computer on exam day.

Exam Results

NCEES will release results 7–10 business days after the exam. This is a dramatic change from the 8-10 weeks in the old format. You will receive an email notification from NCEES with instructions to view your results in your My NCEES account. However, keep in mind that the states have varying guidelines for releasing exam results. To learn more, contact your state board.

Examinee Guide

NCEES lets you download the Examinee Guide which is the official guide to policies and procedures for all NCEES exams. You really need to read this document before starting the exam registration process. It has all the information you ever need to know about approved calculators, procedures, accommodations, policies, etc. Here's the link: https://ncees.org/exams/examinee-guide/

Engineering Forum:

Please join our *Engineering community Forum* on our website: EITFastTrack.com where members can post comments regarding practice problems and general strategy. We have discussions on practice questions, testing strategies, latest news, and other general concerns as well. We also post a "Problem of the Day" where you are invited to work the solutions with us! Join today and be a part of our community.

In addition, if you purchase the paperback on Amazon, please email us (EITFasttrack@gmail.com) and we'll give you a FREE Ebook version of the book!

Why It's Important to Schedule the Exam First Before Studying:

I see a lot of students make this mistake. You should schedule the exam a few months out FIRST before you begin your preparation. It's very important to make it official. Don't start studying with no end goal in mind. That's where people mess up. There's something called Parkinson's Law. It states that "Time expands to fill the time which you allotted for it" – or something like that.

If you don't have an actual exam day booked, you'll tend to study very slowly, without purpose, because you have a free blanket of time. Without an end goal, you have all the time in the world. I see this all the time- it leads to becoming overwhelmed because you are just focusing on all the different topics and just randomly flipping through the FE handbook getting frustrated. Then you will most likely rationalize how you really don't need to pass this exam or how it's not important anymore for your career.

Scheduling the exam FIRST makes it real. I recommend 2 months out. Then back-engineer your game plan to study each day now that you have pressure and a goal set. Doing it this way means that you don't have time to "mess around". You will study with purpose and make it part of your job. That's how it should be. If you get stuck on a problem here and there, just skip it and let it go! You don't get hung up on it or let it bother you. You don't need to get 100% correct during the exam, just need a passing score.

I think somewhere between 5-10 hours per week on average of studying is reasonable. You can't tell me you can't easily find one hour during the day -each day- to crank out some problems. You can probably find a lot more. Try to do 1-3 problems in the morning before work/kids/school (just wake up 30 minutes earlier), a few problems during your lunch time, and then a few more after you put the kids to bed, or go to sleep, etc... maybe can even "sneak" in some studying during work - but I wouldn't broadcast that though to coworkers and don't do it openly. Don't talk about Fight Club. On the weekends, try to maximize your study hours. Wake up very early on Saturday and Sunday mornings and work for 2 or 3 hours.

This is why this EBook version of the paperback, which is on Amazon, is great. You can open the PDF file on your computer during work and no one will even know. They will think you are working hard on a confusing spreadsheet or something. Side note, always have a spreadsheet open in a tab to be able to switch to quickly if someone walks in on you. You can also use the EBook while you are waiting in line at the doctor/dentist.

Bottomline, you need to treat studying like it's your full-time job. You can't have an open blanket of time to study. Because that's not studying. Schedule the exam, and then it's time to get serious. It's like a boxer training for an upcoming fight. He doesn't just train indefinitely because he will get burnt out. Instead, he sets the date and then follows his training plan in a very methodical way leading up to that date.

Computer Based Test Strategy:

1) On exam day, the testing center will provide you with an electronic copy of the *FE Handbook* which will be exactly like the PDF file you used to study. It will be present on your computer screen at all times during the exam. The *FE Handbook* is a "searchable" file. Use this to your advantage! You do not have to memorize equations or page numbers. When trying to find the answer to a specific question, simply "search" for a key word in the problem statement. If the search does not yield any results, you could "search" each of the possible answer choices to reverse engineer the question. This will often allow you to find the answer.

You must become very familiar with the handbook because sometimes it might be hard to find an equation or chart if you aren't familiar with it. For example, if you are trying to solve for the friction head loss through a pipe, and you search for "Moody Diagram" on the electronic pdf, nothing will come up. However, if you search for "Stanton", which is another name for the Moody Diagram, you will be able to find the Moody diagram on page 201. Also, for Geotech problems, if the question is asking about the coefficient of curvature, nothing comes up on that search – you have to search for "coefficient of concavity" on page 260. In addition, if the problem is asking for the angle of internal friction, the actual equation is on the diagram on page 262 but you have to search for "Mohr" – which is the Mohr-Coulomb Failure.

2) On exam day, it is highly recommended that you go through the short tutorial prior to beginning the exam which teaches you how to use the computer. It will teach you how to navigate through the questions, but more importantly, how to mark/flag a question in order to come back to it later. If you have basic computer skills, you will be tempted to skip over the tutorial because it will seem self-explanatory; however, it will be time well spent. Part of your overall exam strategy, which is covered in the next section, will be to mark/flag the harder questions for a later time when you make your second pass. It also shows you how to activate the clock/timer which tracks how much time is remaining on your exam. If you skip the tutorial, you are risking not knowing how to navigate the software. Take this time to relax and go through the short tutorial at the beginning of the exam.

3) Paper and pencils will not be allowed in the testing centers. In addition, scratch sheets will not be allowed to work out problems. All examinees will be provided with dry-erase booklets for problem solving. Expect the booklet to be a spiral bound (at the top) laminated notebook with dimensions slightly larger than a sheet of loose-leaf paper. It will be made up of about ten laminated sheets. Since most of the problems only involve 1 to 3 steps to solve, 10 pages will be enough room, so don't worry about running out of room. If you do run out of space, just simply erase and start over.

4) You will be provided with a fine-tipped marker which will be about the size and weight of a standard ink pen. As soon as you receive it at your work center, remember to **test it** on the laminated notebook in order to verify that it works! You will be surprised that a majority of the dry erase markers might be low on ink, and you do not want to begin your exam only to realize that your pen doesn't work when you reached the first problem where you have to calculate something! The test centers see hundreds of examiners per day (not just EIT/FE examiners) and it really just comes down to one person overseeing the test center. The last thing on their mind is to change out pens, especially while they are responsible for monitoring the entire center. Test your markers; you will be happy that you did.

5) When you are faced with a harder type question which you do not recognize the solution to be immediately solvable, we recommend flagging (skipping) the question in order to go to the next question. You learn how to do this from the tutorial at the beginning. You can press

control + F or just click on FLAG in the upper right of the screen. But since this is a computer-based test, you cannot write notes in the exam booklet. However, you can write notes in small print at top or back of any page in the laminated notebook. Let's say that you know the equation to solve a particular problem is on page # 121, and that one of the variables you need is located in the table on Page #127, however you can't figure it out. You should write the question # and page # (and any notes to yourself) on the back of the last page of the laminate notebook so you can save time when you come back to it at later. This is especially helpful on HVAC type questions where you are trying to read the psychrometric chart but having trouble or on deciding if the way you took a derivative is correct or not. Just designate one section of your laminated notebook to be "mission control" where you keep notes to yourself.

6) As you study, it is highly recommended to have a copy of the *FE Handbook* available and using it as you go through the practice problems in this book– in order to simulate actual exam conditions. The EIT/FE exam mostly tests your ability to quickly find the correct equation in the FE handbook; therefore, it is wise to become familiar with navigating the search tool on the .PDF during your study. I said this earlier, if you know the layout of the handbook by heart, you are already in the 1% of all test takers. The odds are heavily in your favor -before you ever step foot in the testing center-because no one else will do this.

7) We highly recommend that you double check that the clock/timer is activated in the lower right side of the screen before you begin the exam. The timer tells you how much time is remaining on your test. You learn this in the tutorial at the beginning of the exam. It will appear at the bottom right side of your computer screen. However, sometimes you must manually activate it before you begin. Be sure to monitor it as you are answering questions to gage how fast or how slow you are going. Remember, since this is a computer-based exam, there will be no proctor telling you how much time you have remaining on your exam. It is entirely up to you to regularly monitor your time throughout the exam. Don't rely on anyone.

8) We strongly suggest wearing the earmuffs (sound proofing) which will be provided to you at your computer terminal. Please realize that not all examiners in the test center are taking the same exam as you. Some examiners are there for different reasons; such as, continuing education courses, company screening testing, driver's education, etc. The test center works hard to assure that there no distractions, but not all examiners take their exams seriously and may tend make a lot of noise (by eating snacks, talking, listening to music, etc.) at their computer terminal. But this is not you! The FE exam is the first step for you to obtain your Professional Engineering (P.E.) license. You are taking this test seriously because is it important to your career and professional development. In order to drown out background noise and distractions, as soon as you begin the tutorial, you should put on the earmuffs. Once

the test begins, you will not even realize that you have them on. Who cares that they look funny- you are here to pass the exam. Don't worry about it. You may also want to bring a seat cushion.

9) The testing center will be very strict about not bringing any cell phones, personal items, etc. into the testing center. If you do bring personal items in, they will have a locker for you to lock them up in before you will be allowed to enter the area where the computer terminals are located. You will need to lock up your keys, wallet, etc. in the locker. We suggest leaving all other items, including cell phones, in your car. Do not bring anything with you into the test center other than your license and test center confirmation code/paperwork (which you print out after you register with the test center). You worked too hard to get to this point to risk getting caught with your cell phone in your pocket and having your exam disqualified on the spot. Just leave it in your car. You have the rest of your life to look at your cell phone and Apple watches. Don't bring it with you. Remember to get your license back from the proctor after your exam is over. The test center will hold it for you while you take your exam.

10) You will not be allowed to study in the testing center while waiting for your test to begin. They will make you leave the waiting area if they see you studying. Therefore, it is best to sit in your car upon arriving at the test center until about 30 minutes prior to test time. Spend this time flipping through the hard copy of the *FE Handbook* one last time, reviewing problems, and focusing on your game plan. You should feel confident that you prepared ahead of time and are focused on engineering your way through the exam. Be sure to read your confirmation page that you printed out from the testing center; it may require you to check in at least 20 minutes prior to your scheduled test time. **Don't be late!**

11) Visit the testing center's website to learn more about their requirements. Learn the directions to the test center, parking arrangements (do you need money to park?) which floor is the center located on? You want to eliminate all possible distractions on exam day so you can focus on what you have to do.

12) Be prepared for the test center to take your photo and give palm scans every time you enter and leave the actual testing room. You can't have food or water in the test room, but you can raise your hand and leave at any time.

13) One hidden benefit to the new testing format is that the computer randomly selects problems from a "question bank". Unlike the old pencil and paper exam which was curated as a whole, questions can possibly come up which can be similar to one another. Back to back questions can ask you to solve the same question but with slightly different givens. If this happens, it will save you a lot of time searching in the FE handbook.

14) Your computer screen will be split in half, with the FE handbook on one side and the test questions on the right side. The PDF will have two tabs, one with a search bar that returns every location of the keyboard you type in and one with a hyperlinked table of contents. Be careful when using a graph in the handbook, such as the psychometric and Moody graphs, since these are very busy graphs, it will be very easy to lose your place in the graph because you cannot mark your place using a pencil. Take your time and don't lose easy points on reading the graph type problems.

15) When you enter the test room, they will give you a laminated notebook and pen. You should ask for 2 of each just in case you need it later.

16) After about 55 questions, you will be prompted to review those questions and then submit them. You will no longer have access to those questions after you have submitted them.

17) The questions are not visibly broken down into different sections, but the test still loosely groups the questions together. It's not a hard and fast rule, but you can expect subjects to be grouped together.

18) You can't carry time over across the midpoint break. Once you take your break, you forfeit any extra time you may have. Also, after the break you are not allowed to go back and review questions from the first half of the exam. Our recommendation is to aim at finishing both halves in around 2 hours and saving the last 30 minutes or so to check your work and review.

Admission to the exam

You must present a current government-issued ID upon arrival at the test center. Acceptable forms of ID must be government issued and must include a valid expiration date, your name and date of birth, a recognizable photo, and your signature. Your name must be in English. Valid U.S. military IDs that do not include a signature will be accepted. Student IDs will not be accepted.

The first and last name on your appointment confirmation letter and your ID must match. To help speed up the process while checking in, bring a printed copy of your appointment confirmation letter and arrive at the Pearson VUE test center 30 minutes before your scheduled appointment.

What may I bring into the exam room?

- The ID used during the admission process
- A calculator that complies with the current NCEES Calculator Policy

- Key to your test center locker
- Reusable booklet supplied by Pearson VUE
- Eyeglasses (without the case)
- Light sweater or jacket
- Items included in the Pearson VUE Comfort Aid List

The most current version of the appropriate NCEES-supplied reference handbook (FE and FS) will be supplied onscreen as a searchable PDF.

How This Book Works

The problem with most EIT/FE study materials is that they do not teach you how to pass the exam. They contain many different types of questions -ranging from too general to very unrealistic problems- which only waste your time. They tend to deal with theory and the study material ultimately ends up being a book of random practice problems. However, we believe that the best way to prepare for this exam is to develop a specific strategy to pass it. In order to pass the EIT/FE exam, it is not necessary to study everything, but only a fraction of each subject. The EIT Fast Track book will show you how.

Why would studying for the EIT/FE Exam be any different?

The EITFastTrack E-Book is designed **specially** to teach you how to pass the exam. This book does not waste time on theory or obscure problems- which will only confuse you more, but instead, only contains practical questions and ones that are *most likely* to appear on the actual exam based on the percentages which are published by NCEES. Our research team consists of practicing engineers in industry with real life experience, as opposed to theory-based professors who have been out of school for 20 years. The problems were developed using the NCEES percentage breakdowns on each topic area and are presented in a logical order which will allows you to master the *FE Handbook*. This book will serve as your **Game Plan** for exam day.

By utilizing the percentages from NCEES, the book maximizes your exposure to all problem types in the shortest amount of time. And by eliminating obscure and hard problem types that have no logic behind them, this book contains only **realistic problems** and provides excellent practice to prepare you for the ACTUAL exam. I always hated when I was studying using certain prep books, a lot of the problems were ridiculously hard. What's the point of making me feel dumb before my big test? We believe that nothing prepares you better than working through actual exam questions.

Since the *FE Handbook* is the only reference that you are allowed to have in front of you during the exam, this book teaches you how to use the handbook to your advantage. The more familiar you are with the handbook the easier it will be on test day. Every problem's solution is thoroughly explained, in detail, and cites specific pages in the *FE handbook*. They are no mystery equations or magical answers, every equation and variable is fully explained and referenced.

For those of you who do not have the time to devote the recommended study time of 8 weeks, our proven Fast Track™ Section is right for you! Using tips and strategies, it guides you to specific sections in the *FE Handbook* in each topic that are most likely to appear on the actual exam base on the percentage break NCEES provides. It also reviews common engineering formulas and concepts you should know by heart – to help you save time looking up equations. This section is also great for anyone who has been out of school for a long time wanting to brush up on basic engineering skills before starting to work the practice problems in the book. It can serve as a nice refresher course.

This E-Book contains over 330 practice problems compiled in (5) Exams. Exam # 1 problems are organized in topic order – which allows you to become familiar with the *FE Handbook* without having to flip to different areas. The questions will guide you through each section of the handbook so you can learn how every chapter is organized. Exams # 1, 2, 3, 4, 5 are organized in random topic order, simulating the actual exam, allowing you to hone your skills in solving many types of problems thrown at you from all directions. However, since every question in every exam is categorized by topic in the table provided on page 56, you have the option of working on any specific topic if you choose. For example, if you know that your weak area is "Engineering Economics", use the specification chart to find out which question numbers are engineering economics type problems. Flip straight to them and start working.

Don't waste your time any longer! You need to start working problems. This book systematically forces you to work through the *FE Handbook* and only focus on topics with the highest percentage of showing up on the actual exam.

Overall Exam Strategy:

A big part of why standardized tests are so evil is their ability to blind us to the obvious and practical. Students are often misled into thinking that they have to solve every question correctly in order to get a decent score. In reality, you only need to answer about 65% of the questions right in order to pass.

You will find that most of the questions in this book are relatively easy to solve. This is on purpose. Most of the problems on the actual EIT/FE exam will be easy to solve, only requiring 1 to 2 steps in order to solve. There will be some hard questions, but you do not get any extra points for solving the harder problems. Remember, your goal to pass the FE exam, you do not need to score a 100%. In reality, you only need around 65% in order to pass. Since NCEES determines the cut score for each exam, no one knows exactly what the score is since it is determined specifically for each session. Some questions get thrown out if a lot of people miss them. Therefore, you are not only competing against yourself but against other test takers.

You should only focus on maximizing your points. You accomplish this by **not wasting precious time trying to solve harder problems.** There will be a lot of easy questions on the test, but if you waste time solving the challenging ones, you will run out of time to solve the easy ones which could be at the end of the test.

As major league baseball fans, we tend to quote Ted Williams to students in our prep classes in order to make the comparison to the perfect test taker. Ted was arguably the greatest pure hitter who ever lived and he was the first to bring math and statistics into the game of baseball. In his book, <u>The Science of Hitting</u>, Ted explains how to play percentages. He knew the strike zone and disciplined himself not to swing at balls outside it. "Get a good pitch to hit" was the mantra taught to him by Rogers Hornsby, the batting instructor for Minneapolis. By being selective and by learning how to only swing at high percentage pitches, he has one of the highest batting averages ever in the history of baseball. Ted became legendary for his patience at the plate.

It is our desire in writing this book to teach students the art of playing the percentages in order to maximize their score when taking the EIT/FE Exam. You need to be patient while taking the test and search out and find those high percentage questions to answer. Just as Ted Williams only swung at the high percentage pitches, we show you how to identify high percentage pitches (easy and medium questions) on the test and not waste time on outside pitches (hard questions). **You will learn that only spending time on the questions that matter is the key to scoring high**. Students will learn that perfect practice is the key.

We hope that you practice the example problems in this book- they continue to appear time and time again on the actual exam. Follow the tips and advice in this book and you will pass on your first try!

Develop Problem Recognition Skills:

Everyone has the will to win, but you need to have the will to prepare to win. That's what separates winners from losers. You need to put in the hard work up front and prepare by practicing. Wayne Grezky is considered the greatest hockey player ever. He is the leading point-scorer in NHL history, with more assists than any other player has points, and is the only NHL player to total over 200 points in one season – a feat he accomplished four times. However, he was certainly not the biggest or the strongest, but he is considered the smartest player in the history of the game. His size, strength, and basic athletic abilities were not considered impressive but his intelligence and reading of the game were unrivaled, and he could consistently anticipate where the puck was going to be and execute the right move at the right time.

Many sports writers contributed Grezky's success on natural instinct and being a creative genius. However, Grezky admits it has nothing to do with natural instinct and he is far from being a genius. He says that 9 out of 10 people think he's a genius on the ice but says that it is simply not true. He said it has everything to do with how much his dad made him practice as a child and his study of the game. He learned to skate when he was 3 years old and through many hours of practice, he was able to develop a deep understanding of the game's shifting patterns and dynamics. He practiced his entire life until he learned to instantly recognize and capitalize upon emerging patterns of play. On the ice, he never went to where the puck was, but to where the puck was going. He is famous for saying *"that in my own way I've put in almost as much time studying hockey as a medical student puts in studying medicine"*.

The bottom line is that you need to practice. **By practicing, you develop problem recognition skills.** This is the key to scoring high. The only way to do this is to solve as many practice problems as you can. Practice is very much underrated and is a lost art these days. However, don't just practice, practice the right things, and you will do the right things on the test. Perfect practice makes perfect. Many people mistakenly attribute genius qualities when what they are witnessing is just a result of practice. A recent student showed that if a person spends 20,000 hours practicing a single task, they become an expert. As soon as you realize that your score has nothing to do with intelligence and luck, instead; has to do with how well you prepare beforehand, you will be on your way to a high score.

80/20 Principle:

The overall strategy that we recommend is based on the 80/20 principle. The 80/20 principle is named after the Italian economist Vilfredo Pareto, who observed that 80% of income in Italy was received by 20% of the Italian population. The assumption is that most of the results in any situation are determined by a small number of causes and that 80 percent of your outcomes come from 20 percent of your inputs. There are business examples such as 20 percent of employees are responsible for 80 percent of a company's output or 20 percent of customers are responsible for 80 percent of the revenues. You may also notice how you may only wear 20% of the clothes in your closet 80% of the time!

The important thing to understand is that in your life there are certain activities you do (your 20 percent) that account for the majority (your 80 percent) of your happiness and outputs. When you start to analyze and breakdown your life into elements it's very easy to see 80/20 ratios all over the place. The trick, once your key happiness determinants have been identified, is to make everything work in harmony and avoid wasting time on those 80 percent activities that produce little satisfaction for you.

The message is simple enough – **focus on activities that produce the best outcomes for you.**

Don't Waste Time on Hard Problems:

Many students do not get their best possible score because they waste precious time on hard questions. They simply just run out of time and do not get a chance to answer the easy and medium questions that remained. Time management plays an important factor during the test. You don't need to answer all of the questions right to do well. You only need to answer about 65% of the questions right in order to pass! So if you know you aren't going to be able to finish the exam, you can actually focus on just about 65 percent of the questions, and if you get a good amount of them right (and make sure you still use the last few minutes to guess on the rest) you will pass.

Students often tell us that there just wasn't enough time to finish the test, and we always tell them, **"It is supposed to be that way!"** It's completely normal. The FE Exam is designed to be hard and not being able to finish. Do not panic. Go in with the number of questions you need to answer to achieve your goal score (answering 72 of the 110 questions to pass), then in the last minute or two, guess on the rest, and you will likely get some of those right, which will only raise your score. Taking your time on 72 questions will give you a better score than rushing through 110 questions. If there is a question you don't know the answer to, or you know will take a long time to answer correctly, simply just skip it.

Don't Let Them in Your Head:

Like most test, they intentionally contain questions that the test developers know will take a lot of time to answer. Don't fall into their traps. Skip the really tough ones, and if you have time, come back to them, or just guess when you are using your last minute or two to fill in all of the questions. Every test has questions that are not only difficult, but also take a lot of time to answer. **They are testing whether you are smart enough to skip these questions.** Many students do not skip hard questions, but instead, waste quality time and still end up getting it wrong.

Using the 80/20 principle as a tool allows you to spend the most amount of time on the problems that matter - **the easy and medium questions.** We handpicked all of the example problems in this book based on the 80/20 rule – all of which have a high percentage chance of showing up on the exam.   In order to maximize your score, you have to search out and find the easy and medium questions and answer those first. Find the "low hanging fruit" type questions first. This strategy allows you to now have 4.5 minutes per question to answer questions as opposed to a little less than 3 minutes per question. In the last 2 minutes remaining in each section, you can make an educated guess on all the harder type questions. Using this method, you give yourself an extra 1 ½ minutes to focus on each question. Even with a few careless errors—don't set yourself up for perfection—you'll be far more accurate than trying to answer every single question perfectly.

For some reason, the idea that you have to work every single problem correctly gets passed on from generation to generation. It's a vicious cycle. No one is perfect. Hall of Famers, the best baseball hitters of all time, only hit the ball 30% of the time (3 out of 10 times at bat). Conversely, this means they failed 70% of the time. Think about it. The best hitters in history never hit the ball in 7 out of 10 at bats. Don't pressure yourself for perfection, keep it all in perspective.

Remember, we are trying to play percentages here. You are not only competing against yourself, you are also competing against all the other test takers on test day. **On test day, let all the other test takers waste time trying to solve all the hard problems in sequential order** while you stick to your strategy. There are only 2 things that you have control over on this test: 1) How much time you allot to each question, and 2) How you prepare and practice ahead of time. You must manage your time effectively by following the strategies in this book. You will maximize your score by focusing on about 65% of the test questions and answering correctly than attempting to solve every question in the section perfectly.

Maximize Your Time:

Here's how you do it:

On your FIRST PASS, only solve the easier problems first. If the solution only involves a few steps or if a quick "search" of the *FE handbook* reveals the equation to use, or if it is a basic definition type question, go ahead and solve it. However, if at first when you read the question and you don't IMMEDIATELY know how to solve it, then mark/flag it and skip to the next question. You learn how to flag a question in the short tutorial at the beginning of the test. Most of your FIRST PASS strategy should not utilize the search tool on the FE Handbook, you should be able to find questions that are basic and easy to solve. It will be perfectly normal to skip the first 10-20 questions using this strategy, but remember, you are trying to maximize your points. You don't need to solve them in exact order. Don't worry about how many questions that you are skipping. Less experience test takers will be struggling and wasting their time on these harder questions in the beginning while you are answering all the easy questions. Your <u>FIRST PASS</u> is all about answering the "low hanging fruit" types of questions. There will be a lot of them scattered through the exam, the trick is having the patience to skip through the test in order to find them. Go find them and rack up easy points!

On your <u>SECOND PASS</u>, quickly review any notes that you made to yourself in the laminated booklet (see CBT Testing Strategy section) to see if you can now answer any questions that you first skipped. Don't waste a lot of time on problems that you still have no idea how to solve. Remember, a lot of the questions will only require a few short steps to solve, so if the problem appears to be very complex, there is a good chance that there could be extra information in the problem that you do not need in order to solve. Try reading it over and over to try to narrow it down to specifically what they are asking. On this <u>SECOND PASS</u>, you should be using the "search" tool on the *FE Handbook* to look up key works from the problem and the possible answer choices. If you are spending too much time on a particular question, just skip it and go on to the next question. The <u>SECOND PASS</u> is really an iterative approach where you are looking into the problems a little deeper trying to find the correct answer. Do not randomly guess at this point unless you are confident the answer is correct. If there is any time left at the end of the test then the difficult problems can be addressed.

The <u>THIRD PASS</u> begins about 5 minutes prior to the end of the test. Keep an eye on the little timer/clock in the bottom right hand corner of the screen; be sure it is turned on! Try to determine if you can eliminate one possible answer choice based on engineering judgment. If you just totally guess outright, you have a 25% chance of guessing correctly. But if you can eliminate just one answer choice, you then just increased your odds at guessing correctly by 8%! Eliminate 2 answer choices; you now have a 50% chance of guessing correctly. Using this strategy, if you have 15 questions remaining when time is running out, you should at least, based on the odds, guess 3 or 4 correctly. If you can eliminate a few choices, you may be able to guess 7 or 8 correctly - which may be enough to pass the cut score. **Do not leave any question blank!** There is no penalty for guessing. Don't just guess, make an educated guess and use engineering judgment. You can get a lot of questions down to 2 or 3 answers choices by inspection.

- Unofficially, you only need about 65% to pass this exam. Concentrate on the problems you know something about. Guess quickly on the rest.

- Train for a good 8 weeks, getting comfortable working problems. Be sure to use the Fast Track section in this book if short on study time.

- Use the "search" tool to look up the key word in the question, or search for the possible answer choices to see if anything comes up. Reverse engineer it.

- You must build speed, since you're battling the clock more than the complexity of the exam.

- Most of the problems on the FE exam do not require a lot of work. The exam is testing your knowledge of basic engineering topics. If a problem seems really difficult, look for a simple and easy way to solve.

- Watch your units! The question might ask you the volumetric flow rate in ft^3/ sec, but you most probably solved it in ft^3/min. BEFORE you bubble in the answer, reread the question to see what it is asking for. This is a common trick.

- During the exam, you will feel like you aren't getting any of the problems correct and might feel like giving up altogether. When you start thinking this, remember that this is completely normal. Many of the other test takers will be thinking the same thing. You need to push beyond that feeling and just stay in the game and visualize your goal. Don't let your mind wonder off. Stay focused on the problems. Let all the other test takers mentally give up before times up.

- The typical person has up to 50,000 thoughts in a single day. About 95% of those thoughts are the same as the ones we though the day before. Every day your thoughts are a loop, and your life is run according to the tape you play repetitively in your brain, one thought after another, 50,000 times per day, assuring you that you are whatever you think you are. Carefully consider you own 50,000 daily thoughts. What are you telling yourself? Are you giving yourself affirmations for victory or excuses that continuously open the door to failure?

- If you expect the best chances are you will get it. You can do this.

A Final Word:

A word of caution! If you have been out of school for a while or a recent college graduate, do not attempt to read through the *FE Handbook* like a novel because you **WILL** get discouraged! There is enough information in it to discourage anyone, including the brightest engineering professors! Remember, the *FE Handbook* is just an available reference for you to use, it doesn't represent all the information that you must learn in order to pass the exam. Not even close.

You must get in the proper "learning" mindset and realize that this test is an opportunity to develop new skills. No matter how hard it is at first, you'll be able to improve over time through hard work and practice. Your score will reflect the amount of work you put in - not just your raw intelligence. Studying does not have to be a struggle, but a journey of learning increments filled with opportunities for growth as well as gains.

Remember, the problems in this book are handpicked and designed based on playing the percentages – based on the NCEES breakdown. We will not attempt to try to teach you how to solve complex partial differential equations, when there is only a small fraction chance of up it showing up on the actual exam, but you can bet we will show you how to solve basic integrals, which has a good chance of showing up. Similarly, we will not cover structural design using load combinations; however, you can expect to brush up on basic statics, dynamics, and mechanics of materials, etc. You must work on problem-solving speed and **problem-recognition skills**.

The Law of Averages:

(How to Get the Law of Averages to Work for You)

This is a Jim Rohn classic. It gives you a great illustration on how life works and what you can expect. There's actually a bible story called the Parable of the Sower that explains this concept. Success is just a few basic fundamentals practiced every day. Success is also just a numbers game.

If you do something often enough, a ratio will appear. In baseball, we call it batting average. Ask anyone in Sales, and they will tell you the fastest way to get more sales is to get more rejections. It's a rejection game, not a sales game. The more No's you can gather up, the more Yes's you will get. To double your success rate, double your failure rate. Of course, you can improve your skill too and your ratios will improve. But here's what you can do:

You can make up in numbers what you lack in skill.

Even if you can only make 1 sale per every 10 calls (10% closing rate), you can still beat someone who can make 7 sales per 10 calls (70% closing rate). But how? Just by working harder! In a one-month long contest, the better skilled person makes 10 calls and gets his

7 sales, but you make 100 calls and get your 10 sales. 10 beats 7 and you win! You had the same closing ratio of 10%, but you just worked harder than he did by making more calls. Combined with better skills, imagine what you could accomplish! No one said you can only call 10 people. There's no limit on the upper bound.

Success is a numbers game. If you are not good at something, practice it. If you bat 3 out of 10 in major league baseball, you earn $10 million dollars per year. Which means, if you fail 7 times out of 10, still get $10 million per year. You don't have to bat 1000. You don't have to be 100% every single time. Life isn't a "All or Nothing scenario" that you were led to believe in school. In life, you only have to be right one time. You can fail at 6 businesses, but you only need to find one that works. You don't have to bat 1000 to make good money. It's not like in school taking a test where you just have one shot at a good grade. It's not so binary.

In life, you can have multiple shots, you get to choose which pitches to swing at, and you only just need to make one of them to be a success. Also, in life, you are the player, the umpire, the coach, the judge, and the teacher, how can you possibly fail?

In order to win the battle in your own mind, you must trust the law of averages and circumstances will work in your favor and that your life changing efforts will be rewarded. It teaches you that sometimes, you just lose. For no apparent reason you will lose sometimes. It's part of life. Don't ask me why. It's just the way it is. The beautiful part of it is that once you know how it works, you can use it for your advantage! Just keep on going. In life, you will fail more times than you will succeed. Just keep on going. Never stop. I know that if I fail more times than my competitor, I will win in the long game.

The Self-Image:

This concept is the best thing I have ever learned. It's worth the price of this book. It's pure gold. I accidently discovered a book that was written in 1937, called Psycho Cybernetics, written by Dr. Maxwell Maltz, that I believe explains the secret becoming very successful. It changed my life. The book discusses the concept of the Self-Image. Dr. Maltz said that this concept was the greatest discovery in the last century.

Our self-image controls our behavior like a thermostat. The picture you have in your mind is the goal your behavior is programmed to maintain. It can never deviate from this image. **Long term results are always, ALWAYS equal to your self-image.** Your success will never be greater than the image you have of yourself. You can never be more than the picture you have of yourself. Period.

How do you see yourself this summer at the beach? Slim, toned, ripped? Well, no amount of exercise will help you if you can't see it. You might slim up, but you will fall right back to where you started because your self-image is still the same. It will always self-regulate and return to your true self-image. Same with your money blueprint. You will never make more than the money image you have of yourself. Go look up the book "Secrets of the Millionaire Mind".

Can you see yourself passing this exam? If you can't see it – in your mind's eye- it can never happen. Do you see yourself as a great test taker? Or do you believe that you are a poor test taker? This is why I said to hang up a blank certificate frame earlier. It's the first step to changing your self-image.

What is your Current Self-Image?

The self-image of yourself was developed over years and years of your life and reinforced by your habits every day. You will NEVER become "a great test taker" unless you change your self-image. You need to change the paradigm. You must understand that your self-image is not yours. Your thoughts are not yours either. They are created by your old habits, trying to correct the deviation from your self-image. Our self-image was programmed into us when we were children by your parents and teachers. You can have all the knowledge and skills in the world, but if your "Self Image" isn't set up for success, you're doomed.

By learning how to alter your Self-Image, you never have to be the same person again, only by choice. You will be able to become whoever you want to become. You are limitless. The concept of the self-image is extremely powerful. You can read more about it for yourself. I'm just here to present it. Do your own research.

How to Change Your Self-Image:

The trick is to remake your hidden self-image for success or anything that you want to work on. You CAN learn how to alter it. By changing your self-image, you will discover deep reservoirs of talent and ability within yourself. I overcame my fear of public speaking using this method and many other things.

You need to learn how to do self-image visual exercises. There's also a Goal Card Method involves writing your major goal on a card that you can carry loose in your pocket and reading that as many times as possible during the day. Declarations and Affirmations make a powerful paradigm shifts in your life as well as visual boards. Sounds like bullsh$t, I know, but it isn't.

When you visualize something, you are literally creating a new neural network or pattern within your brain that corresponds to what it is you want to achieve. When you practice creative visualization, you are literally wearing grooves in your mind. Use it to picture the way you would like to feel and act. When you think in different ways than you typically think, and entertain new possibilities, you create the what – if possibility. You'll find yourself just taking action.

Check out a book called "With Winning in Mind", written by Lanny Bassham, He's an Olympian rifle shooter and uses this technique in train other Olympians. Trust me. This isn't bullsh$t guys. It absolutely works. It's the single best thing I ever learned. Ever heard of the Law of Attraction? Well, it's not just dumbed down videos on TikTok or YouTube. It's real, in a sense, but it's based on Psycho Cybernetics.

State Management:

In the movie Gladiator, right before the one of the battles, he bends down to scoop the sand & dirt with his hands and rubs it between his fingers. That is State Management. He is doing that to mentally prepare for war and to get into battle mode. He is picking up the sand to trigger the State that he wants to be in. Most people are horrible at managing their State. **Life is really all about having the right mindset.** Managing your internal state is so crucial. Get into the right state, and the right behaviors will pour forth automatically. State Management is so critical.

You might be the best test taker in the world, but how do you feel RIGHT NOW before the test? Do you feel nervous? Anxious? Are you focusing on the fight that you had with your wife last night over dirty laundry or how the bank made a mistake on your online account? Or, do you feel clear, confident, and certain?

You attract the things in life that you focus on. There are certain ways that we hold our body that can instantly put you into a more positive and empowered state. If your physiology is wrong, it will be difficulty if not impossible to pop into a great state. Make sure it supports the trigger of a peak and empowered state. To get into the correct state, you will learn how to fire off a trigger. Look into the Power Poses – the "Champion pose". Walk around like Rocky Balboa and tell me you don't instantly feel great! I do this before work presentations, and it really builds my confidence and laser-like focus when you need it..

Anchoring:

This comes from a body of psychology called NLP. It deals with how people make change in their lives and how to make sure those changes last. And whenever you use it correctly, it can be an incredible potent tool to have. Let me teach you how to manage your state through anchoring. You can fire off the anchor right before your test to get you in the correct state. Anchoring locks in a very specific state that you want to be able to trigger off at will.

You first need to set an anchor for yourself. Try to remember a time when you accomplished something really spectacular. Bring back those feelings. Were you excited, proud, full of joy? Now hold that feeling, really feel it, let it pour through you, and anchor it to a physical movement – I like to raise my arms in victory. Choose whatever you want.

Now, when you want that same feeling to come back, fire off that same anchor. The same feelings should come back. This is how actors get into character right before the big shoot. Also, how do you think someone like Tony Robbins prepares to go onstage? Do you think he just walks out there and starts talking? No, he pumps himself up by firing off an anchor to get into that high energy state. There's no other way. He knows that he must come on stage in a higher state of energy than the audience- in order for the Law of Transference to work. They will feel what he feels. He knows that they aren't buying his product, they are buying his energy.

Go research on YouTube "Wolf of Wall Street Movie Clip-The money Chant" This is the scene with Matthew McConaughey. In real life, that was his unique way to get into character before filming a crucial scene. But the directors loved it so much, they decided to keep it in the actual movie. You need to find your unique way to get fired up.

Second Effort:

This is a concept that Vince Lombardi, former football coach of the Green Bay Packers football team, taught his players. There are usually only about 168 plays in a typical football game. But only 3-4 plays actually determine the outcome of the game. Since you have no idea when those 3-4 plays are coming up, you must give each play 100% effort! By doing this, you'll be guaranteed to take advantage of maximizing every play. This goes back to the Law of Averages.

Razor's Edge:

Here is a concept taught by Bob Proctor. The line which separates winning from losing is as fine as a razor's edge. The real winners in life are, more often than not, only two or three percent more effective than those who lose.

You need to understand that you can be every bit as effective as anyone you read about or even hear about. The Razor's Edge is simply doing a little bit more … a little bit more than others … a little bit more than is expected … and a little bit more than is necessary. And it doesn't really take any special skills or talents to do it. The good news is you can have the Razor's Edge working for you. It can totally change your life. It did for me.

Now, just consider the tremendous difference you could create in your own life if you were to adopt a similar mental attitude. For example, if you are a person who is working in sales and currently selling only three units a week, what would the consequences be for you if you were to decide to make one additional sale per week, through a conscientious application of the second effort concept? Well, on a weekly basis, it might not appear to be a major breakthrough. However, viewed over the time frame of an entire career, it would actually amount to well over two thousand extra sales. Moreover, from a monetary standpoint, it would mean you would actually receive an extra ten years' income over the span of a forty-year career. Yes, that one sale would be the Razor's Edge difference, which could catapult you into "the big leagues" in your chosen career.

I see it every time in pro sports. The "greatest" golfers … like Tiger Woods … are only 3 or 4 strokes better than the "poorest" golfers in the tournament, but their winnings are dozens of times higher than those who come in second, third, or fourth place. Running backs fall forward to pick up a few extra yards each play. What does that do over the course of a game, a season, a career…

How can you get the Razor's Edge working for you?

1) Refuse to Settle for the Basics:

For example, you may have mastered the basics of reading by the fifth or sixth grade. But have you done anything since then to improve your reading skills? And you may have mastered the basics of arithmetic, but have you gone beyond that to master the skills required for saving, investing, and budgeting for your future?

2) Decide to become an expert in Something:

Once people understand the basics of something, they usually stop their learning in that area. Only a small percentage of people ever go on to become the acknowledged experts in a particular area. And they are the ones, of course, who typically receive the largest incomes. That's why you should look at what you're doing and ask yourself, "How good am I at doing it?" and "How much better could I be?"

3) Dedicate Your Time to Study:

All you have to do is study one hour a day in your chosen field, and in five years you will be an expert in that field. In Proctor's words, "If you were to follow this schedule rigorously, in a relatively short span of time you would stand among your peers like a giraffe in a herd of field mice."

4) Turn Your Car into A Library:

Turn your radio off and your CD player or iPhone on. If you drive thousands of miles to work or errands each year, then listen to educational, motivational CDs. You can learn basically just about anything. Make recordings of your Control Sheet I discussed earlier.

5) Add the Razor's Edge Element to Your Job:

Perhaps you're in a customer service position. You will be astounded at what happens if you change your attitude towards your customers. If you tend to see customers as an interruption OF your business ... instead the reason FOR your business ... you're bound to lose some customers. But if you think of ways to sharpen your customer service skills ... and then actually do it ... you'll see an amazing difference in how you feel and in how much they buy. Try smiling at every customer. Give everyone a genuine, welcoming "hello" instead of perfunctory "hi." And make sure you go out of your way to thank them for their business.

Before a work meeting, really prepare for it- strive to be the most prepared person in the room, read all the emails, the manuals, etc.. take notes. You will be seen as the smartest in the room – just by simply preparing for the meeting! Most people don't even bother to read the manual. This takes no extra skill.

You are only one inch ... one step ... one idea ... away from turning onto the boulevard of beauty in your own life... and the inches are everywhere.

How to get this to work for you:

Do one extra problem a day, it will add up over time. Take time to learn the FE Handbook inside and out. My Razor's edge, when I took this exam, was to learn the sections so well that I could flip to any major topic area in less than 3 seconds. Does that take any special skill? No. All it took was a little time each day becoming familiar with its layout. Did most test takers do this too? No. But why? Because it's easy Not to Do. What's easy... is also easy not to do.

Learning Curve of the FE Handbook:

There will be a time during your preparation in which you will start flipping through the *FE handbook* and want to quit because you think that this is too much to learn in this short period of time. **This is completely normal.** You can't expect to get every question correct. This phenomenon is based on the basic learning curve. At one point, the curve plateaus without ever increasing until sometime later down the road. This will seem to happen to you as you begin studying. Realize that everyone needs to study. Do not quit! Don't judge your progress by how many questions you are getting correct in practice. Don't fall into the trap of thinking that you should be getting 60% of all the practice questions right if you want to pass the actual exam. Don't think like that. You don't necessarily need to memorize the problems, but become familiar with the steps it takes to solve different types of problems. More importantly, what you are learning is how the *FE Handbook* is organized. Most of the equations that you will need during the exam can be found in the *FE handbook*.

As stated before, for some reason, the idea that you have to work every single problem correctly gets passed on from generation to generation. It's a vicious cycle. No one is perfect. Hall of Famers, the best baseball hitters of all time, only hit the ball 30% of the time (3 out of 10 times at bat). That's what a batting average of 300 means. Conversely, this means they failed 70% of the time. Think about it. The best hitters in history never hit the ball in 7 out of 10 at bats and still make millions of dollars. Don't pressure yourself for perfection, keep it all in perspective. In basketball, you have to shoot 50% to be considered an average player. If you make an extra 10 shots per hundred, you are an All-Star. In real life, the odds are a little different. You don't have to be right every time. In fact, it doesn't matter how many times you strike out or fail a test. In life, to be a success, you only have to be right once. It doesn't matter how many problems you get wrong in practice; it only matters that get a percentage of the problems correct during the actual exam, and that percentage changes for each exam.

Expect to Struggle:

You should expect to struggle while first starting to work problems in this book. It's normal. You are clearing out the cobwebs, learning how to use the *FE Handbook,* and brushing up on material you learned in college. If you aren't getting problems wrong and doing stupid mistakes with units then something is definitely wrong. You aren't trying hard enough to succeed. Don't be afraid to fail.

Examples of great men and women failing have become emblematic of success: Michael Jordan, the greatest basketball player in the history of the game (sorry Kobe) missed over 9,000 shots in his career and he lost almost 300 games. 26 times he's been trusted to take the game-winning shot and missed. He failed over and over and over again in his life. And that is why he succeeded. Babe Ruth struck out 1,335 times to get his near record 714 home runs. Thomas Edison persisted through 1,300 failed experiments until he finally invented the light bulb. Abraham Lincoln lost over 90% of the debates his participated in but he is still considered the best debater of any president. If you read the biography of any famous actor, you will learn that they did not get the role more often than they did land the role. The best comedians of all time; Richard Prior, Steve Kinison, bombed on stage more often, at least in the beginning, than they killed it. True victory is preceded by defeat.

Only Have to be Right One Time:

Doesn't matter how many times you failed before. You only have to be right one time. If you focus, visualize your goal, and avoid the naysayers, success will come. Progress is never in a straight line. It will have dips. Your criteria for success should be you taking action, not solving practice problems correctly. As you work through your mistakes, it is like swinging a machete through a thick vegetated forest. You are creating new pathways that didn't exist before. As you study, you are forcing yourself to learn new skills by creating new pathways and connections. Once you create the new pathway, it's always there and it cannot be erased. Everyone has a failure curve. But the trick is to exhaust your failure curve during practice (by working as many practice problems as you can) not waiting during the actual exam. In sales, if you want to double your income, you need to double your rejections. It's a numbers game.

Avoid the Naysayers:

Avoid discussing the exam with other people while waiting in line before the exam or even before the exam. There will be some groups of people (I call them the HERD) who say that "this exam is stupid and a waste of time", "it doesn't make you a better engineer", "in the old days they used to just hand these out when you graduated", "you can't make any money as a PE anyway", "bla bla bla" etc. You want to avoid the naysayers and all that negative energy all together.

It's best to try to relax while you are waiting in line for the exam center to open its doors and not get caught up in meaningless discussions about the exam or people's opinions. Stay cool, calm, collected, visualize your goal and stay positive. Use this time to take pride in the fact that you prepared and feel confident about the exam and look forward to the challenge.

Also don't make these grand announcements on social media about taking the exam. If you fail, you will have to relive it all over again when everyone asks if you passed.

Don't be Afraid to Fail:

Don't be afraid to fail. When you tell yourself you are too tired or don't have time to study, realize that someone else out there is working hard and getting stronger at working these problems. Mike Tyson used to wake up to jog at 3 am in the morning when preparing for a boxing match. A reporter once asked him why? Mike simply responded, *because I know that my opponent isn't*. Remember that you are also going up against other test takers the same day. You don't have to get all the problems correct; you just have to be better than about 35 % of all the other test takers. Visualize your goal and stay focused on working the practice problems in this book. Gain every advantage you can over other test takers. Study a little bit each day. Work 1 or 2 problems in the morning, a few at lunch time, and max it out at night. When you start gaining momentum by studying a little bit each day, a compounding effect starts happening. Since compounding is an exponential function, it will seem to get easier, and you will be amazed by how much material you have gone through.

Even on days when you are the most tired and don't feel like studying, try to do just one thing to improve yourself by 1%. Flip through the *FE Handbook* or just do one problem from the book. Improving yourself by just 1% per day for one month is not 30% better… it is much more than that because of the compounding effect. I secret I learned long ago is that **you can make up in numbers what you lack in skill**. Just put in more study time than the rest of the test takers – and you will succeed. You don't have to be some genius engineer, just put in more time practicing the test questions.

I truly believe that we are all so much more capable than what we were led to believe throughout our lives and especially in school. I think this comes from the fact that we were conditioned at a young age to be afraid of failing. We got punished for making mistakes on tests or getting a problem wrong. But failing is the only way to really learn something. Rocky was right, it's not about how many times you succeeded, it's about how many times you failed or got knocked down but got up anyway. That's what separates winners form losers. You have to keep going.

Most people only use a fraction, maybe 5 or 10%, of their potential. It's time to tap into the other 95%. Whether or not you choose to find the time to study is entirely up to you.

Creating Your Own Luck:

Phil Jackson is considered one of the greatest basketball coaches of all time by coaching the Chicago Bills to six consecutive NBA championships. He also has the highest winning percentage of any NBA coach. After winning his sixth NBA title, a reporter asked him how he became so lucky. Phil responded by saying that he doesn't believe in luck. He explained to the reporter, *"When you take care of the little things and pay attention to all the details upfront, luck happens. Luck is what happens when you prepare ahead of time and take care of all the little details in practice, and through the natural laws of cause and effect, things just tend to go your way"*.

Luck has always been known as when preparation meets opportunity. If you work hard by studying and take care of the little details, things will go your way during the test and in life in general. The bottom line is that you **need to practice** in order to develop problem recognition skills. This is the key to scoring high and passing on your first try. That is what the book is all about, maximizing your chances of success. You are an engineer, so you need to engineer your way through the test. How do you accomplish this? By having a game plan, a strategy. If all else fails, use your engineering judgment. Play it smart, and think like an engineer! Stick to your game plan and get to work. The beauty of success, whether it's finding the girl of your dreams, the right job or financial success, is that it doesn't matter how many times you have failed, you only have to be right once. And, then everyone can tell you how lucky you are.

It's time for you to take control of yourself by developing an **internal locus of control** in your life. Most people have an **external locus of control**, meaning that they see forces outside themselves as being in charge of their life. They believe that success is really beyond their control and it gives them something else to blame when things go wrong. For those with an external locus of control, it doesn't matter how hard they try since they see life as a game of luck. They lack control of their emotions; if people around them are in a bad mood, then they're in a bad mood too. They may also not want to put forth the effort to succeed unless they have already been successful in the past. They also tend to be afraid to take risk in life. When they do make mistakes, they assign responsibility to others rather than trying to learn from what they did.

Successful people tend to have an internal locus of control. These people believe that **they make their own luck.** They believe that the more they strive, the more they will succeed. Anything they want to accomplish is totally within the realm of possibility. Having an internal locus of control means being self-confident and self-motivated. It means being optimistic, because you know that your destiny is in your hands.

You can become a person with an internal locus of control. As you go through your process of studying, you need to start attributing internally. Start by changing the way you talk to yourself. You can become a person with an internal locus of control. As you go through your process of studying, you need to start attributing internally. Start by changing the way you talk to yourself.

Old way of talking to yourself	New way of talking to yourself
I got through college because it was easy	I worked hard and did an awesome job
I lost motivation to study because I can't seem to get any practice problems right.	My motivation comes from within, so it's irrelevant that I didn't get the problem correct.
I am not a good test taker	I can learn new skills and strategies to become a great test taker that worked for others in the past.
I feel motivated because I just got a problem correct.	I feel motivated because I choose to.
I only got good grades in school because my professors were merciful and made it easy.	I got good grades because I'm smart and studied hard.
Things work out for me because fate is on my side.	In life, things work out for me because I make good decisions.
I have low self-esteem because I haven't accomplished much in life and barely made it out of school with a low GPA.	I have high self-esteem. I know I can accomplish anything that I put my mind to.
I will feel so nervous during the exam.	I feel nervous during exams only when I (incorrectly) tell myself that I need to pass for approval or validation.
I don't have time to study.	I don't have time not to study. I want to advance my engineering career and preparing for this exam will help me to become a better engineer.
It's not like me to do well on tests	It is like me to do well because I am different now and learned new skills.

Hard Work:

If you want to go through life trying to make other people happy and not taking any risks, then ignore all the advice in this book. But if you want to win, there is no getting around hard, hard work. You should be hungry to make your mark on this world and willing to work towards your goals. The best investment you can make is in yourself. Remember, you are the average of the top 5 people that you hang around. Who are you hanging around with? Where will these people be in 5 years? Are they pushing themselves to be better professionally?

The fact that you invested in this book and are trying to reach your goal, means that you are already 10 times more likely to pass this exam than the average test taker. Remember, every time you work through one of the practice problems in this book or flip through the *FE handbook*, you are **increasing your chances of passing**. If you prepare using this book and understand and practice all of the questions, you will pass on your first try.

The Set of the Sail:

Jim Rohn also taught about this concept.

Your own personal philosophy is the greatest determining factor in how your life works out.

It's not what happens that determines your life. It's what you do about it that determines it. What happens, happens to everybody. What you do about it is key. Don't try to change all the other things out there. Just trim a better sail.... What does that mean? All of us are in a little sailboat throughout life. The difference where you arrive in 1 year, 2 years, etc., is not determined from the blowing of the wind, but the set of the sail. (YOUR SAIL). Therefore, the key to a better life is learning how to trim a better sail.

That's what learning and self-development is all about - to set a better sail. To be better this year than you were last year. Some people blame many different things for their failures or lack of success: For example: Politics, Republicans, Democrats, the economy, their company, the company policy, their supervisor at work, high taxes, stock market, parents, community, preachers, low wage rates. **I'm telling you that it has nothing to do with any of that !!!!**

Throw away this old blame list. I used to have an old blame list too. How do you trim a better sail? Read the books, learn from the past, invest it into tomorrow, into the next day, next week, next year, learn, amend the errors in judgement, learn from other people, walk away from the 97% of people who aren't even trying., study, educate yourself, ask questions, have fun, be present wherever you are. Search and you will find. Save at least 10% of your money and you will become a millionaire.

Your personal philosophy is the greatest determining factor in how your life works out. Don't try to change all the other things out there. Just trim a better sail.

Outcome Independence:

Let go of the outcome. The best coaches do not focus on winning; they focus on systems and processes. You can't control the other team and there are too many variables. It's important to only focus on what you need to do next, and doing it to the best of your ability. The process is really what you have to do day in and day out to be successful. Nick Saban talks about processes all the time. Instead of asking their players to focus on winning the championship or the next big game, the best coaches ask them to focus on what the next action is. The next drill. The next play. The next touchdown. It's not the outcome that's important, but the process.

Stop worrying about if you will pass or fail this exam, just focus on what your next step is…. Did you work any practice problems today? Are you learning the format and layout of the FE Handbook? Do you know where the table is to calculate the polar moment of inertia (J) for problems involving stresses in shafts? Do you know how to read a psychrometric chart yet? Are you reviewing how shear and moment diagrams look for different beam loadings? Do you realize that there is a table which has deflection equations for common beam loadings? Do you know how long you have to solve each problem? Did you work and problems during lunchtime today or did you just surf the web for 45 minutes? Focus on things that you can control.

Eliminate the clutter and all the things that are going on outside and focus on the things that you can control with how you sort of go about and take care of your business. That's something that's ongoing, and it can never change. It's the journey that's important. You can't worry about end results. It's about what you control, every minute of every day. You always must have a winning attitude and discipline, in practices, weight training, conditioning, in the classroom, in everything. It's a process. When you commit to a process over an outcome, you redirect your focus on what is within your inner locus of control; discipline, motivation and organization to name a few, drive the actions needed to necessitate the outcome you're moving towards.

When you're committed to the process, you always win because you're improving daily. You're constantly moving towards what you want because of the tiny actions you're taking. Remember, your criteria for success is taking action each day. You must design and commit to a system for change; an efficient process where positive outcomes are an inevitable outcome. Ask yourself: "What could I do daily that would guarantee extraordinary result results?

Great Tables in the FE Handbook to Know:

1) <u>Table of Material Properties</u>. *Page 138 (144 of 502) – in the FE Handbook*

   This table is good for finding the Modulus of Elasticity (E) for common materials. It also gives the density. You typically use (E) for problems asking for the deflection in a beam (like problems # 44 & #131) and the elongation of an object due to tension (like problem #45).

2) <u>Table of Properties of Water</u>: *Page 199 (SI) & Page 200 (English)*

   This table is great for problems asking you to calculate the Reynolds # (like problems #107, #200, #229). For any temperature of water, is gives you the kinematic viscosity which you need for the Reynolds # equation (Like problem # 11).

   It's also great for problems involving Pump Power (Like problems #51, #71, and #85), Bernoulli Equation (like problem #181). You need the specific gravity for those problems. Also true for a Manometer-type problem (like problem #325)

3) <u>Table for Simply Supported Beam Slopes & Deflections</u>: *Page 140*

   Awesome table for quickly find the formula for the deflection of common beam loadings (like problem #268). Just match the loading with the left picture and find your deflection formula. Also tells you the slope and maximum moment.

4) <u>Table of Centroids, Area Moment of Inertia (I), and Radius of Gyration</u>: *Page 98 & 99*

   This is an extremely useful table for problems asking for the stresses in beams (like problem # 117). For the shape that's given, you can find the Moment of Inertia (I). Make sure you use I_{xc} value which is the first value shown.

The tables on page 115 & 116 are great for problems asking you for the Torsional Stress in a shaft (like Problems #123 and #255) because it gives you the Polar Moment of Inertia (J) for that equation. If it's a solid shaft, use the first top one. If it's hollow with a wall thickness, use the second one from the top.

5) Table for Dynamics: Mass Moment of Inertia: *Page 129*

Good for flywheel problems (Like problem #193) for finding the mass moment of inertia for rotation about a fixed axis.

6) AISC Table 3-2: W Shapes *Page 285.*

Must have for Beam problems (like problems #285, #286, #297, #315, #331)

7) Table for Economics and Interest Rates: *Page 230*

Definitely need to know where these equations are located for engineering economics problems (like #27, #81, #99, #179, #202). The actual interest rate tables start 2 pages from this one.

8) ASTM Reinforcement Bars: *Page 277*

The tables tell you the area of re-bar sizes. (like problem #277

9) ASTM: USCS: *Page 267*

For questions about soil classification (like problem #9, #90)

10) Moody Diagram: *Page 201*

This chart allows you to find the Friction Factor (f) from the Reynolds# and flow. (Like problem #11, #265)

3 Types of Problems:

For any test I take, I like to think that the problems come in 3 main types. That's how I prepare. For each concept/equation, I listed the problems associated with it.

1) Basic Concepts and Equations:

You should know these by heart, so you don't waste time trying to find the equation:

- F = MA: *Problems: #125, #173 Geotech, & #Bonus problem 5,*

- Pressure/Stress = Force / Area: *Problems: #154, #243, #Bonus 2 (pg 169).*

- △ Length = F(L)/ (A)(E): *Problem: #45*

- Truss Diagrams/Basic Statics: *Problem#: #3, #4, #32, #38, #83, #93, #119*

- Q = VA: *Problems: #9, #156, #224, #282, #304*

- Engineering Economics: *Problems: #27, #81, #179*

- Ethics: *Problems: #21,#22, #23, #78*

- Springs: F = k(s) *Problem: #16, 334*

- h = ΔP/ γ   This is a really good common conversion for fluid   problems. If the H isn't given, you can calculate from the pressure difference: *Problem: #72, &#32, #88*

- Problems just using basic engineering reasoning skills: *Problems: #1, #3, #4, #39, #41, #58, #94, #126*

2) Equations to be familiar with and can look up very quickly: Don't have to memorize:

- $h_f = f (L/d) (V^2/2g)$. Darcy-Weisbach Equation: *Problems: #11, #265*

- Power = Qγh/n   Pump Power Equation: *Problems: #51, #71, and #85*

- $Q = -k \cdot A \, (dT/dx)$ Fourier's Law of Conduction: *Problem: #77*

- $v = (k/n) \cdot R^{2/3} \cdot S^{1/2}$ Manning's Equation: *Problem: #76*

- Straight Line Depreciation: *Problems: #29, #136*

- $\sigma_{bending} = M \cdot C / I$ Stresses in Beams: *Problems: #117*

3) **Look-up Type Problems that you have no clue what it means:**

Remember, if you find yourself asking *how in the world* am I supposed to know that? - it's usually a good sign that the answer is stated somewhere in the manual. A good example is an environmental question about lime (page 340 of the FE Handbook) like problem #234.

Problems #95, #234, #267, #300, #376, #332,

Fast Tracking Schedule:

For those of you who do not have the time to devote the recommended study time of 8 weeks, this section is for you! This section is also great for anyone who has been out of school for a long time wanting to brush up on basic engineering skills before starting to work the practice problems in the book. It can serve as a nice refresher course. **The idea behind this section is for anyone who feels completely overwhelmed with starting to prepare for this exam.** The greatest marksmen do not start out shooting bull's-eyes from 100 feet away. First, they bring the target in closer and learn the basics. Then they slowly push the target out. Same for successful businessmen. They don't start out by creating a million-dollar company; instead, they first start up a small business and learn and grow from there. This section attempts to bring the target in closer for you. Refresh yourself on basic engineering principles you learned in school. Throughout the book, we slowly push the target away so you can improve on solving many different types of problems.

Topic # 1: Mathematics:

1) This topic will be about 6-9 questions according to NCEES.

2) Know how to do a basic integral. These are simple points to earn. *For practice, see problem #'s 25,91,225.*

3) Know solve to solve the roots to the quadratic equation: *For practice, see problems # 243, 301*

4) Know how to solve equations of straight lines in standard form and point slope form: *For practice, see problems # 38, 145*

5) Know how to take a basic derivative. *For practice, see problems #6, 186E, 217*

6) Understand your basic trigonometry functions. Very helpful when solving force problems.

7) If you need to calculate the volumes of basic shapes.

8) Know how to solve a matrix type problem. *For practice, see problem # 158.*

9) Know to calculate a dot product. *For practice, see problem #'s 89, and 198.*

Topic # 2: Probability and Statistics:

1) Review permutations and combinations. *For practice, see problem #'s 186D and 208.*

2) Review the definitions for standard deviations. *For practice, see problem #'s 10 and 80*

2) Understand how expected value works. *For practice, see problem # 144.*

3) Understand how linear regression works. *For practice, see problem # 189.*

4) Understand how Hypothesis Testing works. *For practice, see problem # 114.*

5) Understand how Unit Normal Distribution works. These tables are useful. *For practice, see problem # 95.*

6) Understand how Probability Density functions work. *For practice, see problem # 143.*

Topic # 3: Engineering Ethics and Professional Practice:

1) Ethics are the easiest problems to earn points on. This section is only two pages long and you should read through the laws.

2) You must remember that Public Welfare is top priority, along with public safety. You need to be competent in the area that you are working in.

3) When answering these types of questions, you should always play it straight. Do not bend the rules or pretend that a technical issue does not exist, always choose to fix it correctly, especially if your boss pressures you to certify something, a project is behind schedule, funding is low, or if a client desperately needs the project turned over immediately. Do not fall into these common scenarios. ALWAYS choose to be ethical and fix the problem- because it is the right thing to do. Think of the hardest working and honest person you know and think of how they would handle the situation. That's how you should approach these problems.

4) Recommend practicing the followings Problem #'s: 21, 22, 23.

Topic # 4: Engineering Economics:

1) Economic problems are relatively easy points to earn. Learn how to use the interest rate tables in the handbook.

2) Review Break Even Analysis. *For practice, see problem # 30.*

3) Review the equations for straight line depreciation and book value. *For practice, see problem # 29, 136, 178, and 258.*

4) Know how to use the interest tables to do basic problems of moving money around: *For practice, see problem # 27, 28, 81, 99, 102, 118, 146, 179, 190, 202, 217, 222, 261, 299, 326.*

Topic # 5: Statics:

1) You should know how to solve Static problems quickly.

2) Know how to resolve a force into x and y components on page 107 (111 of 498). *For practice, see problem #'s 3, 4, 33, 34, and 128.* Note: A force diagram may not be given, it could just be a picture of an object resting on a table or against a wall, etc., and you will have to draw the force diagram.

3) Know how to solve for reaction forces on a truss on page 110 (114 of 498). *For practice, see problem #'s 36, 83, and 138.*

4) Know how to solve for centroid locations on page 111 (115 of 498). *For practice, see problem #'s 63, and 183.*

5) Know how to use table on page 111 (115 of 498). to calculate the moment of inertia for different shapes. *For practice, see problem #'s 117, and 183.*

6) Know what basic shear and moment diagrams look like. *For practice, see problem # 35.*

Topic # 6: Dynamics:

1) Understand Particle Kinematics. *For practice, see problem # 37.*

2) Know how to do Projectile Motion problems. *For practice, see problem #'s 39, 125, and 167.*

3) Know how to do Potential Energy, Kinetic Energy, and Spring type problems. *For practice, see problem #'s 16, 40, 64, 65, 203, 245, and 289.*

4) Understand Laws of Friction problems. *For practice, see problem #'s 77, 84, 124, 125, 187, 275, 283, and 321.*

5) Know the table on page 128 (132 of 498) for radius of gyration and mass moment of inertia problems. *For practice, see problem # 193.*

<u>Topic # 7: Strength of Materials:</u>

1) Understand definition of Engineering Strain and Uniaxial Loading. *For practice, see problem #'s 45, 92 and 154.*

2) Understand Thermal Deformations. *For practice, see problem # 46.*

3) Understand Pressure Vessels. *For practice, see problem #'s 47, and 101.*

4) Understand Stress Strain. *For practice, see problem # 42.*

5) Understand Torsion. *For practice, see problem #'s 255, and 256.*

6) Understand Beams. *For practice, see problem #'s 35, 36, 44,117, 119, 183, 185, 209, and 335.*

7) Understand Columns. *For practice, see problem # 220.*

8) Understand that common material properties. *For practice, see problem # 268.*

9) Understand common beam deflection formulas. *For practice, see problem # 44, and 268.*

<u>Topic # 8: Material Science:</u>

1) Understand Corrosion. *For practice, see problem #'s 68, 165, 223, 249, and 303.*

2) Understand Thermal and Mechanical Processing and Properties of Materials. *For practice, see problem #'s 49, 277, and 316.*

3) Understand Interior and Exterior Cracks. *For practice, see problem # 43.*

4) Understand the Relationship between Hardness and Tensile Strength. *For practice, see problem # 111.*

5) Understand Impact Tests. *For practice, see problem #'s 166, and 278.*

6) Understand Concrete questions. *For practice, see problem #'s 87, 295, 317, and 322.*

7) Understand Binary Phase Diagrams. *For practice, see problem #'s 159*

Topic # 9: Fluid Mechanics:

This is the largest section on the exam: 12-18 Questions.

1) Understand Pressure in a static Liquid. *For practice, see problem #'s 53, and 88.*

2) Understand how manometers work. *For practice, see problem # 325.*

3) Understand Buoyancy and the Continuity Equation. *For practice, see problem #'s 52, 137, 156, 224, 253, 282, and 327.*

4) Understand the Bernoulli Equation and Reynolds Number. *For practice, see problem #'s 50, 107, 53, and 228.*

5) Understand Head loss Due to Flow and Manning's Equation. *For practice, see problem #'s 11, 76, 134, 247, 265, 272, and 329.*

6) Understand Pump Power Equation. *For practice, see problem # 51, 71, and 285.*

7) Understand Similitude. *For practice, see problem #'s 168, and 269.*

8) Understand Aerodynamics. *For practice, see problem # 109.*

9) Understand how to use the Moody Diagram. *For practice, see problem # 265.*

10) Understand how to use the Drag Coefficient Diagram. *For practice, see problem # 184.*

Civil

(Exam Specifications):

14 Topic Areas	Expected # of Questions	Question # in this Book:
1) Mathematics and Statistics	8-12	6, 10, 12, 15, 25, 38, 67, 80, 89, 91, 95, 96, 114, 116, 123E, 132, 143, 144, 145, 149, 155, 158, 171, 186D, 186E, 189, 194, 197, 201, 207, 208, 218, 221, 225, 243, 251, 262, 264, 267, 274, 276, 280, 286, 291, 292, 293, 301, 320, 327
2) Ethics and Professional Practice	4-6	21, 22, 23, 78, 98, 120, 157, 160, 162, 176, 196, 231, 241, 290
3) Engineering Economics	5-8	27, 28, 29, 30, 81, 99, 102, 118, 136, 146, 178, 179, 190, 202, 217, 222, 258, 261, 299, 326
4) Statics	8 – 12	3, 4, 31, 32, 33, 34, 35, 36, 62B, 62C, 83, 93, 100, 119, 123B, 126, 128, 138, 140, 183, 185, 186, 191, 204, 209, 239, 242B, 335
5) Dynamics,	4-6	7, 16, 39, 40, 62F, 64, 77, 84, 94, 103, 123D, 123F, 123G, 124, 125, 130, 141, 167, 174, 187, 193, 198, 203, 214, 233, 245, 257, 275, 283, 289, 296, 300, 321, 328, 344
6) Mechanics of Materials	7 - 11	1, 42, 43, 44, 45, 46, 63, 70, 92, 101, 117, 123, 133, 154, 164, 215, 216, 220, 236, 255, 256, 268, 318
7) Materials	5-8	47, 48, 49, 68, 87, 111, 122, 159, 165, 166, 175, 195, 212, 223, 238, 249, 278, 295, 309, 310, 316, 317, 322
8) Fluid Mechanics	6-9	11, 50, 51, 52, 53, 65, 71, 76, 88, 107, 108, 109, 112, 123C, 127, 134, 137, 150, 153, 156, 168, 177, 184, 186C, 200, 224, 226, 228, 229, 235, 242C, 247, 250, 253, 259,

		265, 269, 272, 282, 285, 302, 304, 306, 325, 329,
9) Surveying	6-9	2, 20, 110, 129, 172, 186B, 205, 213, 314
10) Water Resources and Environmental Engineering	10-15	8, 37, 57, 61, 62, 73, 74, 75, 79, 97, 115, 151, 163, 170, 181, 199, 211, 234, 246, 252, 254, 263, 266, 277, 287, 294, 330
11) Structural Engineering	10-15	5, 18, 19, 29, 60, 105, 113, 148, 244, 273, 279, 284, 288, 297, 298, 303, 305, 307, 311, 315, 319, 331, 332
12) Geotechnical Engineering	10-15	9, 13, 26, 58, 59, 62D, 85, 90, 131, 135, 142, 152, 161, 169, 173, 180, 182,188, 192, 206, 240, 248, 270, 313, 323, 333
13) Transportation Engineering	9-14	17, 41, 56, 69, 72, 82, 86, 106, 147, 210, 219, 227, 230, 232, 237, 260, 281, 312, 324
14) Construction Engineering	8-12	14, 54, 55, 62E, 66, 104, 121, 139, 242, 271, 308

1) The piston of a hydraulic actuator is 1.5 inches diameter and is subject to a hydraulic line pressure of 1500 psi. Calculate what the cross-sectional area should be (in²) if the design stress for the piston is 20,000 psi:

(A) .132 in²

(B) .232 in²

(C) .332 in²

(D) .432 in²

2) In the following diagram, the survey instrument reads 3.75 on the leveling rod. What is the elevation at the leveling rod at Point A?

H instrument = 7.25

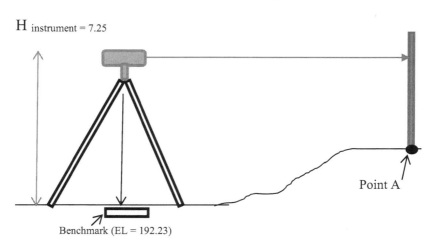

Point A

Benchmark (EL = 192.23)

(A) 202.99

(B) 195.73

(C) 112.56

(D) 219.81

3) Which of the following equations represents the equilibrium of the diagram below?

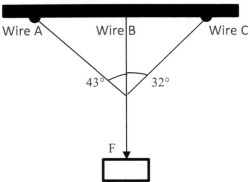

(A) $F = (F_{Wire\,A})^2 + (F_{Wire}\,B)^2 + (F_{Wire}\,C)^2$

(B) $F = F_{Wire\,A}\,(\sin 43°) + F_{Wire\,B} + F_{Wire\,C}\,(\sin 32°)$

(C) $F = F_{Wire\,A} + F_{Wire\,B} + F_{Wire\,C}$

(D) $F = F_{Wire\,A}\,(\cos 43°) + F_{Wire\,B} + F_{Wire\,C}\,(\cos 32°)$

4) Which of the following represents the shear and moment diagram for the beam elow?

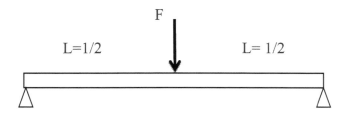

(B) V 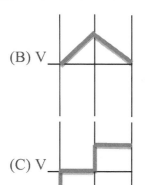 M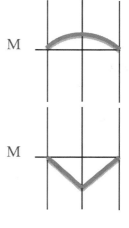

(C) V 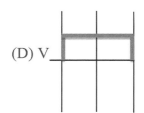 M

(D) V M

5) A beam supports a 4-inch composite wall around an air handler room in a large hospital. If the wall is 8 ft high and 12 feet long, the load on the beam (lb/ft) is most nearly: (Assume the wall has a unit weight of 120 lb/ft³)

(A) 3840

(B) 219

(C) 178

(D) 320

6) Evaluate the Following Limit:

$$\lim_{x \to 2} \frac{x^2 + x - 6}{x^2 - 3x + 2}$$

(A) -5

(B) -3

(C) 5

(D) -9

7) At one section of its track, a roller coaster travels in a straight line so that its distance, D, from a point on the line after time, t, is $D = 10t^4 - t^3$. Calculate its velocity when time = 3:

(A) 1053

(B) 53

(C) 513

(D) 5031

8) A drainage system is to be designed to collect rainwater runoff for a 2.75 acre car dealership lot. Using a rainfall intensity of 7.8 in/hr and a runoff coefficient is 0.85, the peak discharge (ft³/s) is most nearly:

(A) 11

(B) 15

(C) 18

(D) 22

9) The mechanical and plasticity tests of a soil under consideration as a fill material are shown below. The soil may be classified, using the Unified Soil Classification System, as:

Sieve	% Passing
10	17
40	23
200	62

Liquid Limit = 70

Plastic Limit = 20

(A) MH

(B) SM

(C) CH

(D) CL

10) Calculate the Standard Deviation for the values: 3,2,7:

(A) 0

(B) 12.6

(C) 2.6

(D) 4.6

11) For the following pipe section, what is the friction head loss using the Darcy-Weisbach Equation?

V = 10 fps
RE = 10^5
Relative Roughness (E) = .00006

Pipe ID = .5 ft

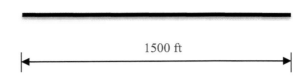

1500 ft

(A) 19 ft

(B) 52 ft

(C) 67 ft

(D) 84 ft

12) Evaluate: $_4P_2 \cdot {}_5P_3$:

(A) 720

(B) 270

(C) 27

(D) 411

13) A field technician obtains a soil sample and brings to the lab. The sample has a cohesion of 32kPA, normal stress of 38kPA, and a shear stress of 52 kPA at the point of failure. The angel of internal friction for the soil is most nearly:

(A) 13°

(B) 18°

(C) 21°

(D) 28°

14) A project schedule is shown in the following table, how many weeks long is the critical path?

Activity	Preceding Activity	Duration (weeks)
Start		0
A	Start	6
B	A,E	2
C	B	2
D	C	3
E	Start	1
F	A, E	1
G	F,B	7
Finish	D, G	0

(A) 10

(B) 12

(C) 15

(D) 17

15) The equation of a line is $3y + 2x = 6$. What is the slope of the line perpendicular to the given line?

(A) m = 3/2

(B) m = 7/8

(C) m = -3/2

(D) m = 2/3

16) A 1,800 lbf boulder traveling at 7 fps passes point A, rolls down a ramp towards Indiana Jones, and is stopped by a spring bumper which compresses 3 feet. A constant frictional force of 5 pounds acts on the ball. What is the spring modulus required?

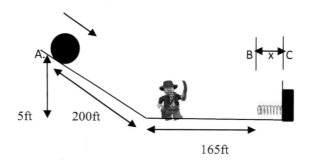

(A) 179 lb/ft

(B) 1,896 lb/ft

(C) 311 lb/ft

(D) 541 lb/ft

17) A vertical alignment for a proposed amusement park ride is shown below. The horizontal distance (ft) between P.V.I $_1$ and P.V.I $_2$ is most nearly:

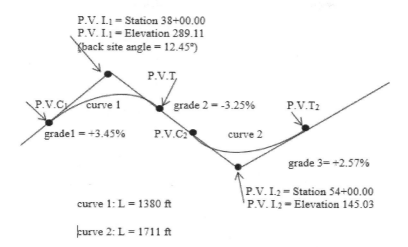

P.V. I.$_1$ = Station 38+00.00
P.V. I.$_1$ = Elevation 289.11
(back site angle = 12.45°)

P.V.T.

P.V.C$_1$ curve 1   grade 2 = -3.25%   P.V.T$_2$

grade1 = +3.45%   P.V.C$_2$ curve 2

grade 3= +2.57%

P.V. I.$_2$ = Station 54+00.00
P.V. I.$_2$ = Elevation 145.03

curve 1: L = 1380 ft

curve 2: L = 1711 ft

(A) 1,470

(B) 1,600

(C) 1,711

(D) 1800

18) The total axial load per linear foot (lb/ft) at the bottom of each wall is most nearly:

Materials:
Residential construction. Brick façade.

Loads:
Roof dead load = 10 psf
Roof live load = 5 psf
Snow load = 0 psf
Average wall dead load = 45 psf
Not in seismic location.
Do not use load combinations.

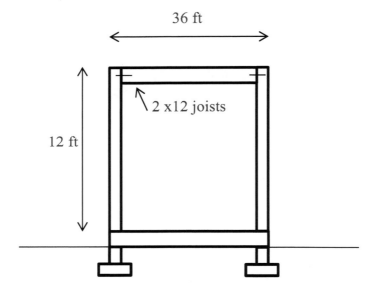

(A) 754

(B) 810

(C) 989

(D) 1051

19) You are designing a retaining wall for client and will use Rankine's Theory. Boring log results indicate that the proposed sandy material has a friction angle of 34°. The Rankine active lateral earth coefficient (k_a) is most nearly.

(A) .19

(B) .21

(C) .28

(D) .32

20) The elevation at point B is most nearly:

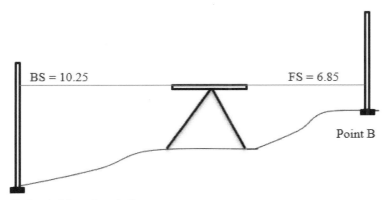

BS = 10.25   FS = 6.85

Point B

Point A (elevation: 3 ft)

(A) 4.7 ft

(B) 5.1 ft

(C) 5.8 ft

(D) 6.4 ft

21) You are the engineer of record on a construction project which is currently behind schedule and is urgently needed by your clients. Your supervisor instructs you to certify the structural steel gusset plate connections as properly completed, even though you know that quality control weld testing identified several welds which have failed and require reworking. What should you do?

(A) Certify it and then ask your supervisor for a bonus.

(B) Explain the situation to your supervisor and refuse to certify it.

(C) Certify it but keep a close eye on the welds for any visible signs of emanate failure, retest the welds a year from now.

(D) Explain the situation to the clients and ask them if they want the failing welds to be fixed.

22) You are the quality control engineer responsible for monitoring pollution levels associated with a burn disposal site. A routine test shows levels of pollution which are slightly higher than legally allowed. What should you do?

(A) Tell your supervisor and let him decide whether or not to fix it.

(B) Ignore the issue, since the levels are only slightly higher.

(C) Only fix the problems if it can be done very cheaply.

(D) Fix the problem, no matter what it costs, and even if your supervisor tells you to ignore it.

23) What is the first obligation of a licensed engineer?

(A) To work on your next promotion

(B) To put your company's mission statement first

(C) To the federal Government

(D) Public welfare

24) Which of the following is a comprehensive approach to communicating hazardous information?

(A) Bill of lading

(B) GHS

(C) SDSs

(D) MSDS

25) Solve the following integral:

$$V = \pi \int_{0}^{1} (x^2 - x^4)\, dx$$

(A) 2π

(B) $\pi/15$

(C) $2\pi/7$

(D) $2\pi/15$

26) The effective stress at point P in the diagram below is most nearly:

The boring log indicated that no water present was present.

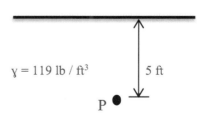

$\gamma = 119\ \text{lb} / \text{ft}^3$ 5 ft

P

(A) 595 lb/ft²

(B) 612 lb/ft²

(C) 748 lb/ft^2

(D) 801 lb/ft^2

27) $100 today is equivalent to how much a year from today at an interest rate of 6% per year?

(A) $94.75

(B) $106

(C) $110

(D) $214.05

28) How much should an engineer put in an investment with a 10% effective annual rate today to have $10,000 in five years?

(A) $7,209

(B) $6,209

(C) $10,209

(D) $6,902

29) A beam segment in an apartment building design has the following loads:

Distributed Dead Load, w = 750 lb/ft @ 10 ft

Concentrated Live Load, F_1 = 7 kips.

Concentrated Live Load, F_2 = 3 kips.

Concentrated Live Load, F_3 = 2 kips.

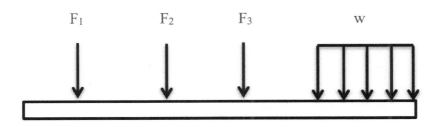

If the dead load factor is 1.3 and the live load factor is 1.8, the total factored and un-factored load acting on beam, respectively is?

(A) 32 kips, 14 kips

(B) 20 kips, 32 kips

(C) 32 kips, 20 kips

(D) 20 kips, 14 kips

29B) An engineering company purchases a piece of machinery that costs $9,000. It has a 10-year life and salvage value of $200. Find the straight-line depreciation:

(A) $8,120 / yr

(B) $840 / yr

(C) $800 /yr

(D) $880 /yr

30) The cost of producing a product from a factory is:
C= $15,000 + 0.03 • P (P is the number of items produced) If the items sell for $2.50 each, how many items must be produced to break-even?

(A) 8,071

(B) 6,073

(C) 12,079

(D) 2,076

31) A force is a vector quantity and is defined when which of the following conditions are specified:

(A) Magnitude

(B) Point of application

(C) Direction

(D) All of the above

32) The reaction force at By is most nearly: (Neglect the mass of the beam.)

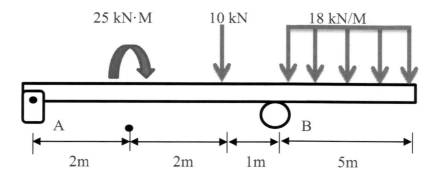

(A) 87 kN

(B) 148 kN

(C) 207 kN

(D) 566 kN

33) Calculate the magnitude of the resultant of the 3 forces in the following diagram:

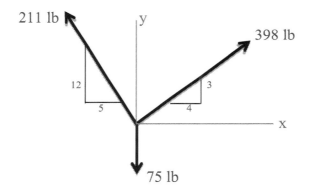

(A) 612 lb

(B) 209 lb

(C) 429 lb

(D) 581 lb

34) A 185 lb person stands on a balcony supported by only one diagonal support. Calculate the force in the support from the force diagram below:

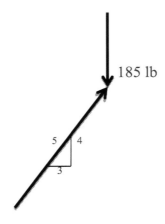

(A) 172 lb

(B) 305 lb

(C) 271 lb

(D) 232 lb

35) Analyze the truss shown below. The force in member AH is most nearly:

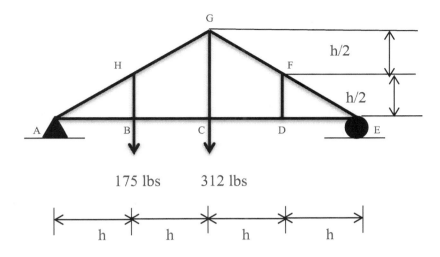

175 lbs   312 lbs

(A) 588 lbs (Compression)

(B) 644 lbs (Tension)

(C) 588 lbs (Tension)

(D) 644 lbs (Compression)

36) If the weight of the beam is 100 N/m, find the support reactions at Points A and B:

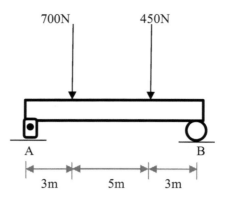

(A) Not enough information to determine

(B) Ay = 1,072N, By = 1,068N

(C) Ay = 1,182N, By = 1,068N

(D) Ay = 1,182N, By = 1,034N

37) In general, converting an area of light underbrush woods to a ½ acre lot multi housing apartment complex will have what effect on time of concentration and amount of runoff?

(A) Increase time of concentration and decrease runoff.

(B) Decrease runoff and increase time of concentration

(C) Increase time of concentration and increase runoff.

(D) Decrease time of concentration and increase runoff.

38) One line passes through the points (0, –4) and (–1, –7) while another line passes through the points (3, 0) and (–3, 2). What can be determined about these lines?

(A) Parallel

(B) Perpendicular

(C) Not enough information to determine

(D) The lines intersect

39) A particle's motion is tracked and plotted in the following diagram. Calculate the particle's acceleration between points
B & C?

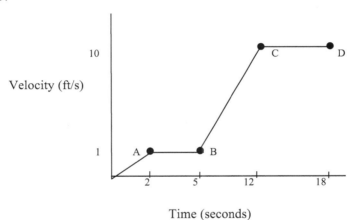

Time (seconds)

(A) 12 ft/s²

(B) 1.3 ft/s²

(C) 2.5 ft/s²

(D) .7 ft/s²

40) The car in the following diagram collides with the spring. If the spring deflects 1.5 meters, what was the velocity of the car before impact?

Velocity =?

Mass of Car = 75 kg
Spring constant = 10 kN/m

(A) 13 m/s

(B) 21 m/s

(C) 17 m/s

(D) 39 m/s

41) The station of the P.I. is most nearly:

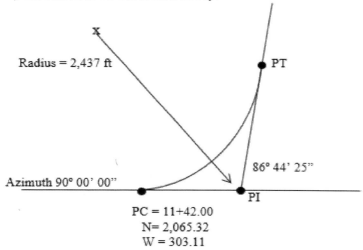

Radius = 2,437 ft

PT

86° 44' 25"

Azimuth 90° 00' 00"

PI

PC = 11+42.00
N= 2,065.32
W = 303.11

(A) 34+44.14

(B) 32+41.18

(C) 37+14.12

(D) 31+39.78

42) The maximum tensile principal stress in MPa for the two-dimensional stress state given is:

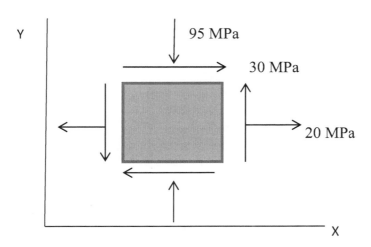

(A) 20

(B) 27.5

(C) 40

(D) 102.5

43) A brittle specimen is loaded in tension in the figure below with an applied stress of 250 psi, what is the resulting stress intensity for the crack?

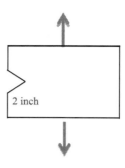

2 inch

(A) 978 psi • in$^{1/2}$

(B) 688 psi • in$^{1/2}$

(C) 88 psi • in$^{1/2}$

(D) 458 psi • in$^{1/2}$

44)   Find the tip deflection of the cantilevered beam shown from the distributed load of 11,379 N/m. The beam is 3.7 m long. Assume $E{\cdot}I$ is 3.47×10^6 N • m^2

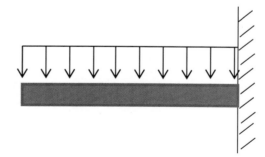

(A) .0007 m

(B) .007 m

(C) .077 m

(D) .7 m

45) A titanium rod with a cross sectional area of 20 in² is shown in the figure below. When the rod is placed under the tension force shown, what is the elongation (inches)? (Modulus of elasticity (E) = 16 x 10⁶ lb/in²)

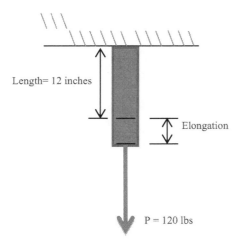

(A) .00045 in

(B) .000045 in

(C) .0000045 in

(D) .0000054 in

46) A steel beam with a length of 3 m is heated from 45 °C to 55 °C. If the coefficient of thermal expansion of steel is 0.000016 (m/m°C), what is the thermal deformation due to the change in temperature?

(A) .048 m

(B) .00048 m

(C) .0048 m

(D) .000048 m

47) Calculate the tangential (hoop) stress for a thick-walled cylinder pressure vessel shown below that is subject to an internal pressure of 5,000 psi: (Assume it is not a thinned-walled vessel) $r_i = .25$ inch, $r_o = .45$ inch

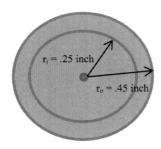

(A) 6,490 psi

(B) 4,950 psi

(C) 10,000 psi

(D) 9,450 psi

48) The standard tensile test curve can determine all the following, except:

(A) S-N plot

(B) Yield strength

(C) % Elongation

(D) Ultimate tensile strength

49) Which of the following processes is a technique used to increase the strength and lower the ductility of a metal by plastically deformation.

(A) Annealing

(B) Stress relieving

(C) Cold working

(D) Differential hardening

50) In a flow through a straight, smooth pipe, the Reynolds number for transition to from laminar flow to turbulence flow is generally taken to be:

(A) 1500

(B) 2100

(C) 4000

(D) 250,000

51) Select the most efficient horsepower pump that can lift water against a head of 25 feet flowing at 5 ft³/s. (Assume pump efficiency = .72, and γ = 62.4 lb/ft³. Neglect all friction losses)

(A) 10 horsepower

(B) 19 horsepower

(C) 30 horsepower

(D) 20 horsepower

52) Find the velocity (ft/s) of the fluid in the pipe shown below?

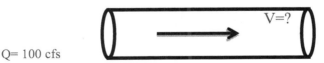

Q= 100 cfs

Area = 5 feet²

(A) .5 ft/s

(B) 20 ft/s

(C) 10 ft/s

(D) 15 ft/s

53) What is the pressure P_a just upstream of the pipe exit? (Assume: $x_1=$ 50m, $x_2=$ 15m, $x_3=$ 0, $\gamma = 9800$ N/m³)

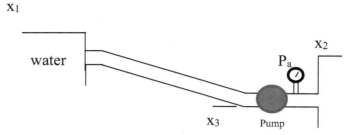

(A) 47,000 Pa

(B) 147,000 Pa

(C) 247,000 Pa

(D) 347,000 Pa

54) (1) Foreman, (2) Laborers, (1) Finisher are part of a concrete crew. The Foreman gets paid $65/hr., the laborer gets paid $28/hr, and the finisher gets paid $30/hr. The crew is able to place 38 CY of concrete per day. A work day is 8 hours per day.

For a certain project, the crew has to place 5,216 cubic feet of concrete. Find the total cost of labor?

(A) $3,678

(B) $5,931

(C) $7,248

(D) $9,042

55) For the given mass diagram below, which statement is correct?

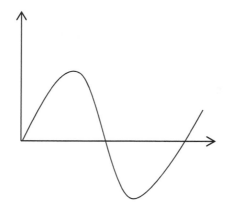

(A) Is a deficit earthwork operation

(B) Is an excess earthwork operation

(C) Is a balanced earthwork operation

(D) Cannot determine from the diagram

56) Mass haul diagrams help determine which of the following:

(A) Stations

(B) Cut

(C) Fill

(D) All of the above

57) If the depth of flowing water in a channel with Manning's roughness of .03 and an average bed slope of .65% is 3 feet, the velocity (ft/s) of the water would be most nearly:

Assume: Wetted perimeter: 220 ft
Area = 1,200 ft²

3 ft

2 feet

Channel Section:

NTS

(A) 1.8 ft/s

(B) 2.4 ft/s

(C) 9.1 ft/s

(D) 12.4 ft/s

) A retaining wall is being designed for the soil below. The effective horizontal force is most nearly:

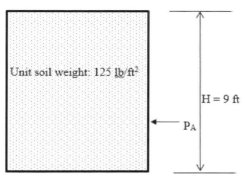

Unit soil weight: 125 lb/ft²

H = 9 ft

P$_A$

Angle of internal friction: 80°

(A) 12 lb

(B) 20 lb

(C) 32 lb

(D) 41 lb

59) Given a sand sample with a V$_V$ = 120 and V$_S$ = 105, the void ratio of the sand is most nearly:

(A) 0.2

(B) 1.14

(C) 2.5

(D) 3.18

60) The weight of the steel in the building below is most nearly:

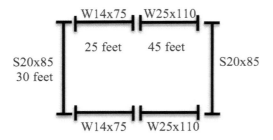

Building Plan View:
(Not to scale)

(A) 14,950 lbs

(B) 16,150 lbs

(C) 18,750 lbs

(D) 22,450 lbs

61) A sewerage treatment plant has an average flow of 15 M-gal/day and a peak to average flow ratio of 2.75. Determine the total volume of an aerated wash chamber if detention time is 2 min.

(A) 6,620 ft³

(B) 7,620 ft³

(C) 8,620 ft³

(D) 9,620 ft³

62) CO_2 is being released at a rate of 650 ppb from a certain manufacturing company as part of its internal processes. If the pressure is 3 (atm) at a temperature of 145°C, the Air Pollution (ug/m³) is most nearly:

(A) 11,901

(B) 17,998

(C) 19,352

(D) 21,794

62B) A sign is supported by a diagonal cable and a rigid horizontal bar. If the sign has a mass of 35 kg, then determine the tension in the diagonal cable that supports its weight?

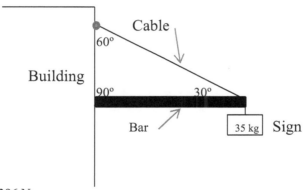

(A) 396 N

(B) 400 N

(C) 590 N

(D) 686 N

(E) 829 N

62C) If the sign in the diagram below has a mass of 18 kg, then what is the tensional force in each cable?

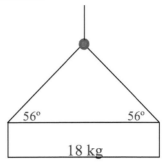

(A) 345 N

(B) 18 N

(C) 598 N

(D) 212 N

(E) 106 N

62D) For the footing shown below, the equation which represents the Factor of Safety against Overturning is:

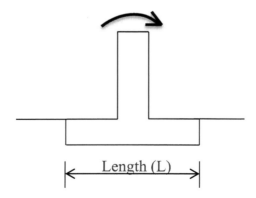

(A) FS$_{overturning}$ = ΣF$_R$/ F$_O$

(B) FS$_{overturning}$ = ΣM$_R$/ M$_O$

(C) FS$_{overturning}$ = ΣV(tanØ +BC$_a$ +P$_{p)}$

(D) FS$_{overturning}$ = Q$_{ULT}$ / Q$_{TOE}$

62E) The volume (CY) of soil is most nearly:

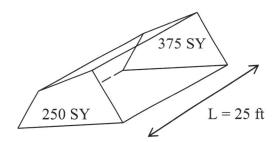

(A) 7,813

(B) 3,564

(C) 4,959

(D) 2,604

62F) A bike tire has a radius of 50 cm. If the tire is rotating at 350 rpm, the ratio of the tangential velocity at the midpoint of any spoke with the tangential velocity at the tire's circumference is most nearly:

(A) Half

(B) Triple

(C) Quadruple

(D) Zero

Solutions to Exam # 1:

Solution to Question # 1:

You do not need the handbook for this type of question. It's simply testing your basic engineering skills. Don't run off searching for formulas, think like an engineer first! This is one of those problems that you can just reason it out. Don't freak out because it looks like a mechanical engineering problem.

What is the problem really asking me? What is it testing me on that I should know? This is the first type of problem categories I was referring to on page 42. The FE Exam might be loaded with this type of question.

Pressure = Force / Area *(refer to page 131 (137 of 502) of the FE Handbook):*

This is one of those basic equations you just need to know.

Therefore:

1500 psi = Force / $[\pi (1.5)^2/4]$ (Area of a circle is $\pi d^2/4$)

1500 psi (1.76 in^2) = Force

Force = 2640 lb (acting on the piston)

Therefore:

Pressure = Force / Area

20,000 psi = 2640 lb / Area

Area = 2640 lb / 20,000 psi

Area = .132 in^2

The answer is (A) .132 in^2.

You do not need the handbook to solve this type of problem. It only involves basic math. Time to think like an engineer!

Don't run off searching for formulas. Draw what you know from the information given:

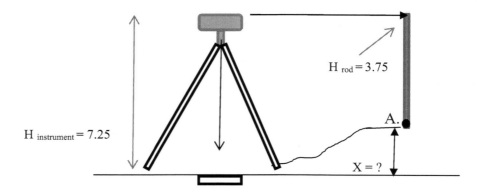

$H_{rod} = 3.75$

A.

$H_{instrument} = 7.25$

$X = ?$

Benchmark (EL = 192.23)

You would like to find the distance "X" so it can be added to the benchmark elevation to get the elevation at Point A.

X = Instrument height – Rod height (Obvious from the picture)

X = 7.25 – 3.75

X = 3.5

Therefore:

Point A = 192.23 + 3.5

= 195.73

The answer is (B) 195.73.

Solution to Question # 3:

Don't run off looking for equations again. Just think about this like an engineer. No work is required. Very basic engineering fundamentals here you'll be tested on.

It's testing to see if you understand that only the y-components of the tension in the cables relate to the Force of the box – since the Force is pointing down.

Let's sum forces in the Y-Direction:

The y-component of $F_{wire\ A}$ = F $_{Wire\ A}$ $(\cos 43°)$

(use cos not sine here. 90-43 = 47. Or you can take the sin 47)

(Note: the x-component is F $_{Wire\ A}$ $(\sin 43°)$)

The y-component of $F_{wire\ B}$ = F $_{Wire\ B}$ (It's already pointing down, no angle)

The y-component of $F_{wire\ C}$ = F $_{Wire\ c}$ $(\cos 32°)$

Therefore,

The answer is (D) F = F $_{Wire\ A}$ $(\cos 43°)$ + F $_{Wire\ B}$ + F $_{Wire\ C}$ $(\cos 32°)$

Solution to Question # 4:

No calculations are needed for this type of questions. Just reason through it.

The simply supported beam with only one force at mid-span acting downwards will have reactions at the supports acting upwards.

Therefore, the shear diagram will rise at the supports, be constant across until mid-span where the force is located. The shear diagram will drop vertically at mid span and then be constant again until the support at the end. Remember, shear is zero at the maximum moment in this example at mid span.

The moment diagram is a diagonal line, since the shear diagram was vertical and horizontal lines.

(Note: If the beam had a distributed load across it, the shear diagram would have a diagonal line, and then the moment diagram will be a parabola)

Answer is (A).

Solution to Question # 5:

Did you choose (A) 3,840? 3,840 is the total load on the beam, but the problem is looking for the load per foot (lb/ft) on the beam!

Don't need the handbook for this question. It's basic. Think like an engineer. Draw a simple picture of what this looks like because this is a straightforward problem. They give you the dimensions of the wall and the unit weight. Therefore, you can find the total weight on the beam.

The problem is looking for the load per foot (lb/ft).

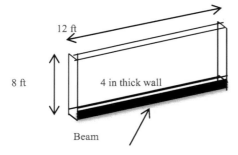

12 ft

8 ft

4 in thick wall

Beam

The volume of the wall is:

V = Height x Length x thickness

V = (8ft) (12ft) (4 in) (1ft/12in)   (Note: convert inches to feet)

V = 32 ft^3

Since the unit weight is given as 120 lb/ft^3, the total load is:

Total Load = 120 lb/ft^3 (32 ft^3)

= 3,840 lb   (The beam is 12 ft long, therefore, the load per foot is)

= 3,840 lb / 12 ft

= 320 lb/ft

Before choosing your answer, reread the question to make sure you know what they are looking for…

The answer is (D) 320

Solution to Question # 6:

Refer to page 47 (53 of 502) of the FE Handbook: L'Hospital's Rule

Just take the derivative and then plug in 2.

$$\lim_{x \to 2} \frac{x^2 + x - 6}{x^2 - 3x + 2}$$ (*Remember x becomes 1 and a constant becomes 0*)

$$= \frac{2x + 1}{2x - 3} \quad = \frac{2(2) + 1}{2(2) - 3} \quad = \frac{4 + 1}{4 - 3} \quad = 5$$

The answer is (C) 5

Solution to Question # 7:

Refer to page 101 (107 of 502) of the FE Handbook: Particle Kinematics:

Realize that Velocity is a derivative of distance, and that acceleration is just a derivative of velocity. Jerk is a derivative of acceleration. Yes, that's a real thing.

Find the velocity (which simply means take a derivative of the distance equation which is given)

$D = 10t^4 - t^3$

$V = (4)10t^3 - (3)t^2$

Now, when t = 3: (substitute "3" in for time)

$V = 40t^3 - 3t^2$

$V = 40(3)^3 - 3(3)^2$

$V = 40(27) - 27$

$V = 1,053$

The answer is (A) 1053.

(Note: If the question wanted to know the acceleration after a certain time, just simply take another derivative of the velocity to find the acceleration)

Solution to Question # 8:

Refer to page 290 (296 of 502) of the FE Handbook: Rational Formula

You bet this is on the exam.

$Q_p = CIA$

Plug and chug. But watch units if the problem gives you weird units.!

$Q_p = .85(7.8 \text{ in/hr})(2.75 \text{ Acre})$

$Q_p = 18 \text{ ft}^3/\text{s}$

The answer is (C) 18

Solution to Question # 9:

Refer to page 267 (273 of 502) of the FE Handbook: USCS.

USCS Table. Make sure that you use the Unified Soil Classification System as the question stated. Do not use the AASHTO Soil Classification System on the previous page.

62% pass the 200 sieve, therefore the material is a Fine-grained soil. The liquid limit is given as 70; therefore the material has to be MH, CH, or OH.

To determine the material, you must use the Atterburg plot on the same page – the chart at the bottom.

To find the plasticity index, use the equation:

PI = LL- PL

PI = 70 – 20

PI = 50

Plot LL of 70 versus PI of 50 and the result is above the "A" line. The symbol is CH. (CH is a high plastic clay and sandy clay).

The answer is (C) CH

Solution to Question # 10:

Refer to page 63 (69 of 502) of the FE Handbook: Sample Standard Deviation: Middle of page.

This problem is testing to you see if can decipher the complicated looking Standard Deviation equation in the handbook. It's simple and easy to set up using a table:

X = each number
M = mean of the all the values: 3+2+7= 12/3 =4

X	M	$(X - M)$	$(X - M)^2$
3	4	-1	1
2	4	-2	4
7	4	3	9

Now, apply the formula:

S^2 = 1/ (n-1) (sum $(X - M)^2$)   (Note: N-1 = 3 -1 = 2)

S^2 = (1+4+9) / (2)

S^2 = (14) / (2)

S^2 = 7   (Now, take square root of each side)

SD = 2.6

The answer is (C) 2.6.

Solution to Question # 11:

Refer to page 183 (189 of 502) of the FE Handbook: Head loss due to Flow.

This is the second type of problem I said to know how to look up the formula quickly.

h_f = fLv^2/ 2Dg

What do we know from the problem?

We know:

L = 1500 ft

(Be sure to look at the schematic for extra information! Not just the word problem)

V = 10 fps
D = .5 ft   (The Inner Diameter is shown on the schematic)
E = .00006
RE = 10^5

All we have to do now is find the Friction Factor, f, using the Roughness (E) and the RE.

Refer to page 201 (207 of 502) of the FE Handbook: The Moody Diagram.

Moody, Darcy, or Stanton Friction Factor Diagram

f = .018   E = .00006

RE = 10^5

(Note: Once you find E, just follow its curve upwards until you reach the RE value going up vertical, then read to the left side of the chart for f)

Now it's just plug & chug:

$h_f = fLv^2 / 2Dg$

$h_f = (.018)(1500 \text{ ft})(10 \text{ fps})^2 / 2(.5 \text{ ft})(32.2 \text{ ft/s}^2)$

$h_f = 83.85$ ft

= 84 ft

Note: This was a warmup problem. I could have given you Q but not the Velocity. You would need to calculate V by the formula Q = VA. I gave you the diameter, remember.

Step Further: If I didn't give you the Reynolds #, You would need to use the formula:

RE = VD/v which is underneath the Moody Diagram on the x-axis. To find little v, which is the Kinematic Viscosity, use the Chart on page 200 (206 of 502) of the FE Handbook. Go look at that chart now…It's a great chart.

In order to know what that is you must have the temperature of the water. The problem will give it to you. Slick, right? But I made it easy and just gave you the RE. Also note, page 200 is in English units, the SI chart is on the page before.

Even Step Further: I gave you the Relative Roughness (E)- but if I didn't, the formula is:

E = e/D, It's also shown on the Moody Diagram on the right hand side and e can be found on the table below the Moody Diagram for different types of pipe.

Now you know how to work many variations for Darcy Equation problems.

The answer is (D) 84 ft

Solution to Question # 12:

Refer to page 64 (70 of 502) of the FE Handbook: Permutations and Combinations:

The number of different *permutations* of *n* distinct objects *taken r at a time* is:

$P(n, r) = n! / [(n-r)!]$

$P(4, 2) / = 4! / [(4-2)!)]$

$P(4, 2) / = 4! / (2!)$

$= 4(3)2! / (2!)$ (note: the 2! cancel out on top and bottom)

$= (4)(3)$

$= 12$

$P(5, 3) = n! / [(n-r)!]$

$P(5, 3) / = 5! / [(5-3)!)]$

$P(5, 3) / = 5! / (2!)$

$= 5(4)(3)2! / (2!)$

$= 5(4)(3)$

Therefore: 12•60 = 720.

The answer is (A) 720.

Solution to Question # 13:

Refer to page 262 of the FE handbook: Mohr-Coulomb Failure.

Those sneaky test developers hid this at the bottom of the page. And also, if you searched for "angle of internal friction" it doesn't find a match. You need to search for "internal friction" to find it on the next page which shows you what the variables mean. But look at the equation in the diagram on page 262. See the games they play.

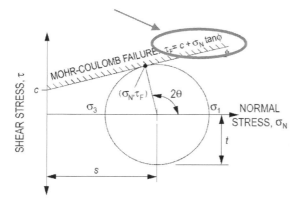

$t_f = C + Theta_n \tan\emptyset$

$52kPa = 32kPA + 38kPA \tan\emptyset$

All you have to do is rearrange the equation to solve for the internal friction.

$\tan \emptyset = 52 -32/38$

Now take the arc tan of this:

$\emptyset = \tan^{-1} (52 -32/38)$ (make sure you press 2nd on your calculator to get $\tan^{-1}$)

$\emptyset = 27.8°$

The answer is (D) 28 °

Solution to Question # 14:

Refer to page 310 of the FE Handbook: Construction. CPM Precedence Relationships.

This is a construction management critical path problem. These are easy to solve if you set up a simple diagram. Draw a network logic diagram. From the problem, you should have drawn something similar to this: Just note which activities are preceding.

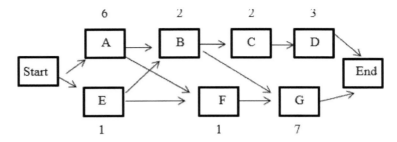

The next step is to list tour all paths through the network. The longest path is the critical path.

Path	Durations	Total
Start-A-B-C-D-Finish	6+2+2+3	13
Start-A-B-G-Finish	6+2+7	15
Start-A-F-G-Finish	6+1+7	14
Start-E-B-C-D-Finish	1+2+2+3	8
Start-E-B-G-Finish	1+2+7	10
Start-E-F-G-Finish	1+1+7	9

The answer is 15 weeks, based on the fact that Start-A-B-G-Finish has a duration of 15 weeks, and that is the longest durations of any path – which is the critical path.

The answer is (C) 15 weeks.

Solution to Question # 15:

Refer to page 35 of the FE Handbook: Straight Line: Top of Page. But you shouldn't need it.

Let's put the equation that's given, $3y + 2x = 6$, in the general form $y = mx + b$ so we can find the slope. (m = the slope).

$3y + 2x = 6$
$3y = -2x+6$
$y = -2x/3 + 6/3$
$y = -2x/3 + 2$

ok, so the slope of this line is -2/3. (The slope is what # is in front of the x)

The problem asks for a line that is **perpendicular** to this line, therefore, by definition, the slopes of these two lines are negative reciprocals of each other.

Since we now know that -2/3 is the slope of the line, the negative reciprocal of + 3/2.

If the problem stated that the lines were parallel to each other, the slopes would have been the same, not negative reciprocals.

The answer is (A) m = 3/2

Solution to Question # 16:

Refer to page 107 (113 of 502) of the FE Handbook: Potential Energy:

They are testing your understanding that the total Energy of the ball before hitting the spring has to equal the total Energy after compressing the spring. Energy is conserved.

Let's figure out the ball's total energy at Point A:

The Total E is equal to the Kinetic Energy (because it's moving) and the Potential Energy (because it's 5ft off the ground)

E total = ½ MV² + MgH
E total = ½ (1800/32.2)(7²) + (1800/32.2)(32.2)(5ft)
E total = 1370 ft lbs + 9000 ft lbs
E total = 10,370 ft lbs

At Point B, there will be negative Frictional Force, so = -5(200 + 165) = -1825 ft lbs

Energy (Point B) = 10,370 ft lbs -1825 ft lbs

  = 8,545 ft lbs

At Point C, when the spring compresses to its max point, the energy went into compressing the spring and also a small amount of frictional force.

8545 = ½ kx² + 5x (The spring compresses 3 feet -from the problem, x = 3ft)
8545 = ½ k 3² + 5(3) (Most people miss the 5(3) here)
8545 = 4.5(k) +15
8545 = 4.5(k) + 15
k = 1,896 lb/ft

The answer is (B) 1,896 lb/ft

Solution to Question # 17:

At first glance, it looks like a very hard problem, doesn't it? Looks like a vertical curve design on page 300 (306 of 502).

Well, time again to start thinking like an engineer on each of these problems.

The problem wants to know the horizontal distance between PVI 1 and PVI 2. Since the stations are given at each point, just simple subtract the stations to find the distance. In surveying, to find the linear distance between two points, you just subtract the station numbers.

Distance = 54+00 - 38+00

D = 5400 – 3600 = 1600.

= 1,600 feet

Don't be psyched out by how complicated the problem appears to be at first. Look at the drawing and think first before writing it off as being too difficult.

The answer is (B) 1,600

Solution to Question # 18:

Use basic engineering on this one.

Load on EACH wall from dead and live loads is:

$L_1 = (36 \text{ ft}/2)(10 \text{ psf} + 5 \text{ psf})$

(Note: each wall only sees half of the 36 ft – to get the load per foot on the outside wall edge- That's the trick on this problem.)

$L_1 = 18 \text{ ft} (15 \text{ psf})$
$L_1 = 270 \text{ lb/ft}$

The wall itself also has a dead load:

$L_2 = 45 \text{ psf} (12 \text{ ft})$
= 540 lb/ft

Total load: 270 + 540 = 810 lb/ft

The answer is (B) 819

Solution to Question # 19:

Refer to page 263 of the FE Handbook. Horizontal Stress Profiles and Forces.

$K_a = \text{Tan}^2 (45 – Ø/2)$

$K_a = \text{Tan}^2 (45 – 34/2)$

$K_a = \text{Tan}^2 (28)$ (take the Tan on the calculator)

$K_a = .5317$ (now square it)

= .2827

The answer is (C) .28

<u>Solution to Question # 20:</u>

This is basic surveying. Not in the handbook but you should know.

Height of Instrument (HI) = Known elevation + Back sight (BS)

HI = 3ft + 10.25 FT = 13.25 ft

Turning Point (TP) = Height of Instruction (HI) – Foresight (FS)

 Point B = 13.25 ft – 6.85 = 6.4 ft

The answer is (D) 6.4 ft

<u>Solution to Question # 21:</u>

<u>Refer to page 4 (10 of 502) of the FE Handbook</u>: Code of Ethics

Read the Fast Track Section on Ethics to see how to solve these types of problems. Basically, this should be common sense, but you should always do what is right- what your heart says to do. It is your duty as an engineer to be ethical and never succumb to pressure from the schedule, taking short cuts, clients, or your boss. NEVER! It is your job to provide safety to the public as the engineer of record or any design that you do. Always play it straight in these problems.

The answer is (B) Explain the situation to your supervisor and refuse to certify it.

<u>Solution to Question # 22:</u>

<u>Refer to page 4 of the FE Handbook</u>: Code of Ethics

Always choose to fix the problem. Do not take short cuts! Always go by the book.

The answer is (D) Fix the problem, no matter what it costs, and even if your supervisor tells you to ignore it.

 <u>Solution to Question # 23:</u>

<u>Refer to page 4 of the FE Handbook</u>: Code of Ethics

Answer is (D) Public welfare.

<u>Solution to Question # 24:</u>

<u>Refer to page 15 (21 of 502) of the FE Handbook:</u> GHS. Top of Page.

Look up question.

The answer is (B) GHS

Solution to Question # 25:

Refer to page 47 of the FE Handbook (Page 53 of 502 on the PDF): Integral Calculus.

$$V = \pi \int_{0}^{1} (x^2 - x^4)\, dx$$

$$V = \pi \left[(x^3/3) - (x^5/5) \right] \Big|_{0}^{1}$$

(Note: Remember to add 1 to the exponent and then divide by the same number: x^2 becomes $x^3/3$ and x^4 becomes $x^5/5$)

$$V = \pi \left[(1^3/3) - (1^5/5) \right] - \left[(0^3/3) - (0^5/5) \right]$$

(Note: Now plug in the values, subtract from each other, and solve)

$$V = \pi \left[(1/3) - (1/5) \right]$$

$$V = 2\pi/15$$

The answer is (D) $2\pi/15$.

Solution to Question # 26:

Refer to page 263 of the FE Handbook: Effective Stress.

The effective vertical stress at point P = 119 lb/f^3 x 5 ft = 595 lb/ft^2

Note: since no water is present, there's no uplift, the total effective stress is the same as total effective.

The answer is (A) 595 lb/ft^2

Solution to Question # 27:

Refer to page 230 (236 of 502) of the FE Handbook: Economics:

The table at the top of the page. There are two ways to approach solving these type questions. You can use the formula or the symbol to solve this kind of problem. We recommend to use the symbols.

Method 1 (Using Symbols and the compound interest rate tables, *the Preferred Method*)

Right off the bat you can eliminate answer choice (A) of $94.75 because you will not have LESS THAN $100 -the amount that you originally had. The question does not assume inflation or stock market losses.

The question gives you the present value (P) of the amount that you invest today, which is $100. The question wants to know what the future value (F) will be worth a year from now if the interest rate is 6%.

Therefore, you know P=$100, i% = 6%, n= 1 year

We are trying to calculate the future value (F).

Using the symbol from the table which falls under the "Convert" column "F given P":

(Note: It makes sense to read "F/P" as "I'm trying to calculate what the future value "F" will be if I already know what the present value "P" is. Or simply "I want to know F if I am given P". It does not mean F is divided by P. Come on! I hope you didn't think that 😊.)

The equation for F given P is:

(F/P, i%, n)   (n = # of years)

Therefore:

 (F/P, 6%, 1 yr)

Now, using the compound interest rate Factor Table at the bottom of the page 235 (241 of 502) for I = 6% , find the value of "F/P", which is the 4th column over, that corresponds with n = 1.

The value from the chart is 1.0600   (Don't continue until you really find it. These problems are so easy)

Therefore:

Future value (F) = $100(F/P, 6%, 1 yr)

(F) = $100 (1.0600)   (Note: just plug in the value we found from the table:)

(F) = $106

Method 2 (using the equation on page 230)

From the table, 4th column from the left, the formula is:

$(1+i)^n$

$(1+6\%)^1$

(1+.06)

(1.06)

Now, multiply that value by the present value:

F = $100 (1.06)

F = $106

The answer is (B) $106.

Solution to Question # 28:

Refer to page 236 (242 of 502) of the FE Handbook: 10% Interest Table: Bottom Table.

You should be able to determine that answer choice (C) can be eliminated because the amount has to be LESS THAN $10,000 -the amount will have in 5 years.

Method 1: The symbol for P given F is: [Note: We are using "P given F" because we are trying to calculate P and we were given F (=$10,000)]

(P/F, i%, n) (Now, plug in what we know)

(P/F, 10%, 5)

Using the factor table for 10% on page 236, Look for the value of P/F for: i=10% and n = 5 years. You should see that P/F = .6209   (Don't continue until you really find it.)

Therefore:

F = $10,000 (given in the question):

$P = F (P/F, i\%, n)$
$P = (\$10,000)(0.6209)$
$P = \$6,209$

Method 2: Using equation on page 230 of the FE Handbook, under P given F

$P = F (1 + i)^{-n}$
$P = (\$10,000) (1 + 0.1)^{-5}$
$P= \$6,209$

The answer is (B) $6,209

Solution to Question # 29:

Just use basic engineering on this problem:

Factored load:

Dead load = 750(10)(1.3) = 9,750 lb = 9.8 kips

Live load = (7 + 3+ 2)(1.8) = 21.6 kips = 22 kips

Total: 9.8 kips + 22 kips =31.8 kips = 32 kips

Unfactored load:

Dead load = 750(10) = 7500 lb = 7.5 kips

Live load = (7 + 3+ 2) = 12 kips

Total: 7.5 kips + 12 kips = 19.5 kips = 20 kips

The answer is (C) 32 kips, 20 kips

Solution to Question # 29B:

Refer to page 231 (237 of 502) of the FE Handbook: Straight-line depreciation. Middle of page.

The equation is:

$$D_j = (C - S_n)/n$$

Givens:

Cost (C) = $9,000
n = 10 year life
S_n = Salvage value = $200

Therefore:

D = ($9000-$200) / 10

D =$880 per year

*(Note: Be careful, this equation gives you the depreciation value **per year**)*

(Also Note: If the question wanted to know the "Book Value", the formula is on the same page, BV = initial cost – D_j)

The answer is (D) $880/ year

Solution to Question # 30:

Refer to page 231 of the FE Handbook: Break–even: Top of Page.

Break even means that "Earnings = Cost"

(Read that paragraph, it says income will just cover the expenses)

C= $15,000 + 0.03 • P

(2.5P) = 15000 + 0.03 • P   (substitute 2.5P for C, because it says each item P is $2.5)

Solve for P:

(2.5P) - .03P = $15,000

2.47P = $15,000

P = 6,072.87

The answer is (B) 6,073

Solution to Question # 31:

Refer to page 94 (100 of 502) of the FE Handbook: Force: Top Left of Page.

The answer is **(D) All of the above.**

Solution to Question # 32:

Refer to page 94 of the FE Handbook: Statics.

You shouldn't need to use the handbook for basic statics problems. Just one of those things you must know by heart. It's easy but takes some practice.

Just draw your reaction forces (Remember: a hinge like on the left side will have a X and Y reaction force; a Roller like on the right side will only have a Y reaction. Also, assume its direction up/down/right/left, if your answer comes out positive then you chose the correct direction, but if it comes out negative, then you need to reverse your direction. Don't worry I'll show you everything you need to know in this one problem).

Here's the problem drawn again:

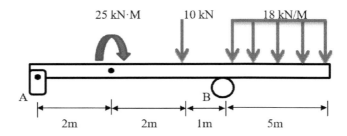

Ok, Let's draw a force diagram: Next Page.

First step is to draw Ay and By acting upwards. I'm assuming the direction is up at this point. I would also redraw the beam with just a line to make it easy to see. Also, I drew Ax acting to the right. It doesn't matter right now which way it goes.

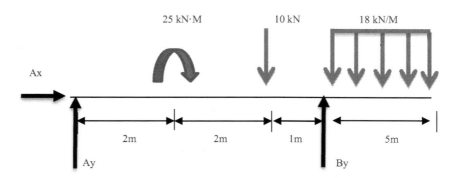

Before you can begin solving this, you need to notice that there is a distributed load on the right of 18kN/M. This must be simplified into a point load first before moving on.

Multiply: The distributed load times its distance.

18kN/M (5M) = 90kN.   (90kN is now the force acting down on the beam)

But where does it go?   The new distance is equal to half of its original length:

5m/2 = 2.5m

You need to draw the 90kN acting down at half of the 5m which is shown. So 90kN is 2.5m away from By.

Like this:

We just simplified a distributed load into one single force acting at halfway of its length. Now, we can solve the problem.   Be careful, if it were a triangular load, the new single load would not be at half the distance, it would be at 1/3 the distance – which is a triangle's centroid. We'll do a problem like that later)

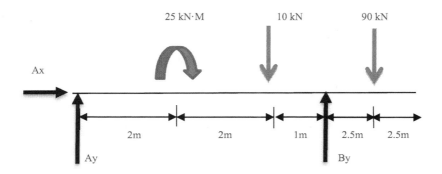

Now, I like to take moments about point A. That way, Ax and Ay cancel out. I'm assuming clockwise is positive. See my directional arrow below.

 $M_A = 0$

Here's the way you set it up:

The 25kNM is already a moment acting clockwise. So it's positive.

The 10kN force is 4m away from point A acting clockwise. (2m+2m = 4m)

By is 5m away from point A and acting counterclockwise so it's negative.

90kN is 7.5M away from point A and acting clockwise. (2m+2m+1m+2.5m)

Here's the equation: *(Don't move on until you know how I set this up)*

+25kNm + 10kN (2m+2m) -By (2m+2m+1m) + 90kN(2m+2m+1m+2.5m) = 0

Now simplify:

+25kNm + 10kN (4m) -By (5m) + 90kN(7.5m) = 0

Simplify again:

+25kNm + 40kNm -By (5m) + 675kNm = 0

Simplify again:

740kNm – By(5m) = 0   (Now solve for By)

740kNm = By(5m)

740kNm / 5m = By

By = 148kN   (Notice how it came out positive. That means we chose the correct direction which is up)

The answer is (B)148 kN

Ok, but let's go a step further. Let's say we want to know the value of Ay:

Let's just sum the forces in the Y-direction:

All the forces going up is positive while forces going down are negative.

Ay + 148kN – 10kN – 90kN = 0

Ay + 48kN = 0

Ay = -48kN   (ok, see how the answer came out negative! That means we assumed the wrong direction. It should be pointing down. So if the question wanted to know the direction of Ay, it's downwards).

Let's also find Ax.   Let's sum the forces in the X direction.

Ax = 0   (There are no other forces in the x direction)

Solution to Question # 33:

Refer to page 94 of the FE Handbook: Resolution of a Force: Middle of Page.

Simply solve for the component forces in both the x and y directions, square them, and take the square root to find the resultant force.

Pay extra attention to the direction of the forces, some may be positive or negative, we'll see this below.

First, since they didn't give us the angles, you need to use the slopes. The slopes are given for the 2 sides, so just solve for the hypotenuse for each triangle:

For the 211 lb force: $H = \sqrt{5^2 + 12^2} = 13$

For the 398 lb force: $H = \sqrt{4^2 + 3^2} = 5$

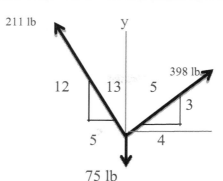

211 lb

y

12 13 5 398 lb

3

5 4

75 lb

Let's sum forces in the y-direction:

$\Sigma F_y = 0$: $R_y = 12/13(211) + 3/5(398) - 75 = 0$ (note how the components are positive except the 75 lb force because it is pointing down)

$R_y = 194.7 + 238.8 - 75 = 0$

$R_y = 358$ lb

In the x-direction:

$\Sigma F_x = 0$: $R_x = -5/13(211) + 4/5(398) = 0$ (notice how there is a negative sign in front of the 211 lb force because it is pointing to the left, Also the 75 lb does not have a x-component)

$R_y = -81 + 318 =$

$R_y = 237$ lb

Therefore:

$R = \sqrt{R_y^2 + R_x^2}$

$R = \sqrt{(358)^2 + (237)^2}$

$R = \sqrt{(358)^2 + (237)^2}$

$R = 429$ lb

The answer is (C) 429 lb.

Solution to Question # 34:

Refer to page 94 of the FE Handbook: Resolution of a Force: Middle of Page.

Since the person only exerts a force in the vertical direction, only the vertical component of the force in the support needs to be calculated, since that is the component which resists the person's weight. That's what they are testing you on.

Therefore:

$\Sigma F_y = 0$: -185 lb + 4/5(Force $_{support}$) = 0

(The vertical component is the sine of the angle. They didn't give the angle, so use the slope – opposite divided by hypotenuse)

4/5(Force $_{support}$) = 185 lb

Force $_{support}$ = 232 lb

The answer is (D) 232 lb.

(Note: Answer (A) could have been eliminated right away; the force in the support cannot be less than the person's weight. Since it is on a diagonal, the support must be working harder to support the weight.)

Solution to Question # 35:

Shouldn't need the Handbook. You went to engineering school. Think.

Let's sum forces in the horizontal direction:

$\Sigma x = 0$:   Ax = 0.

(There are no other forces in the x direction so Ax = 0, There is no X-component in the x direction at Point E because it is a roller. It only has a y-component)

If you sum forces in the vertical direction:

$\Sigma y = 0$:   Ay + Ey – 175 lb – 312 lbs = 0

However, this equation has 2 unknowns, Ay & Ey. We need to do something else. We only showed you this because sometimes you can quickly solve for a reaction just by summing forces.

We can use the method of joints very easily to solve this. Since the question asks for the force in member AH, we would like to know the forces Ax, Ay, AB, which are intersect at point A.

Therefore, let's take moments about point E. Force Ey goes directly through point E so it does not have a moment. It cancels out. The two forces acting down in the middle of the truss will have a moment. Ay will have a moment also. Ax and AB act directly through point E, so they will not have a moment. We can solve for Ay then!

Take moments about point E.

Everything clockwise will be positive:

 $M_E = 0$: Ay (4h) -175lb (3h) – 312lb (2h) = 0

$M_E = 0$: Ay (4h) -525h – 624h = 0

Ay (4h) -1149 = 0

Ay (4h) = 1149

Ay = 287.25 lb

(Since the answer came out positive, we picked the correct direction of force Ay)

Now, let's draw a free body diagram at point A.

Point A:

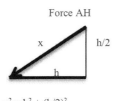

We drew Force AH acting downwards to counter act force AY acting upwards.

Now, let's sum forces in y direction to find Force AH:

$\Sigma\, y = 0$:   Ay – Force AH = 0

We simply need to find the y (vertical) component of Force AH. We need to take the sine of the angle. Not the cos like we did in the previous problem. It all depends on where the angle is that you are using. In this case, since they didn't give us the actual angle, just use opposite side divided by hypotenuse. h/2 comes from the original diagram, see the length on the right-hand side of the page.

First, let's use Pythagorean theorem to find x.

Force AH

$x^2 = h^2 + (h/2)^2$

$x^2 = h^2 + (h^2/4)$ (basic math)

$x^2 = 4h^2/4 + (h^2/4)$ (note: be careful with adding fractions)

$x^2 = 5h^2/4$

$x = 1.12h$

Now, we can sum forces. We only did the first step because they didn't give us the angle

$\Sigma\, y = 0$:   Ay – Force AH = 0

         287.25 – Force AH (h/2 / 1.12h) = 0   (y-component is opposite/ hypotenuse)

         287.25 – Force AH (1/2 / 1.12) = 0   (can cancel out the h)

         287.25 – Force AH (.446) = 0

         287.25 = Force AH (.446)

         287.25 / .446 = Force AH

         644 lbs = Force AH   (compression)

Since it came out positive, we picked the correct direction.

Here's the part to remember: Since Force AH is pointing into point A, member AH will be in compression! Not tension. If the direction of Force AH was acting away from point A, then member AH would have been in tension.

Practice this problem again without looking to get used to the mechanics.

The answer is (D) 644 lbs (Compression)

Solution Question # 36:

You don't need the handbook for this: This is one of those things you just NEED to know how to do. The first step is to always draw a free body diagram (FBD) of all the forces. Obviously, you see the two forces of 700N & 450N on the beam. So, draw those first.

They are testing to see if you know how to set up the reaction forces at both ends. On the left side, it's pinned, so there's 2 components of the reaction, let's call it Ax and Ay. Ay will point up; it doesn't matter the direction of Ax. On the right side, it's a roller, so there's only 1 reaction in the y direction going up. Since it's rolling, there's no force in the x direction. Now, we're not done yet, there's one more force. What is it? The problem said that the beam weighs 100N per meter. This is called a distributed load. The weight is distributed across the entire length of the beam. The way you deal with distributed loads is by converting it to a point load at the center of the beam. A point load is one single load, like the 700N and the 450N.

So, if the weight is 100N per meter, and the total length of the beam is 11m, (look at the bottom of the diagram, add up: 3m + 5m + 3m = 11m. Always look for extra info on diagrams that might not be in the problem!), then the point load is: 100N/m (11m) = 1,100N   You need to place this load at the very center of the beam, which is half of 11m, and is 5.5m from the left side of the beam.

Ok, before you move on, please make sure you understand how to set this FBD up.

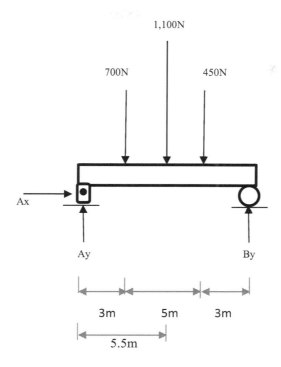

Now we can take Moments about the Points A and B to find it's reaction forces. Let's take a Moment about Point A. It's just the force x (times) the distance away.

$\Sigma Ma = 0$. (I'm assuming Clockwise rotation is +). Remember since we are taking Moments at point A, Ax and Ay do not induce a Moment at point A, only the 3 points loads on the beam and By.

$= 700N(3m) + 1100N(5.5M) + 450N(8m) - By(11m) = 0$

(Note: By has a negative sign because it's trying to rotate the beam counter-clockwise. It has a negative Moment).

Just do some math now, multiply $= 2100Nm + 6050Nm + 3600Nm - By(11m) = 0$

Add like terms: $11,750Nm - By(11m) = 0$

Add By(11m) to both sides in order to solve for By. $11,750Nm = By(11m)$

Divide by 11m both sides: $11750Nm/11m = By$

By= 1,068N

Now we need to find Ay. There's 2 ways to do this. I'll show you both ways. Since we know all the known forces except Ay, we do just sum forces in the Y-direction to find Ay. The other way is to just take another Moment about Point B this time.

First way: $\Sigma Fy = 0$.   Ay -700N – 1,100N – 450N + 1,068N = 0

Ay – 1,182N = 0

Ay = 1,182N

Let's sum Moments about point B to prove we get the same answer for Ay.

$\Sigma Mb = 0$.

= -450N(3m) – 1,100N(5.5m) – 700N(8m) + Ay(11m) = 0

(Note: Ax doesn't cause a Moment at point B)

= -1350Nm – 6050Nm – 5600Nm + Ay(11m) = 0

= -13,000Nm + Ay(11m) = 0

Ay (11m) = 13,000Nm

Ay = 1182N   (It's easier to just sum the Moments in the Fy direction)

The answer is (C) Ay = 1,182N, By = 1,068N

Solution to Question # 37:

Common sense also tells you that converting a wooded area to an area with concrete parking lots and apartments will increase runoff (the ground will not soak up the rainwater)

The answer is (D) Decrease time of concentration and increase runoff.

Solution to Question # 38:

Refer to page 35 of the FE Handbook: Straight Line:

The "Point Slope Form" of the equation for straight line ($m = y_2-y_1 / x_2-x_1$)

The first step is to find the values of the slopes.

If given 2 sets of points for a line, the slope (m) can be calculated by the equation:

$m = y_2-y_1 / x_2-x_1$

Therefore, the slope for the first line is calculated as:

$m_1 = (-7)-(-4) / -1 - 0$ (*Note: be careful adding and subtracting with negatives!*)

$m_1 = (-7) + (4) / -1$

$m_1 = (-3) / -1$

$m_1 = 3$

Now, the slope for the second line is calculated as:

$m_2 = (2)-(0) / (-3) - (3)$

$m_2 = (2) / (-3) + (-3)$

$m_2 = (2) / (-6)$

$m_2 = -1/3$

Notice how m_1 and m_2 are negative reciprocals to each other. (Meaning: The fraction is flipped upside down and changed signs). By definition, lines that have negative reciprocals slopes are perpendicular to each other. (Note: if m_1 and m_2 were equal, then the 2 lines would be parallel to each other)

The answer is (B) Perpendicular.

Solution to Question # 39:

Refer to page 101 of the FE Handbook: Particle Kinematics:

Acceleration is defined as:

$a = dv/dt$ (Note: "dv/dt" means the change in velocity divided by the change in time)

$a = \Delta v / \Delta dt$

$a = (V_{final} - V_{intial}) / (T_{final} - T_{intial})$

Given:

From the diagram between points B & C:

$V_{final} = 10$ ft/s

$V_{initial} = 1$ ft/s

$T_{final} = 12$ s

$T_{intial} = 5$ s

Therefore: just plug and chug from here. Watch units!

$a = (V_{final} - V_{intial}) / (T_{final} - T_{intial})$

$a = (10$ ft/s $- 1$ ft/s$) / (12$ s $- 5$s$)$

$a = (9$ ft/s$) / 7$ s

$a = 1.3$ ft/s^2

The answer is (B) 1.3 ft/s^2.

Solution to Question # 40:

Refer to page 107 of the FE Handbook: Potential Energy:

It doesn't seem like enough information to solve this problem, however, let's equate the kinetic energy of the car and the potential energy of the spring. (This can be done because energy cannot be created nor destroyed; only transferred from one form to another)

The spring's potential energy is:

$U = k\, x^2/2$ (Given: k = 10kN/m, x = 1.5 meter)

Therefore:

$U = k\, x^2/2$

$U = [(10kN/m)\ (1.5\ meter)^2]\ /\ 2$

$U = 11.25$ kN•m = 11,250 N•m

The Kinetic energy of the car is on the same page: Kinetic Energy:

$KE = \frac{1}{2}\, mv^2$

$KE = \frac{1}{2}\, (75\ kg)\ v^2$

Therefore, equating the 2 formulas:

$KE = PE$

$\frac{1}{2}\, (75\ kg)\ v^2 = 11,250$ N•m

$v^2 = 11,250$ N•m $/\ [\frac{1}{2}\, (75\ kg)]$

$v^2 = 300$ N•m / kg

$v = 17.3$ m/s

The answer is (C) 17 m/s.

Solution to Question # 41:

Refer to page 301 of the FE Handbook: Horizontal Curve

This problem is a very straight forward horizontal curve. But the handbook doesn't good a very good job of explaining this.

Station PC = Station PI – T

Station PI = Station PC + T

Let's calculate T:

$T = R \tan (I/2)$

$T = (2437 \text{ ft}) \tan (86° \ 44' \ 25'' \ / \ 2)$

Be careful, we need to convert the angle into decimal form FIRST:

86° 44' 25'':

$25''/60 + 44' = 44.42'$

$44.42'/60 = .74$

$86° + .74 = 86.74°$

Now,

$T = (2437 \text{ ft}) \tan (86.74° \ / \ 2)$

$T = (2437 \text{ ft}) (.945)$

$T = 2302.14 \text{ ft}$

Therefore:

Station PI = Station PC + T

Station PI = 11+42.00 + 2302.14

= 1142 +2302.14

= 3444.14

= 34+44.14

The answer is (A) 34+44.14

Solution to Question # 42:

Refer to page 132 of the FE Handbook: Stress and Strain, Principal Stresses: Middle of Page.

The equation to calculate the principal stress is:

$\sigma_x = 20 \text{ MPa}$

$\sigma_y = -95 \text{ MPa}$

$\tau_{xy} = 30 \text{ MPa}$

$$\sigma_{M_-} = \frac{\sigma_x + \sigma_y}{2} \pm \sqrt{\left(\frac{\sigma_x - \sigma_y}{2}\right)^2 + \tau_{xy}^2}$$

Compare the figure in the problem with the figure in the handbook to determine the variables. Notice how Theta y = -95 MPa, that is because the arrow is pointing down. Pay attention to the direction of the arrows to make them positive or negative.

$\sigma_m = = [(20 + (-95))/2] +/- \sqrt{[(20 - (-95)/2)^2 + 30^2]}$

$\sigma_m = = [-37.5] +/- \sqrt{[(3306.25) + 900]}$

$\sigma_m = = [-37.5] +/- \sqrt{[4206.25]}$

$\sigma_m = = [-37.5] +/- 65$

Therefore:

-37.5 + 65 = 27.5

-37.5 - 65 = -102.5

The answer is (B) 27.5 MPa.

Solution to Question # 43:

Refer to page 123 (129 of 502) of the FE Handbook: Fracture Toughness:

$K_i = y \cdot \sigma \cdot \sqrt{\pi (a)}$

Given:

y = 1.1

(from the figure in the problem statement, this is an exterior crack, not an interior crack in which y = 1)

σ = 250 psi

a = 2 inch (from the figure in the problem statement)

Therefore:

$K_i = y \cdot \sigma \cdot \sqrt{\pi (a)}$

$K_i = (1.1) \bullet (250 \text{ psi}) \bullet \sqrt{\pi (2 \text{ in})}$

$K_i = 275 \text{ psi} \bullet (2.5) \text{ in}^{1/2}$

$K_i = 688 \text{ psi} \bullet \text{in}^{1/2}$

The answer is (B) 688 psi • in$^{1/2}$.

Solution to Question # 44:

Refer to page 141of the FE Handbook: Cantilevered Beam Slopes and Deflections:

Recognize that the *FE Handbook* has common Beam loading diagrams with formulas for deflection already calculated for you! You **Do NOT** need to solve this from scratch! Find the figure on the left which matches the problem that has a cantilevered support with a distributed load across it. It is the 2rd figure down from the top.

Simply locate the reference loading diagram and just plug and chug. Pay special attention to units!

The equation from the handbook is:

$v_{max} = -w \bullet (L^4) / 8EI$

$v = \dfrac{-11,379 \text{ N/m} \bullet (3.7 \text{ m})^4}{8 (3.47 \times 10^6 \text{ N} \bullet \text{m}^2)}$

$v = -.077$ m (Note: the minus sign (-) means pointing downwards, which is common sense)

(Also note: If the problem didn't give you the E (Modulus of Elasticity), just look on page 138 (144 of 502) for the E of common materials!)

The answer is (C) .077 m.

Solution to Question # 45:

Refer to page 131 of the FE Handbook: Uniaxial Loading and Deformation:

The equation is:

Elongation = P (L) / (A) (E)   (This is one of those basic engineering formulas to memorize)

Given:

P = 120 lbs

L = 12 inches

A = 20 in^2

E = 16 x 10^6 lb/in^2

Now, plug in the values into the equation:

Elongation = (120 lbs) (12 inches) / (20 in^2) (16 x 10^6 lb/in^2)

Elongation = .0000045 in

Answer is (C) .0000045 in.

(Note: If the modulus of elasticity was not given in the problem, you can look up the value on page 138.)

Solution to Question # 46:

Refer to page 131 of the FE Handbook: Thermal Deformations: Bottom of Page.

The equation is:

Thermal Deformation = $\alpha \cdot L \cdot (T-T_0)$

Given:

L = 3m

T = 55 °C

T_0 = 45 °C

α = 0.000016 (m/m°C)

Substitute the values into the equation:

Thermal Deformation = $\alpha \cdot L \cdot (T-T_0)$

Thermal Deformation = 0.000016 (m/m°C) $\cdot$ (3m) $\cdot$ (55 °C - 45 °C)

Thermal Deformation = 0.000016 (m/m°C) $\cdot$ (3m) $\cdot$ (10 °C)

Thermal Deformation = .00048 m

Answer is (B) .00048 m.

(Note: If the coefficient of thermal expansion was not given in the problem, you can look up the value on page 138 for various types of materials.)

Solution to Question # 47:

Refer to page 131 of the FE Handbook: Cylindrical Pressure Vessel: Bottom of page.

For internal pressure only, the stresses at the inside wall are:

Hoop stress (tangential): $\sigma_t = P_i [(r_o^2 + r_i^2) / (r_o^2 - r_i^2)]$

$\sigma_t = 5000$ psi $[((.45 \text{ inch})^2 + (.25 \text{ inch})^2) / ((.45 \text{ inch})^2 - (.25 \text{ inch})^2)]$ (just substitute values from the problem statement)

$\sigma_t = 5000$ psi $[(.2025 \text{ inch}^2 + .0625 \text{ inch}^2) / ((.2025 \text{ inch}^2) - (.0625 \text{ inch}^2))]$

$\sigma_t = 5000$ psi $[(.265 \text{ inch}^2 / (.14 \text{ inch}^2)]$

$\sigma_t = 5000$ psi $[(1.89)]$

$\sigma_t = 9,450$ psi

The answer is (D) 9,450 psi.

(Note: If the vessel was thinned-walled, you can use the equation on page 132)

Solution to Question # 48:

Refer to page 122 of the FE Handbook: Tensile Test Curve:

Tensile Test determines the elastic modulus, Ductility, Tensile Strength, and Yield Strength.

The answer is (A) S-N plot

Solution to Question # 49:

Refer to page 117 of the FE Handbook Thermal and Mechanical Processing. Bottom of Page.

The answer is (C) Cold working.

Annealing consists of heating a metal to a specific temperature and then cooling at a rate that will produce a refined microstructure. It is most often used to soften a metal for cold working, to improve machinability, or to enhance properties like electrical conductivity.

Stress relieving is a technique used to remove or reduce the internal stresses created in a metal.

Differential hardening is a technique that allows different areas of a single object to receive different heat treatments. It is common in high quality knives and swords.

Solution to Question # 50:

Refer to page 182 of the FE Handbook Reynolds number.

The answer is (B) 2100. Although the critical Reynolds number sometimes varies, it is generally accepted as 2100.

Solution to Question # 51:

Refer to page 192 of the FE Handbook: Pump Power Equation:

Power (ft lb/s) = Q • γ • h • / n

Given:

Q = 5 ft³/s

h = 25 ft

n = .72

γ = 62.4 lb/ft³

(if γ was not given, simply look it up on the table on *page 199 (*Properties of Water)

If they gave you the temperature of the water, use it to find the specific weight for that temperature

Therefore:

Power (ft lb/s) = (5 ft³/s • 62.4 lb/ft³ • 25 ft) / .72

Power (ft lb/s) = 10,833.33 ft lb/s

However, be careful! The equation solved for the power in ft lb/s, not horsepower.

Let's convert to horsepower:

Refer to page 3 of the FE Handbook: Conversion Factors:

10,833.33 ft lb/s • (1.818 × 10⁻³)

= 19.69 horsepower   (therefore, select the 20 horsepower pump)

The answer is (D) 20 horsepower.

Solution to Question # 52:

Refer to page 181 of the FE Handbook: Fluids, One–Dimensional flows. Top of Page.

$Q = V \times A$

This is a basic equation you should know. Where Q is the flow rate of the fluid through the pipe, V is velocity of the fluid flow, and A is the cross-sectional area of the pipe.

Since Q and A were given in the problem, simply solve for V.

Q = V x A

100 ft³/second = V (5ft²)   (Watch your units, make sure they are consistent and will cancel out)

$$V = \frac{100 \text{ ft}^3/\text{second}}{(5 \text{ ft}^2)}$$

$V = 20$ ft/s

The answer is (B) 20 ft/s.

(Note: sometimes the problem will give you Q in (cfm) or the Area of the pipe in (in²), if so, pay attention to your units. May have to convert minutes to second and inches to feet in order to get a velocity in feet per second. In addition, sometimes the problem might give you Q in terms of a mass flow rate, (lbs/sec). In this case you have to divide by the fluids density in order to convert to a volumetric flow rate Q. This equation is also on *page 181 of the FE Handbook*.

Solution to Question # 53:

Refer to page 178 of the FE Handbook: Characteristics of a Static Liquid

Realize that the pressure at P_a inside the pipe is the same pressure outside the pipe at the same elevation: The pressure is simply due to static head pressure.

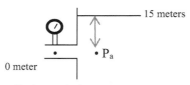

$P_a = \gamma \cdot h$ (Basic equation)

$P_a = 9800 \text{ N/m}^3 \cdot (15 \text{ meters} - 0 \text{ meters})$

$P_a = 9800 \text{ N/m}^3 \cdot (15 \text{ meters} - 0 \text{ meters})$

$P_a = 147,000 \text{ N/m}^2$

$P_a = 147,000 \text{ Pa}$ (Remember that N/m² = Pa)

The answer is (B) 147,000 Pa.

Solution to question # 54:

This is a basic quantity take off construction problem. Think. Be ready for easy questions like this on the exam. The crew can place 38 CY of concrete per day, convert this to cubic feet.

$38 \text{ yd}^3 (3^3 \text{ ft}^3/\text{yd}^3) = 38 \text{ yd}^3 (27 \text{ ft}^3/\text{yd}^3) = 1,026 \text{ ft}^3$

If the job requires 5,216 ft³, it will take them 6 days to complete:

$5,216 \text{ ft}^3 / 1,026 \text{ ft}^3 = 5.08$ days, so 6 days.

6 days (8 hr/day) = 48 hrs are required.

Total cost per hour: $65/hr + $28/hr (2) + $30/hr = $151/hr

Total labor:

$151/hr (48 hrs) = $7,248

The answer is (C) $7,248

Solution to Question # 55:

Refer to page 309 of the FE Handbook: Mass Haul Diagram.

The line continues up towards the end of the diagram which indicates excess. If it ends at the line, it would be balanced. If it ends below the line, it would be a deficit.

The answer is (B) Is an excess earthwork operation

Solution to Question # 56:

Refer to page 309 of the FE Handbook: Mass Haul Diagram.

The answer is (D) All of the above

Solution to Question # 57:

Refer to page 185 in the FE Handbook: Manning's equation.

$$V = (1.49/n)\ R^{2/3}\ \sqrt{s}$$

We know everything except R_H.

Givens:

n = .03

base (b) = 2 ft

depth (d) = 3 ft

slope (s) = .0065

Let's find R, the hydraulic radius.

R_H = A/P (on page 185 in the list of variables)

$R_H = 1{,}200 \text{ ft}^2 / 220 \text{ ft}$

$R_H = 5.5 \text{ ft}$

Therefore,

$$V = (1.49/n) \, R^{2/3} \, \sqrt{s}$$

$$V = (1.49/.03) \, (5.5)^{2/3} \, \sqrt{.0065}$$

$V = 49.6 \, (3.1) \, (.0806)$

$V = 12.4 \text{ ft/sec}$

(Note: make sure you use the x^y button on calculator to solve $(5.5)^{2/3}$

$V = 12.4 \text{ ft/s}$

The answer is (D) 12.4 ft/s

Solution to Question # 58:

Refer to page 263: Horizontal Stress Profiles and Forces:

$$P_A = 1/2 K_a \, \gamma \, H^2$$

We don't know K_a

$$
\begin{aligned}
K_a &= \text{Tan}^2 \, (45 - \varnothing/2) \\
&= \text{Tan}^2 \, (45 - 80/2) \\
&= \text{Tan}^2 \, (45 - 40) \\
&= \text{Tan}^2 \, (5) \\
&= .008
\end{aligned}
$$

$$P_A = 1/2 K_a \, \gamma \, H^2$$
$$P_A = 1/2 (.008)(125 \text{lb/ft}^2) \, (9\text{ft})^2$$
$$P_A = 41 \text{ lb}$$

The answer is (D) 41 lb

Solution to Question # 59:

Refer to page 259: Phase Relationships:

Void Ratio: Simple plug and chug. But for the exam, refer to the chart if the problem gives you Va or Vw in order to calculate Vv.

$e = V_v / V_S$

$e = 120 / 105$

$e = 1.14$

The answer is (B) 1.14

Solution to Question # 60:

This is a basic structural problem that you should know how to do. No equations. Don't run off searching for an equation, think like an engineer.

Step 1: Find the weight of each beam:

(S20x85 means that the beam weighs 85 lbs per ft)

S20x85(30ft) = 85lbs per foot x 30 ft = 2,550 lbs
W14x75(25ft) = 75lbs/ft x 25 ft = 1,875 lbs
W25x110(45ft) = 110lbs/ft x 45 ft = 4,950 lbs

Because the other three beams are the same size you can add the three beams and multiply by 2 to get the total weight of steel.

Total weight of the beams = (2550 + 1875 + 4950) x 2 = 18,750 lbs

The answer is (C) 18,750 lbs

Solution to Question # 61:

This is basic type question and there is no special formula to solve it.

We know the volumetric flow rate:

Q average =15 mgd,   (mgd = million gallons per day)
Detention time, td = 2 min.

We can calculate peak flow since they gave us the ratio of 2.75:

Q =15 x 2.75=41.25 mgd

Let's convert mgd into ft³/sec:

Engineering Conversions:

41.25 mgd = 45,250,000 gpd (.134) = 6,063,500 ft³ per day.

5,527,500 ft³ per day (1 day/ 24 hours)(1 hour/60 min)(1 min/ 60 sec) =

= 64 ft³/sec

Volume of chamber:

V=Q td   (watch your units)

64 ft³/sec (2 min) x (60 sec /1 min)

= 7,620 ft³

The answer is (B) 7,620 ft³

Solution to Question # 62:

Refer to page 312 of the FE handbook: Air Pollution:

= ppb x P(MW)/RT

The problems gives us ppb, T, and P. T has to be converted to K.

R is also known as .0821 Latm/ (mole*(K)) as you can see below the equation.

We can use the table on page 343 to find the MW of CO_2.
That's the trick.

MW = 44.0

= ppb x P(MW)/RT
= 650 ppb x (3 atm)(44.0)/ .0821 Latm/ (mole*(K)) (273.15 +145)
= 2,500 ug/m³

The answer is (D) 2,500 ug/m³

Solution to 62B:

Refer to page 94 of the FE Handbook: Resolution of a Force.

Since the mass is 35 kg, the weight is 343 N.   [Note: 35 kg (9.8) = 343 N]

Since there is only one "upward-pulling" cable (in the vertical direction), it must supply all the upward force. This cable pulls upwards with approximately 343 N of force. Thus,

Fy = F (tension) (sin 30°) = 343 N

F (tension) = 343 N / (sin 30°)

F (tension) = 343 N / (.5)

F (tension) = 686 N

The sign is only 343 N, but since the cable is on a diagonal, it has to work twice as harder to hold it up.

The answer is (D) 686 N.

Solution to 62C:

Refer to page 94 of the FE Handbook: Resolution of a Force.

Since the mass is 18.0 kg, the weight is 176.4 N. [Note: 18 kg (9.8) = 176.4 N]

Therefore, each cable must pull upwards (vertical component) with 88.2 N of force.

F_y = Force in Cable (Sin 56) = 88.2 N

Force cable = 88.2 N / sin 56

= 106.4 N

The answer is (E) 106 N

Solution to 62D:

Refer to page 264 of the FE Handbook: Retaining Walls:

The answer is (B) $FS_{overturning} = \Sigma M_R / M_O$

Solution to 62E:

Refer to page 309 of the FE Handbook: Earthwork Formulas

Average End Area Formula:

$V = L (A_1 + A_2) / 2$

Be careful with units here. The problem wants the volume in cubic yards (CY).

$V = 25$ ft (1yd / 3 ft) (250 yd^2 + 375 yd^2) / 2

$V = 8.3$ yd (625 yd^2) 2

$V = 2,593.75$ yd^3

= 2,604 yd^3

The answer is (D) 2,604 yd^3

Solution to 62F:

Refer to page 103 (109 of 502).

Plane Circular Motion: $V = rw$ (Important: w has to be in radians per second, not RPMs)

The radius of the tire is 50 cm, let's convert cm to m. .5m

The angular velocity of the tire is 350 revolutions per minute. So, let's convert rpm to radians per second.   Just multiple by $2\pi/60$.

350 (rev/minute) x 2π (radians/minute)(1 min/60 seconds) = 37 rad/sec.

The tangential velocity of a point on the midpoint of any spoke is:

$V = R/2$ x w

V = .5m / 2 x (37 rad/sec) = 9.25 m/s

The tangential velocity of a point on the rim or circumference is simply:

V = R x w

V = .5m x (37 rad/sec) = 18.5 m/s

Since the problem asks for the ratio of the velocities just divide:

Ratio = V tangential midpoint / V tangential circumference

Ratio = 9.25 m/s / 18.5 m/s

Ratio: .5 (or half)

The answer is (A) Half.

Note: I showed you how to convert, but if you notice, you didn't have to in this problem since we were looking at Ratios. But it's good practice to know how to do it.

Ratio = 50cm/2 (350 rpm) / 50cm (350rpm)

Ratio = .5 (half).   Same answer.

This is the end of Exam 1.

Go back and review the problems that you got stuck on. Make notes to yourself of all the things you learned on your mission control sheet.

By the end of this book, hopefully you have several pages. This is great! It will allow you to review later. I always keep a running log of anything I discovered during study.

Keep working hard and don't give up!

Successful people are willing to do what unsuccessful aren't willing to do.

That's the razor's edge.

63) What is the y–coordinate of the centroid of the following shape?

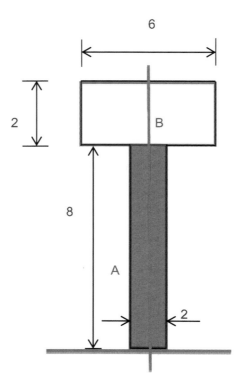

(A) 6.81

(B) 5.83

(C) 6.14

(D) 9.34

64) A car weighing 25 kN is traveling at 125 kilometers per hour as shown in the figure below. What is its kinetic energy?

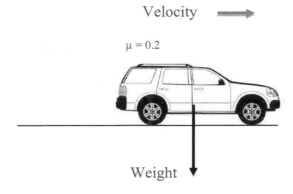

(A) 1,534 kJ

(B) 44.3 kJ

(C) 3,069 kJ

(D) 195,312.5 kJ

65) A fish aquarium is filled with water to a depth of 12m. The total force on the gate is most nearly:

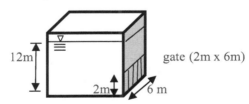

(A) 530 kN

(B) 780 kN

(C) 952 kN

(D) 1,295 kN

66) Total float in a project schedule is:

(A) Early Start + Duration (ES + D)

(B) Late Finish - Duration (LF - D)

(C) Late Finish - Early Finish (LF - EF)

(D) Late Start + Early Start (LS + ES)

67) Determine y   if
$$x - y + z = 2$$
$$x \quad - z = 0$$
$$x + y \quad = -3$$

(A) -2/3

(B) -8

(C) -4/3

(D) -8/3

68) All of the following statements about metallic corrosion are true except:

(A) Corrosion requires simultaneous oxidation and reduction reactions

(B) Iron does not rust if it is kept underwater.

(C) Iron corrodes substantially when in contact with zinc, in a wet environment.

(D) Magnesium is protected by aluminum in a corrosive environment.

69) A certain intersection has a crash rate per million of .82 and an average daily traffic (ADT) entering intersection of 19,920. The number of crashes occurring in a single year at this location is most nearly:

(A) 6

(B) 16

(C) 26

(D) 36

70) A steel bar is subjected to a 950 kN force. The ultimate strength of the material is 80 MPa. What is the factor of safety if the cross sectional of the bar is 520 cm^2?

(A) 4.4

(B) 4.8

(C) 5.2

(D) .4

71) If the pump in the diagram below is 89% efficient, what is the minimum power required if the pressure at the pump inlet (P_i) is 441,000 Pa and the pressure at the pump outlet (P_o) is 147,000 Pa?

(Assume: $Q = 7$ m^3/s, $y = 9800$ N/m^3)

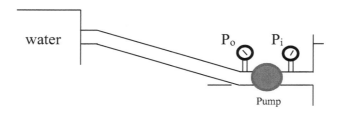

(A) 5.5 x 10^6 watts

(B) 1.5 x 10^6 watts

(C) 2 x 10^6 watts

(D) 2.3 x 10^6 watts

72) An engineer is designing a roadway with a Radius (R) of 320 feet and a sight distance (S) of 75 feet. The Horizonal sight line offset is most nearly:

(A) 2.19

(B) 3.19

(C) 4.19

(D) 5.19

73) A BOD sample was incubated at 22 °C for 9 days and the ultimate BOD was found to measure 147 mg/L.

Given the decay rate of = .306 d^{-1}, base e, the amount of BOD exerted at time t is most nearly:

(A) 103 mg/L

(B) 157 mg/L

(C) 211 mg/L

(D) 911 mg/L

74) The discharge through a weir with a V-notch varies as:

(A) $H^{1/2}$

(B) $H^{3/2}$

(C) $H^{4/2}$

(D) $H^{5/2}$

75) An unconfined aquifer is shown below. Using a hydraulic conductivity of $K = .05$ (ft/sec), the drawdown (MGD) is most nearly:

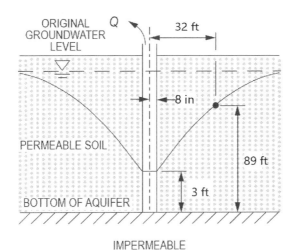

(A) 51

(B) 75

(C) 175

(D) 208

76) What is the velocity of water in a 1-inch diameter pipe that has a slope of 2%, assuming that the pipe is flowing full? (Assume the roughness coefficient (n) for the pipe = 0.013)

(A) .23 ft/s

(B) 1.23 ft/s

(C) 2.23 ft/s

(D) 3.12 ft/s

77) A 300 lbm box is pushed 32 feet across a floor with a constant velocity. What work is done if the coefficient of sliding friction between the crate and floor is .375?

(A) 3166 ft lbs

(B) 3600 ft lbs

(C) 4234 ft lbs

(D) 7699 ft lbs

78) You are an engineer responsible for the design and installation of the HVAC system for a large public-school building. The project is behind schedule and over budget and there is pressure to complete the job. Recently, the supplier has not delivered the specified air handlers because they are on backorder. The project manager of the job orders you to allow a different model air handler which is available in order to not delay the project any further. However, you know that the available model is of a lesser quality and has a history of occasional failure and will likely need replacement only after a few years.

What should you do?

(A) Accept the available model but tell the project manager that it is not right.

(B) Accept the available model and tell the school board that they will likely have to replace it in a year.

(C) Accept the available model and say nothing so the project will look good.

(D) Do not accept the available model, wait for the specified model on back order, and explain the issue with the project manager and the school board.

79) An engineer is designing an activated-sludge treatment municipal wastewater system. If a Step Aeration process is chosen for the design basis, the operational parameter for volumetric loading ($kgBOD_5/m^3$) is most nearly:

(A) 0.3- 0.6

(B) 0.8 - 2.0

(C) 0.6 - 1.0

(D) 1.6 - 4

80) Find the Sample Standard Deviation of the 1,2,6,3:

(A) 16

(B) 1.61

(C) 2.16

(D) 5.61

81) Find the amount which will accrue at the end of year 6 if $1,500 is invested now at 6% compounded annually.

(A) $1,228

(B) $2,128

(C) $2,000

(D) $1,750

82) The curve radius (ft) for a 4.5° (arc basis) horizontal curve is most nearly?

(A) 1273

(B) 1271

(C) 1268

(D) 1277

83) Calculate the vertical reaction force at point C in the frame below.

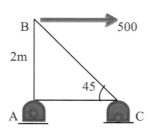

(A) 300 N

(B) 400 N

(C) 500 N

(D) 100 N

84) Which one of the following statements is true?

(A) The coefficient of friction is dependent to the area of contact.

(B) The coefficient of friction is a function of material surfaces.

(C) The coefficient of friction can be greater than 1.

(D) Selections (A) and (B).

85) The effective stress at point P in the diagram below is most nearly:

The ground water is 1 ft below the surface.

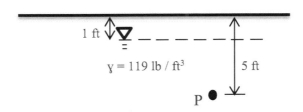

1 ft $\gamma = 119 \text{ lb} / \text{ft}^3$ 5 ft

P

(A) 603 lb/ft²

(B) 312 lb/ft²

(C) 354 lb/ft²

(D) 579 lb/ft²

86) Which of the following is the cumulative total of excavation and embankment at a given station?

(A) Mass haul ordinate

(B) Free haul ordinate

(C) Quantity haul ordinate

(D) Balance point

87) What is the primary factor that affects the strength of concrete?

(A) Water cement ratio

(B) Temperature

(C) Quality control procedures

(D) Rate of hydration

88) Below is a diagram of a fresh water supply system which is used for an illegal moon shine operation. If the valve at the outlet is closed allowing no flow, the gage pressure (kPa) at the valve is most nearly: (Assume tank and piping are completely full)

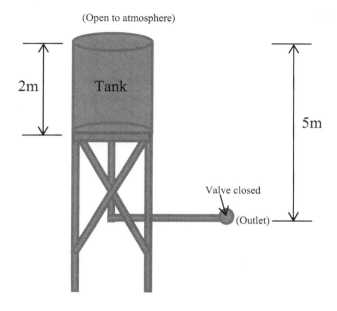

(A) 61 kPa

(B) 49 kPa

(C) 49,050 kPa

(D) 29 kPa

89) Find the Dot Product of [V • W]:

$$V = 2i + 4j$$

$$W = i + 5j$$

(A) 22

(B) 44

(C) 88

(D) 10

90) Laboratory gradation analyses and Atterberg Limits were performed on a soil sample and the results are shown below. During testing no organic odor or materials were noted in the sample.

U.S. Sieve Size	Percent Passing
No. 4	107
No. 10	90
No. 40	79
No. 200	53

liquid limit (LL) = 35%
plastic limit (PL) = 22%

What is the classification of the Soil according to the Unified Soil Classification System?

(A) Silty Gravel

(B) Poorly Graded Sand

(C) Lean Clay

(D) Fat Clay

91) Find the integral:

$$\int_{-1}^{2} \left(4x^3 - x + 1\right) dx$$

(A) 16.5

(B) 17.5

(C) 18.5

(D) 19.5

92) A 2.5 cm diameter by 25 cm long steel rod is shown in the figure below. When the rod is placed under the tension force shown, it elongates by 0.025 cm. What is the strain in the rod?

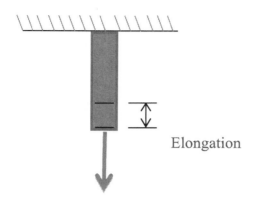

Elongation

F= 110 kN

(A) 0.0001

(B) 0.001

(C) 0.01

(D) 0.005

93) A simply supported beam is loaded with a force as shown in the following diagram. The reaction at point B in the vertical direction is most nearly:

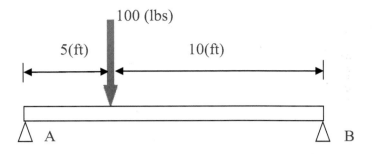

(A) 66 lb

(B) 50 lb

(C) 33 lb

(D) 100 lb

94) A solid aluminum shaft (Assume friction = .3) operates at 1000 rpms and produces 1,650 ft•lb/sec of energy per unit time. Assuming a variable speed reducer with 92 teeth, calculate the horsepower produced by the shaft.

(A) ¾ hp

(B) 3 hp

(C) 10 hp

(D) .5 hp

95) A software company designs a computer circuit in which the wave lengths of the infrared signals form a normal distribution with a mean length of 7 and a standard deviation of 1.5. What is the probability that an infrared signal selected at random will be more than 10 wave lengths long?

(A) .0711

(B) .0228

(C) .0569

(D) .1901

96) Differentiate the following:

$$y = 5x^{-3} + \frac{7}{x} + \frac{2x^6}{3} - 9x + 26$$

(A) $-15x^{-4} + 7x^{-2} + 4x^5 - 9$

(B) $-15x^{-4} - 7x^{-2} + 4x^5 + 9$

(C) $-15x^{-4} - 7x^{-2} + 4x^5 - 9$

(D) $15x^{-4} - 7x^{-2} + 4x^5 - 9$

97) You have been consulted to design wastewater treatment plant using a design flow rate > 1 MGD. The weir overflow rates should not exceed which of the following?

(A) 2,550 gpd/ft

(B) 5,000 gpd/ft

(C) 10,000 gpd/ft

(D) 15,000 gpd/ft

98) Why should engineers act ethically?

(A) Because they can get fired if they don't.

(B) Their supervisors might want them to act this way.

(C) To get a possible promotion out of it.

(D) Because responsible engineers act this way.

99) A hardware upgrade to landing gear costs $1,200 and its salvage value after 3 years is $250. Annual maintenance is $35. If the interest rate is 6%, calculate equivalent uniform annual cost:

(A) $305.39

(B) $405.39

(C) $505.39

(D) $605.39

100) A concurrent-force system is one in which lines of action of the applied forces all meet at:

(A) Perpendicular planes

(B) Two points

(C) Parallel coplanar triangles

(D) One point

101) Calculate the tangential (hoop) stress for a thin-walled cylinder pressure vessel with an inner radius of ½" shown below:

Wall Thickness = .05 inches
Internal Pressure = 1,000 psi

(A) 5,000 psi

(B) 20,000 psi

(C) 10,000 psi

(D) 15,000 psi

102) Below are the cash flows for 2 projects which are being considered. Each project has a life of 4 years. Assuming a discount rate of 10%, select the more preferable project and by how much:

Parameter	Project A	Project B
Initial Costs:	$32,000	$28,750
Annual Costs:	$2,000	$5,500
Salvage Costs:	$1,000	$1,200

(A) Project A by $7,708.05

(B) Project A by $8,708.05

(C) Project B by $9,708.05

(D) Project B by $10,708.05

103) A soccer player kicks a ball at an angle of 53° to horizontal. If its initial velocity is 10 m/s, calculate the horizontal velocity:

(A) 6 m/s

(B) 8 m/s

(C) 10 m/s

(D) 12 m/s

104) A construction project has a planned value (BCWS) of $22,500,000. If the Actual Cost (ACWP) is $23,734,000 and has a Earned value of $21,983,000, the CPI and SPI are most nearly:

(A) .93, .95

(B) .97, .93

(C) .95, .97

(D) .93, 97

105) Assume that the basement wall shown below is supported by the first floor and basement footing. The maximum wall bending moment (ft-lb/ft) is most nearly:

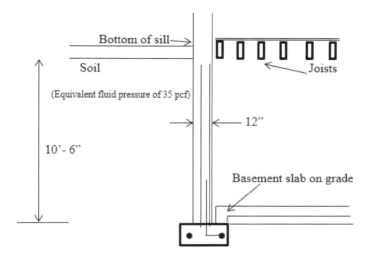

(A) 2400

(B) 2520

(C) 2600

(D) 2860

106) A curving roadway has a design speed of 120 km/hr. At one horizontal curve, the superelevation has been set at 5.0% and the coefficient of side friction is found to be 0.15. The minimum radius (m) of the curve that will provide safe vehicle operation is most nearly:

(A) 1

(B) 2.1

(C) 3.7

(D) 4.8

107) Calculate the Reynolds number for water at a temperature of 60°F flowing through a 1-foot diameter pipe with a velocity of 5ft/s:

(A) 210846

(B) 410846

(C) 510846

(D) 710846

108) The Pitot tube is used to measure which of the following parameters?

(A) Stagnation pressure

(B) Surface tension

(C) Atmospheric pressure

(D) Discharge velocity

109) Air moving at 5 ft/s flows over an air foil with a project area of 35 ft^2, what is the lift force created? (Assume the lift coefficient = .06, ρ_{mass} = 0.074887 lb·sec²/ft⁴).

(A) 3.9 lb

(B) 2.7 lb

(C) .79 lb

(D) 1.9 lb

110) For the profile grade line shown below, the correct mass diagram is most nearly:

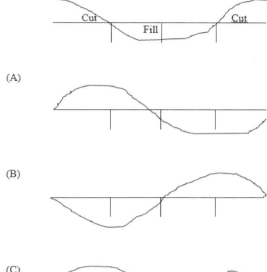

(A)

(B)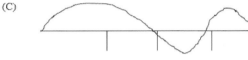

(C)

(D)

111) A steel specimen has a Brinell hardness of 5, therefore, the tensile strength (psi) can be roughly calculated as:

(A) 3500

(B) 2500

(C) 500

(D) No relation between hardness and tensile strength.

112) The flow upstream of a normal shock wave can be described by which of the following parameters?

(A) Re > 2100

(B) Ma < 1

(C) Re < 20,000

(D) Ma > 1

113) A wood (fir) beam with a length of 3 m is heated from 45 °C to 55 °C. The thermal deformation due to the change in temperature is most nearly:

(A) .09 m

(B) .009 m

(C) .0009 m

(D) .00009 m

114) In hypothesis testing, the probability symbol "β" usually indicates this type of error?

(A) Type I

(B) Type III

(C) Type IV

(D) Type II

115) What is the value of the Hazen Williams Coefficient, C, for 5-year-old cast iron piping?

(A) 150

(B) 120

(C) 130

(D) 140

116) You decide to play an amusement park game. Calculate the probability of a quarter landing on heads exactly 5 times if it is flipped 25 times.

(A) .001583

(B) .002742

(C) .009481

(D) .017534

117) A 89 mm×300 mm beam supports a concentrated load 150 mm from the bottom edge. The maximum bending moment is 13.32 x 10^6 N • mm. Find the maximum bending stress (MPa).

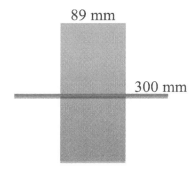

89 mm

300 mm

(A) 6.9

(B) 7.9

(C) 8.9

(D) 9.9

118) A construction company is considering installation of a new accounting system which will cost $4,200, but provide a net annual operational savings of $2,349. As project manager, calculate the payback period.

(A) 1.8 years

(B) .8 years

(C) 3.8 years

(D) 2.8 years

119) Find the tension in the wire which is suspended from the ceiling in the following diagram:

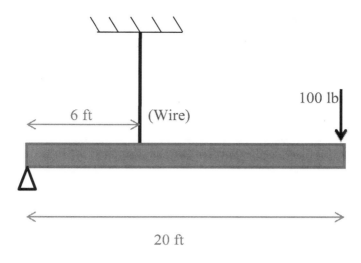

(A) 398 lb

(B) 333 lb

(C) 302 lb

(D) 679 lb

120) An engineer is acting ethically when:

(A) The engineer values his own self-interest first.

(B) The engineer follows the majority.

(C) The engineer does what is best for everyone

(D) The engineer tries to make the most money.

121) A construction project has a planned value (BCWS) of $15,700,000 and a project estimate of $27,500,000. If the Actual Cost (ACWP) is $25,734,000 and currently has an Earned value of $21,451,000, the Estimate at completion (EAC) is most nearly:

(A) $31,021,951.80

(B) $33,021,951.80

(C) $35,021,951.80

(D) $37,021,951.80

122) The property of a material due to which it breaks with little permanent distortion, is called:

(A) Plasticity

(B) Ductility

(C) Brittleness

(D) Flexible

123) How much torque can be applied to a 4 inch outer diameter pipe that has a wall thickness of 0.25 inches when the maximum shear stress is 20,000 psi?

(A) 5700ft lbs

(B) 8600 ft lbs

(C) 9200 ft lbs

(D) 1288 in lbs

123B) In a strength competition, two muscle men pull with two large forces F1 and F2 in order to lift a 125 kg weight by two chains. If the chains make a 2-degree angle with the horizontal, then what is the tension in the chain?

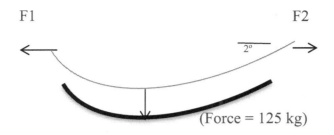

F1   F2

(Force = 125 kg)

(A) 125 kg

(B) 17,536 N

(C) 10,000 N

(D) 27,541 N

123C) If $P_A = P_B$, in which direction will the piston move?

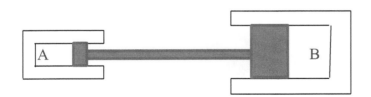

A   B

(A) To the right

(B) To the left

(C) Will not move

(D) Not enough information to determine

123D) Two cars of equal mass are traveling down the street with equal velocities. They both come to a stop over different lengths of time. The ticker tape patterns for each car are shown in the attached diagram.

At what approximate location on the diagram (in terms of dots) does each car begin to experience the impulse?

Which car (A or B) experiences the greatest acceleration? Explain.

Which car (A or B) experiences the greatest change in momentum? Explain.

Which car (A or B) experiences the greatest impulse?

Car A:

Car B:

123E) What is the equation of a circle whose center is at (3,-2) and has a radius of 11:

(A) $(x+3)^2+(y-3)^2 =121$

(B) $(x-2)^2+(y+3)^2 =121$

(C) $(x-3)^2+(y-2)^2 =121$

(D) $(x-3)^2+(y+2)^2 =121$

123F)   A 0.50-kg sled (#1) is pulled with a 1.0-N force for 1 second; another 0.50 kg sled (#2) is pulled with a 2.0 N-force for 0.50 seconds.

Which sled (#1 or #2) has the greatest acceleration?

Which sled (#1 or #2) has the greatest impulse?

Which sled (#1 or #2) has the greatest change in momentum?

123G) A 800 kg car is pulled up a slope as shown in the diagram. Calculate the potential energy it gains at the top.

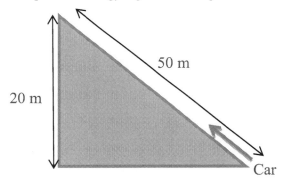

(A) 40 kJ

(B) 157 kJ

(C) 183 kJ

(D) 211 kJ

Exam # 2 Solutions:

Solution to Question # 63:

Refer to page 108 of the FE Handbook: Centroid of Masses, Areas, Lengths, and Volume.

Always spilt the object up into basic shapes (square, rectangle, triangle, etc.) The problem already did that for you.

$y = (A_a \cdot y_a) + (A_b \cdot y_b) / (A_a + A_b)$,   (Note: $A_a = 8x2$, $A_b = 2x6$, $y_a = 4$ (from the origin to the middle of object A), $y_b = 9$ (from original to middle of object B))

$y = [(8x2) \cdot 4] + [(2x6) \cdot 9] / [(8x2) + (2x6)]$

$y = [(64)] + [(108)] / [(16) + (12)]$

$y = [(172)] / [(28)]$

$y = [6.14]$

The answer is (C) 6.14.

Solution to Question # 64:

Refer to page 107 of the FE Handbook: Kinetic Energy.

This is one of those you really need to know by heart.

Kinetic Energy is calculated from the formula:

$KE = \frac{1}{2} (Mass) (Velocity)^2$

(Note: The values must be in the correct units! It is easy to get this type of problem wrong if you don't watch your units!)

In the problem, the weight of the car is given as a weight (kilo newtons). So, we need to convert 25 kN from a *force* into a *mass* so it can fit into the equation.

$F = MA$ (you should also memorize this equation)

$25kN = M (9.81 \text{ meter/second}^2)$

$M = 25,000 \text{ N} / [9.81 \text{ meter/second}^2]$

$M = 2,548.42 \text{ kg}$ (Note: kg meter/second^2) is a Newton)

Now, convert velocity into (meters/second)

$V = 125 \text{ km/hour}$

$V = 125 \text{ km/hour} (1000 \text{ meter/km})(1/3600 \text{ hour/second})$

$V = 34.7 \text{ meter/second}$

Therefore,

KE = 1/2 (Mass) (Velocity)^2

= 1/2 (2,548.42 kg) (34.7 meter/second)^2

= 1,534,263.5 kg m^2/s^2

= 1,534,263.5 J   (Note: 1 Joule= kg m^2/s^2)

KE = 1,534 kJ

The correct answer is (A) 1,534 kJ.

(Note: The coefficient of friction, μ = 0.2, shown in the problem is extra information and is not used to calculate Kinetic Energy.)

Solution to Question # 65:

Refer to page 180 of the FE Handbook: Forces on submerged surfaces.

This is one of those classic fluid problems that you should know how to immediately solve.

The Force on the gate is the average pressure x the Area of the gate.

Remember that the density of water at standard conditions is 1000 kg/m^3.

F = (1000 kg/m^3)(9.81 m/s^2)(1/2)(10m+12m) x (2m x 6m)

Note: The 10m came from the fact that the top of the gate is 10m below the surface. 12m = the bottom of the gate below the surface.

F = (1000 kg/m^3)(9.81 m/s^2)(1/2)(10m+12m) x (2m x 6m)

F = 1,294,920 kg m / s^2

F = 1,294,920 N (1 newton is a "kg m / s^2")

F = 1,295 kN   (convert to kN, move the decimal over to the left 3 times)

Note: If this equation is confusing you, another way to look at it is what is the pressure at the middle of the gate? What is the depth of water at the middle of the gate? 12-1 = 11m. (the gate is 2m high, so midway is 1m).

So, the pressure at the middle of the gate is:

F = (1000 kg/m^3)(9.81 m/s^2)(11m)x (2m x 6m)

F = 1, kN   (same answer)

The answer is (D) 1,295 kN

Solution to Question # 66:

Refer to page 310 of the FE Handbook: Nomenclature: This is Construction Scheduling.

Remember that float is equal to zero along the critical path. If there is a question about Critical Path, just remember that it's the longest path through the network.

The answer is (C) Late Finish - Early Finish (LF - EF)

Solution to Question # 67:

This is a simple algebra problem. You shouldn't need the handbook for this type of problem. First, solve the middle equation for x. I put this in there to keep your guard up for math problems. Don't overlook them.

$x - z = 0$, therefore, $x = z$.

Now, substitute "x" instead of "z" in the first equation and solve for x:

$x - y + z = 2$

$x - y + (x) = 2$

Now, combine like terms:

$2x - y = 2$

$2x = 2 + y$

$x = (2 + y)/2$

$x = 1 + (y/2)$, Now, this with equation, substitute it into the 3rd equation to solve for y.

3rd equation:

$x + y = -3$

$(1 + (y/2)) + y = -3$

Now, combine like terms:

$y/2 + y = -4$
$3y/2 = -4$
$3y = -8$

Therefore, $y = -8/3$

The answer is (D) -8/3.

(Note: It is highly recommended to be able to work through this problem all the way until the end to get the correct answer. On the actual FE Exam, you cannot afford to make mistakes on easy algebra type problems. Now is you time to make the simple mistakes, during practice, so you do not make them on exam day!)

Solution to Question # 68:

Refer to page 117 of the FE Handbook: Corrosion

The answer is (C) Iron corrodes substantially when in contact with zinc, in a wet environment.

The reason that (C) is incorrect is because Iron will actually be protected by zinc. Zinc is designed to be a sacrificial electrode and will corrode first - since it is more anodic in galvanic series than Iron- while the Iron is protected.

Solution to Question # 69:

Refer to page 306 of the FE Handbook: Traffic Safety Equations:
Crash Rates at Intersections:

RMEV = A x 1,000,000/V

The problem is looking for A.

We know:

RMEV = .82

V = ADT x 365
V = 19,920 x 365 = 7,270,800

.82 = A x 1,000,000/7,720,800
A = 5.96
= 6

The answer is (A) 6

Solution to Question # 70:

Let's go back to the basic equation for stress:

Stress = F/A , but you can't just divide 950 kN/ 520 cm^2 because you'll get weird unit of kN/ cm^2 which doesn't make any sense. When dealing with SI units, the answer will probably be in Pascals, Pa. (1 Pascal is N/M^2 :see page 3 of the handbook)

F = The Force is given, but need to convert it to N. 950kN (1000N/kN) = 950,000 N

Now, let's convert the cm^2 to m^2:

Area = 520 cm^2 (1 m/100cm)^2 = 520 cm^2 (1^2 m^2/ 100^2 cm^2)   (don't forget basic math)

Area = .052 m^2

Now, we are ready to divide:

Stress = F/A = 950,000 N / .052 m^2

Stress = 18,269,231 N/m^2 (Remember, a pascal is 1 N/m^2)

Stress = 18,269,231 Pa   (Let's convert to mega pascals, because the problem has the ultimate strength as 80 MPa)

Stress = 18 MPa   (page 1 (7 of 502), just divided by 10^6)

So the Factor of Safety (FOS) = Ultimate Strength / Stress you calculated

FOS = 80 MPa / 18 MPa

The answer is (A) FOS = 4.4

Solution to Question # 71:

Refer to page 192 of the FE Handbook: Pump Power Equation:

Power (watts) = Q • γ • h • / n

Given:

Q = 7 m³/s

n = 89% = .89

γ = 9800 N/m³

h = not given, however, you can calculate from the pressure difference:

h = ΔP/ γ

h = (441,000 N/m²) - (147,000 N/m²) / (9800 N/m³)   (Note: this equation is very useful and a common conversion)

h = 30 meters

Therefore:

Power (watts) = (7 m³/s • 9800 N/m³• 30 meters) / .89

Power = 2.3 x 10⁶ watts

The answer is (D) 2.3 x 10⁶ watts.

Solution to Question # 72:

Refer to page 302 of the FE Handbook: Horizontal Curves Table. At Bottom.

HSO = R [1 – cos (28.65 S / R)]

HSO = 320 [1 – cos (28.65(75)/320)]

HSO = 320 [1 – cos (6.714)]

HSO = 320 [.00685]

HSO = 2.19

The answer is (A) 2.19

Solution to Question # 73:

Refer to page 322 of the FE Handbook: Microbial Kinetics: BOD Exertion.

$BOD_t = L_O / (1-e^{-.k(t)})$
$BOD_t = 147 / (1-e^{-.306(9)})$
$BOD_t = 147 / (1-e^{-2.754})$ (note: use $e^x = e^{-2.754}$ on calculator)
$BOD_t = 147 / (.936)$
$= 157$ mg/L

The answer is (B) 157 mg/L

Solution to Question # 74:

Refer to page 296 of the FE Handbook: Weir Formulas.

The answer is (D) $H^{5/2}$

Solution to Question # 75:

Refer to page 292 of the FE Handbook: Well Drawdown.
Unconfined Aquifer.

Basic plug and chug, just watch your units! So many ways here to mess up.

From the diagram:
r_2 = 32 ft

r_1 = 8 in   (but convert to ft) (1ft/12in) = .67 ft

h_2 = 89 ft

h_1 = 3 ft

$Q = \pi K[(h_2)^2 - (h_1)^2] / \ln (r_2/ r_1)$
$Q = \pi(.05)[(89)^2 - (3)^2] / \ln (32/ .67)$
$Q = \pi(.05)[(7921 - 9] / \ln (47.76)$
$Q = \pi(.05)[(7912] / (3.87)$
$Q = 321.14$ ft^3/sec

However, the problem is asking for MGD, not CFS.

321.14 ft^3/sec x (.646317) = 207.55.

The answer is (D) 208 MGD.

Solution to Question # 76:

Refer to page 185 of the FE Handbook: Open Channel Flow: Manning's Equation:

$v = (k/n) \cdot R^{2/3} \cdot S^{1/2}$

Given:

k = 1.486 *(given in handbook)* (be careful, *k = 1 for SI units*)
n = 0.013
S = 2% = 0.02
R = hydraulic radius = *also on page 185 of the FE Handbook*

R = Area/Perimeter = $[(pi)D^2/4]/ (pi)D$

Reduces to:

R = D/4 *(Note: If the pipe is flowing full, you can always just use R = D/4, Refer to page 184 of the FE Handbook: Flow through noncircular conduits.)*

R = (pipe full) = D/4 = [(1 inch)•(1 ft/12 in)]/4
R = 0.021 ft

Therefore:

$v = (k/n) \cdot R^{2/3} \cdot S^{1/2}$

$v = (1.486/.013) \cdot (.021)^{2/3} \cdot (.02)^{1/2}$
v = (114.307) • (.076116) • (.1414)
v = 1.23 ft/s

The answer is (B) 1.23 ft/s.

Solution to Question # 77:

This is basic physics and should not need the Handbook. *Page 107.*

Work = Force (Distance) , we know the distance so let's find out the Force.

$F_f = f (M)g/ gc$

F= (.375) (300) (32.2) / (32.2)   (Remember, in English Units you have to divide by gc)

F= 112.5 lbf

Work = 112.5(32) = 3600 ft lbs

The answer is (B) 3600 ft lbs

Solution to Question # 78:

Refer to page 4 of the FE Handbook: Ethics

Remember how to answer every ethical question. Never feel pressured to do something that isn't the right thing to do. Public safety is first priority.

Answer is (D) Do not accept the available model, wait for the specified model on back order, and explain the issue with the project manager and the school board.

Solution to Question # 79:

Refer to page 335 of the FE Handbook: Table: Design and Operational Parameters for Activated Sludge.

Find the Step Aeration process on the left side, so the volumetric loading is 0.6 – 1.0.

The answer is (C) 0.6-1.0

Solution to Question # 80:

Refer to page 63 of the FE Handbook: Sample standard deviation:

The equation for *Sample Standard Deviation* is:

$$S = \sqrt{[1/(n-1)] \Sigma (X_i - X_{avg})^2}$$

Given:

n = number of values = 4

$X_{avg} = (1+2+6+3) / 4 = 3$

Therefore:

$$S = \sqrt{[1/((4)-1)] \Sigma (X_i - (3))^2}$$

$$S = \sqrt{[1/(3)] \cdot [(1-(3))^2 + (2-(3))^2 + (6-(3))^2 + (3-(3))^2}$$

$$S = \sqrt{[1/(3)] \cdot [(-2)^2 + (-1)^2 + (3)^2 + (0)^2}$$

$$S = \sqrt{[1/(3)] \cdot [4 + 1 + 9 + 0]}$$

$$S = \sqrt{[1/(3)] \cdot [14]}$$

$$S = \sqrt{4.6}$$

$$S = 2.16$$

The answer is (c) 2.16

Solution to Question # 81:

Refer to page 235 of the FE Handbook: 6% Interest Rate Table: Bottom Table on Page.

We know: P=$1,500, i% = 6%, n= 6 years

We are trying to calculate the Future value (F).

Using the table for 6% interest and n= 6 years, find the value of "F/P". Remember, we are trying to find the Future (F) given the present value (P) of $1,500. So we say "F given P".

The value from the chart for F/P is <u>1.4185</u>

Therefore:

F = P (F/P,i,n)
F = \$1,500 (F/P, 6%, 6)
F = 1500 (1.4185)
F = \$2,128

The answer is (B) \$2,128

<u>Solution to Question # 82:</u>

Refer to page 301 of the FE Handbook: Horizontal Curves

R = 5729.578 / D

R = 5729.578 / 4.5°

R = 1273.24 ft

R = 1,273 ft

The answer is (A) 1273

<u>Solution to Question # 83:</u>

Statics: Just need to know how to do this.

Draw a free body diagram of the <u>External Forces</u>:

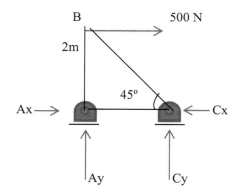

(Note: Point C and Point A are fixed supports, so they both have x and y components.

Since the problem asks to find the vertical reaction at point C, let's take moments about Point A:

$+ \left(\sum M_A = 0 \right.$

$+ \bigcap \sum M_A$: 500N (2m) – Cy (2m) = 0 ·

(Note: 500N force is 2m away from point A.
Cy is 2m away from point A. Cx,Ax,Ay cancel out since they go through point A.

$+ \sum M_A$: 1000N· m – Cy (2m) = 0

$+ \sum M_A$: 1000N· m = Cy (2m)

$+ \sum M_A$: Cy = 500 N

The answer is (C) 500 N.

Solution to Question # 84:

Refer to page 109 of the FE Handbook: Laws of Friction:

The correct answer is (B). The coefficient of friction

Solution to Question # 85:

Refer to page 263 of the FE Handbook: Effective Stress.

The total vertical stress at point A = 119 lb/cf x 5 ft = 595 lb/sf

The pore pressure is:

$$u = \gamma_w (h - h_w)$$

= 62.4 lb/cf (5ft –1 ft)

= 249.6 lb/sf

The effective vertical stress = Total vertical stress – pore pressure

σ' = σ – u = 595 lb/sf – 240.6 lb/sf

= 354.4 lb / sf

The answer is (C) 354 lb/ft^2

Solution to Question # 86:

Refer to page 309 of the FE Handbook: Diagram at the bottom.

The answer is (A) Mass haul ordinate.

Solution to Question # 87:

Refer to page 126 of the FE Handbook: Concrete: Top left of page.

The answer is (A) Water cement ratio.

Solution to Question # 88:

Refer to page 179 of the FE Handbook: The Pressure Field in a Static Liquid:

$P = \gamma \cdot h$

Given:

h = 5m (total height of the liquid)

γ_{water} = 9,810 N/m^3

(Refer to Fluid Mechanics: Definitions: page 177 of the FE Handbook)

Therefore:

$P = \gamma \cdot h$

$P = 9,810$ N/m^3 (5m)

$P = 49,050$ N/m^2 (Note: the problem statement wants the answer to be in kPa, which is a kilo Pascal. 1 Pascal = N/m^2)

(Refer to page 3 of the FE Handbook) Conversion Factors:

(1 Pa = 1 N/m^2 Write this on your Mission Control Sheet)

49,050 N/m^2 = 49,050 Pa

= 49 kPa

The answer is (B) 49 kPa.

Solution to Question # 89:

Refer to page 59 of the FE Handbook: Vectors:

If v = ai + bj and w = ci + dj,

then v · w = ac + bd

Therefore:

v · w = (2)(1) + (4)(5)

= 22

The answer is (A) 22.

Solution to Question # 90:

Refer to page 267 of the FE Handbook: Table.

Since 53% passing #200 sieve that makes it a Fine-grained soil.

LL is 35 which is < 50 so follow the top row of the chart
No organic odor or color so follow the inorganic follow at the top.

Find PI;

PI = LL – PL

= 35 – 22

= 13 ….so PI > 7 and plots above the "A" line.

The answer is (C) Lean Clay.

Solution to Question # 91:

Refer to page 47 of the FE Handbook: Integral Calculus:

$$\int_{-1}^{2} \left(4x^3 - x + 1\right) dx$$

$$= 4x^4/(4) - x^2/(2) + x \Big|_{-1}^{2}$$

(Add one to the exponent and then divide by the same new number, remember that numbers become variables)

= [4(2)^4 / (4) – (2)^2/ 2 + (2)] – [4(-1)^4 / (4) – (-1)^2/ 2 + (-1)]

= [4(16) / (4) – (4)/2 + (2)] – [4(1) / (4) – (1)/2 + (-1)]

= [(16) – (2) + (2)] – [(1) – (1/2) + (-1)]

= [16] – [(– 1/2]

= 16 + ½

= 32/2 + ½

= 33/2

= 16.5

The answer is (A) 16.5

Solution to Question # 92:

Refer to page 119 of the FE Handbook: Under Definitions: Engineering Strain.

Strain is the change in length per unit length.

The equation for Strain = $\Delta L / L_0$

Strain = 0.025 cm /25 cm = 0.001

Answer is (B) 0.001.

(Note: Read the entire question! It is only asking for the calculated strain. You do not have to solve for elongation nor use the Force value.).

Solution to question # 93:

Refer to page 107 of the FE Handbook: Statics

The applied force is **NOT** at the midpoint of the beam in the drawing! The drawing shows the force at the midpoint; however, the distances are not the same. Pay attention to detail! Therefore, you cannot just simply take half of the applied force!

To find the reaction R_b, take moments about Point A. Convention is to always assume clockwise direction for the positive moment.

$+\;\Sigma\, Ma = 0$: $+100(\text{lb})\,(5\text{ft}) - R_b\,(15\text{ft}) = 0$

$+100(\text{lb})\,(5\text{ft}) = R_b\,(15\text{ft})$

$$\frac{+100(\text{lb})\,(5\text{ft})}{(15\text{ ft})} = R_b$$

$R_b = 33.3$ lb

The correct answer is (C) 33 lb.

Solution to question # 94:

You do not need the handbook to solve this type of problem. The question is testing basic engineering skills. The problem tells you that the shaft produces 1,650 ft•lb/sec of energy. Horsepower is energy per time! You simply have to convert to horsepower. All the other information is totally useless.

Refer to page 3 of the FE Handbook: Conversion Factors:

Horsepower = (1,650 ft•lb/sec) • (1.818 × 10⁻³)

Horsepower = 3 hp

The answer is (B) 3 hp.

(Note: if the problem statement asked for the torsional stress on the shaft, you would *refer to handbook page 134 and do question #123 and #255.*)

Solution to Question # 95:

Refer to page 76 of the FE Handbook: Unit Normal Distribution:

Bet you didn't know you can use these charts to solve this kind of problem:

$7 - 10 = 3$

$3/ 1.5 = 2$

Using the chart, for x = 2, find R(x) = .0228

The answer is (B) .0228.

Solution to Question # 96:

Refer to page 45 of the FE Handbook: Differential Calculus:

$$y = 5x^{-3} + \frac{7}{x} + \frac{2x^6}{3} - 9x + 26$$

$= 5x^{-3} + 7x^{-1} + 2x^6/3 - 9x + 26$ (any variable in the dominator should be brought up to the numerator)

$= 5(-3) x^{-4} + (-1)7x^{-2} + [2(6) x^5/3] - 9(1) + 0$ (the exponent comes down to the front to multiply, and then the new exponent equals the previous exponent minus 1)

$= -15x^{-4} -7x^{-2} + (12x^5/3) - 9$

$= -15x^{-4} -7x^{-2} + 4x^5 - 9$

The answer is (C) -15x⁻⁴ -7x⁻² + 4x⁵ – 9.

Solution to Question # 97:

Refer to page 341 of the FE Handbook: Weir Loadings.

For flow > 1 MGD, weir overflow rates should not exceed 15,000 gpd/ft

The answer is (D) 15,000 gpd/ft

Solution to Question # 98:

Ethics – use common sense. Always do what is right.

Answer is (D) Because responsible engineers act this way.

Solution to Question # 99:

Refer to page 235 of the FE Handbook: 6% Interest Table:

$1200 (A/P, 6%, 3) + $35 - $250(A/F, 6%, 3)

$1200 (.3741) + $35 - $250(.3141)

$448.92 + $35 - $78.53

$405.39

The answer is (B) $405.39.

Solution to question # 100:

Refer to page 97 of the FE Handbook: Concurrent Forces:

The answer is (D) One point.

Solution to Question # 101:

Refer to page 131 of the FE Handbook: Cylindrical Pressure Vessel:

When the thickness of the cylinder wall is about one-tenth or less of inside radius, the cylinder can be considered as thin walled. In which case, the internal pressure is resisted by the hoop stress and the axial stress:

$\sigma_t = P_i (r) / t$ and $\sigma_a = P_i (r) / 2t$ (see the previous page for definitions of σ_t and σ_a)

Hoop stress (tangential) =

$\sigma_t = P_i (r) / t$
$\sigma_t = 1000$ psi (.5 inch) / (.05 inch)   (just substitute values from the problem statement)
$\sigma_t = 10,000$ psi
The answer is (C) $\sigma_t = 10,000$ psi.

Solution to Question # 102:

Refer to page 236 of the FE Handbook: 10% Interest Table:

The more preferable project is the one with the lowest "Present Value":

Therefore:

Project A:

$32,000 + $2,000(P/A, 10%, 4) -$1,000(P/F, 10%, 4)

$32,000 + $2,000(3.1699) - $1,000(0.6830)

$32,000 + $6,339.8 - $683

$37,656.8

Project B:

$28,750 + $5,500(P/A, 10%, 4) -$1,200(P/F, 10%, 4)

$28,750 + $5,500(3.1699) - $1,200(0.6830)

$28,750 + $17,434.45 - $819.60

$45,364.85

Project A is more preferable by $45,364.85 - $37,656.8 = $7,708.05

The answer is (A) Project A by $7,708.05.

Solution to Question # 103:

Refer to page 105 of the FE Handbook: Projectile Motion:

The velocity can be separated into x and y components:

The horizontal velocity, $V_x = V \cdot \cos\Theta$

Therefore: plug and chug:
$V_x = V \cdot \cos\Theta$

$V_x = (10 \text{ m/s}) \cdot \cos53°$

$V_x = 6 \text{ m/s}$

The answer is (A) 6 m/s

Solution to Question # 104:

Refer to page 310 of the FE Handbook: Earned Value Analysis.

These problems are very easy. EVMS is only useful for Cost Reimbursable construction contracts – meaning, when the project scope is undefined and you would like to track the cost (CPI) and schedule (SPI). It's not useful on Firm fixed priced construction contracts in my opinion because the risk is on the contractor and liquidated damages in the contract.

Given:

BCWS = $22,550,000
ACWP = $23,734,000
BCWP = $21,983,000

Equations on page 311:

CPI = BCWP/ACWP
CPI = $21,983,000 / $23,734,000
CPI = .93.   (Meaning the project is over budget. Only getting 92 cents of value from every $1 spent. If the CPI > 1, the project is under budget.)

SPI = BCWP/BCWS
SPI = $21,983,000 / $22,550,000
SPI = .97. (Meaning the project is behind schedule. You want SPI > 1, just like the CPI)

The answer is (D) .93, .97

Solution to question # 105:

This may first seem like a geotech problem. But it's actually just a structural problem.

Think!

It's basically a beam with a triangular loading. The width of the wall (12") doesn't matter.

Draw a force diagram from the problem:

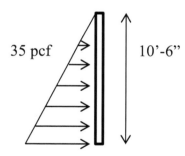

The equivalent fluid pressure is 35 lb/ft³ from the figure but this needs to be converted.

35 lb/ft³ (10.5 ft) height of the wall   (note: 10 feet 6 inches = 10.5 feet)

= 368 lb/ft²

Page 140: Simply Supported Beam Slopes and Deflections:

The diagram at the bottom shows a Triangular load:

$$M_{max} = \frac{w_0 L^2}{9\sqrt{3}}$$

= .0642 (368 lb/ft²) (10.5 ft)²

= 2601

The answer is (C) 2600

Solution to Question # 106:

Refer to page 302 of the FE Handbook: Horizontal Curves:

Side friction factor (based on superelevation)

.01(e) + f = V² / 15R

.01(5) + .15 = (120 km/hr)² / 15R

.2 = 14,400 / 15R

15R = 72,000

R = 4,800 km

R = 4.8m

The answer is (D) 4.8

Solution to Question # 107.:

Refer to page 182 of the FE Handbook: Reynolds number:

Reynolds # = $\dfrac{v \cdot D}{v}$

Given:

V = 5 ft/s

D = 1 ft

v = *find on chart on page 199 of the FE Handbook: Properties of Water: Table*:

For water at 60°F (given in the problem), the kinematic viscosity is:

v = 1.217 x 10⁻⁵ ft²/s

Now, just plug the values into the equation:

Reynolds # = (5 ft/s) • (1 ft) / (1.217 x 10⁻⁵ ft²/s)

= 410846

= (Note: Reynolds number is dimensionless, it has no units)

Answer is (B) 410846.

Solution to Question # 108:

Refer to page 195 of the FE Handbook: Fluid Measurements: Pitot Tube:

The answer is (A) Stagnation pressure.

Solution to Question # 109:

Refer to page 198 of the FE Handbook: Aerodynamics: Air foil theory:

Search for "Air Foil".

The lift force equation is:

$F_L = (C_L \cdot \rho \cdot V^2 \cdot A_p) / 2$

Given:

$C_L = .06$

$A_p = 35$ ft²

$\rho = 0.074887$ lb•sec² /ft⁴ (Note: This is the mass density. If air temperature were given, find its corresponding mass density on table page 200.

Therefore:

$F_L = (C_L \cdot \rho \cdot V^2 \cdot A_p) / 2$

$F_L = (.06)(0.074887 \text{ lb•sec}^2 /\text{ft}^4) \cdot (5 \text{ ft/s})^2 (35 \text{ ft}^2)/2$

$F_L = 1.9$ lb

The answer is (D) 1.9 lb.

Solution to Question # 110:

Refer to page 309 of the FE Handbook: Profile: Mass Haul:

Remember the profile is the cumulative total of excavation and embankment at a given station.

Answer is (A)

Solution to Question # 111:

Refer to page 123 of the FE Handbook: Relationship Between Hardness and Tensile Strength. Left Top of Page.

TS (psi) = 500 BHN

TS psi = 500 (5)

TS psi = 2,500

The answer is (B) 2500.

Solution to Question # 112:

Refer to page 190 of the FE Handbook: Normal Shock Relationships: Bottom Left of Page.

Search for the key work "normal shock wave".

The flow upstream of a normal shock wave is always supersonic, Ma > 1.

The answer is (D) Ma > 1.

Solution to Question # 113:

Refer to page 131 of the FE Handbook. Thermal Deformations:

$\alpha \cdot L \cdot (T-T_0)$

But we need to find α for wood (fir)

See table on page 138 for different materials:

$\alpha = 3 \times 10^{-6} /°C$

Thermal Deformation = $\alpha \cdot L \cdot (T-T_0)$

Thermal Deformation = $(3 \times 10^{-6} /°C) \cdot (3m) \cdot (55 °C - 45 °C)$

Thermal Deformation = .00009 m

Answer is (D) .00009 m.

Solution to Question # 114:

Refer to page 70 of the FE Handbook: Hypothesis Testing:

Search for the key word "hypothesis testing"

The answer is (D) Type II.
(Note: You are not expected to memorize these types of answers; this question is teaching you how to look up the answer quickly in the handbook).

Solution to Question # 115:

Refer to page 297 of the FE Handbook: Values of Hazen-Williams Coefficient C. Table.

The answer is (B) 120

Solution to Question # 116:

Refer to page 66 of the FE Handbook: Binomial Distribution. (Bottom of page)

X is a binomial with n = 25 (since we're flipping the quarter 25 times)
p=q= .5 (since there is a 50% chance each time of landing on heads)
x = 5 (5 possible outcomes)

Just plug and chug into the equation at the bottom of the screen:

$n! / x! (n-x)! \cdot (p^x q^{n-x})$

$25! / 5! (25-5)! \cdot (.5^5 .5^{25-5})$

$25! / 5! (20)! \cdot (.5^5 .5^{20})$

$25! / 5! (20)! \cdot (.5^{25})$ (basic math- add exponents when multiplying base numbers)

$25! / 5! (20)! \cdot (.5^{25})$

(Just use your calculator to figure out the factorials. Use the x^y function to figure out $.5^{25}$)

= .001583

The answer is (A) .001583

Solution to Question # 117:

Refer to page 135 of the FE Handbook: Stresses in Beams:

$\sigma_{bending} = M \cdot C / I$

Given:

M =13.32 x 10^6 N • mm

C = 150 mm

(Value of C is ½ the depth of the beam to the neutral axis, 300 mm / 2 = 150 mm)

I = moment of inertia for rectangular shape.

(See page 93 Table of different shapes: for a rectangle, (I = b • h³ / 12))

Therefore:

I = b • h³ / 12

I = 89 mm • (300 mm)³ / 12

I = 200,250,000 mm⁴

Therefore:

$\sigma_{bending} = M \cdot C / I$

$\sigma_{bending} = (13.32 \times 10^6 \text{ N} \cdot \text{mm}) \cdot (150 \text{ mm}) / (200,250,000 \text{ mm}^4)$

$\sigma_{bending} = 9.9 \text{ N} / \text{mm}^2$

(Note: The question wants the answer in MPa)

9.9 N / mm² ˙ (1000 mm / 1 m)²

9.9 N / mm² ˙ (1000² mm² / 1 m²)

9.9 x 10⁶ N / m²

See page 1 (5 of 498)) Metric Prefixes: M = 1 x10⁶

9.9 M N / m²

9.9 M Pa (Remember 1 N / m² = Pa)

The answer is (D) 9.9.

Solution to Question # 118:

Refer to page 231 of the FE Handbook: Payback period.

$4,200 / $2,349 = 1.8 years

The net annual savings is divided into the initial cost.

The answer is (A) 1.8 years.

Solution to Question # 119:

You shouldn't even need the handbook for this type of question. This is basic statics.

Batting practice let's go.

The first step is to draw a force diagram of all the forces acting on the beam.

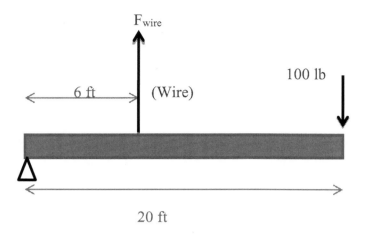

Let's take moments at the wall:

$\Sigma M_{wall} = 0$: (assume clockwise is positive):

100 lb(20ft) – F_{wire}(6ft) = 0

100 lb (20ft) = F_{wire} (6ft)

2,000 ft lb / 6ft = F_{wire}

F_{wire} = 333 lb

The answer is (B) 333 lb.

Solution to Question # 120:

Refer to page 4 of the FE Handbook: Ethics.

Always choose the most righteous/moral answer.

Answer is (C) The engineer does what is best for everyone.

Solution to Question # 121:

Refer to page 311 of the FE Handbook: Forecasting:

EAC = (ACWP + ETC)

Givens:

BAC = $27,500,000
BCWP = $21,451,000

ACWP = $25,734,000
BCWS = $15,700,000

EAC = ($25,734,000 + ETC)   (Let's find ETC)

ETC = (BAC − BCWP) / CPI.
ETC = ($27,500,000 − $21,451,000) / CPI   (Let's find CPI)

CPI = BCWP / ACWP
CPI = $21,451,000 / $25,734,000
CPI = .83   (project is over budget since CPI < 1)

ETC = ($27,500,000 − $21,451,000) / .83
ETC: $7,287,951.81

EAC = ($25,734,000 +$7,287,951.81)
EAC = $33,021,951.80

The answer is (B) $33,021,951.80

Solution to Question # 122:

Refer to page 448 of the FE Handbook: Brittle Materials:

The answer is (C) Brittleness.

Solution to Question # 123:

Refer to page 134 of the FE Handbook: Torsion:

$t = T r / J$

Rearrange the equation for T:

$T = t \ J / r$

Let's find the value of J:

J = polar moment of inertia for a hollow cylinder: See FE handbook page 99. Hollow cylinder is the 2nd column, 2nd row.

$J = \pi / 2 \ (r_2{}^4 - r_1{}^4)$ (a = outer radius, b = inner radius)

r_2 = (outer diameter) / 2

 = 4 in / 2

= 2 in.

r_1 = (r_2 − wall thickness) = 2 in - .25 in = 1.75in

$J = \pi / 2 \ (2 \ in^4. - 1.75in^4 \ )$

$= \pi / 2 \ (\ 16 - 9.38)$

$= 10.47 \ in^4$

Therefore:

$T = 20,000 \ psi \ (10.4 \ in^4) / 2in$

$= 104,000 \ in \ lbs$ (lets convert this to foot pounds)

$= 104,000 \ in \ lbs$ (1 ft/ 12in)

$= 8600 \ ft \ lbs$

The answer is (B) 8600 ft lbs

Solution to 123B:

Refer to page 94 of the FE Handbook: Resolution of a force:

Since the mass is 125 kg, the weight is 1225 N.   [Note: 125 kg (9.8) = 1225N]

Each side of the chain must pull upwards with 612.5 of force.

$Fy \ (sin \ 2^\circ) = 612.5 \ N$

$Fy = 17,536 \ N$

The answer is (B) 17,536 N.

Solution to 123C:

You do not need the handbook to solve this problem. Think like an engineer!

Pressure = Force / Area

Force = Pressure (Area)

The pressure is constant in both sides. From the diagram, the area of a is smaller than the area of b.

Therefore, the Force is greater acting on the right side of the piston, which is pushing to the left.

Force A is less than Force B.

The answer is (B) To the Left.

Solution to 123D:

You do not need the handbook to solve this problem.

The collision occurs at approximately the ninth dot (plus or minus a dot). The diagram shows that it is at that location that the cars begin to slow down.

Car A has the greatest deceleration. The velocity change of each car is the same. (They start with the same velocity and each finish with zero velocity.) Yet car A accomplishes this change in less time. Car A accelerates "most rapidly."

The momentum change is the same for each car. The velocity change of each car is the same (they start with the same velocity and each finish with zero velocity), and the mass of each car is the same. Thus, the momentum change is the same for each car.

The impulse is the same for each car. The impulse equals the momentum change. If the momentum change is the same for each car, then so must be the impulse.

Solution to 123E:

Refer to page 44 of the FE Handbook: Case 4, Circle: Middle of Page.

$(x-h)^2 + (y-k)^2 = r^2$ [the circle is centered about (h,k)]

So for the point (3,-2):

$(x-3)^2 + (y-(-2))^2 = 11^2$
$(x-3)^2 + (y+2)^2 = 121$ *(Note: -(-2) = +2)*
The answer is (D) $(x-3)^2+(y+2)^2 = 121$

Solution to 123F:

Refer to page 109 of the FE Handbook: Equations of Motion.

You don't need the handbook for this question. You need to know basic physics principles.

Sled #2 has the greatest acceleration. Recall that acceleration depends on force and mass. (F=MA) They each have the same mass, yet sled #2 has the greater force.

The impulse is the same for each sled. Impulse is force*time and can be calculated to be 1.0 N*s for each sled.

The momentum change is the same for each sled. Momentum change equals the impulse; if each sled has the same impulse, then it would follow that they have the same momentum change.

Solution to Bonus 123G:

Refer to page 107 of the FE Handbook: Potential Energy:

This is also one of those you really need to know by heart.

In potential energy problems, we are only interested in vertical distances: So, the slope and the angle does not mean anything.

$U = mgh$

$U = (800 \text{ kg}) \cdot (9.81 \text{ m/s}^2) \cdot (20 \text{ m})$ (Note: the value of "g" comes from page 3: Conversion Factors. But if you don't know this then you really need to practice more….)

$U = 156{,}960$ Joules

$U = 157$ kJ

The correct answer is (B) 157 kJ.

End of Exam 2. What did you learn?

Probably that is you search "manning Equation" you couldn't find the equation. Need to use "Manning's Equation".

Great chart on page 199 & 200 for properties of water. Also, page 297 Valves of C.

If you're looking for J the polar moment of inertia, hollow shafts, see page 99.

Keep moving forward soldier. Success is the ability to keep moving forward when you got knocked down. The odds will forever be in your favor.

Success is always the margins.

124) Considering the forces acting on the block shown in the figure below. If the pulling force (**P**) equals the friction force (F$_{friction}$), which of the following is true?

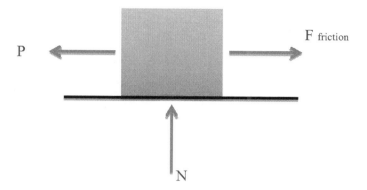

(A) The block will remain stationary if the friction force is static.

(B) The block will accelerate if the friction force is kinetic.

(C) The block will move at constant velocity if the friction force is static.

(D) The block will begin to move if the friction force is static.

125) A car is coasting in a straight line on a horizontal road at 10 mph. If the coefficient of rolling friction between the car's tires and road is 0.03, how far will the car travel before it comes to a stop?

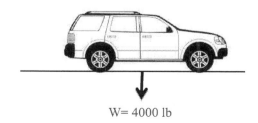

W= 4000 lb

(A) 89.5 ft

(B) 106.5 ft

(C) 118.5 ft

(D) 112.5 ft

126) A flange weighing 150 lbs is resting on a table. If the diameter of the flange is 10 inches what pressure does the flange exert on the table?

(A) 13,101 Pa
(B) 18,706 Pa
(C) 19,191 Pa
(D) 23,101 Pa

127) The discharge through a weir with a V-notch varies as:

(A) $H^{1/2}$

(B) $H^{3/2}$

(C) $H^{4/2}$

(D) $H^{5/2}$

128) Two ropes connect to an eye hook in a rafter. One rope pulls with a force of 270 N at an angle of 55° from the horizontal while the second rope pulls with a force of 180 N at an angle of 110° from the horizontal. Calculate the resultant force on the hook:

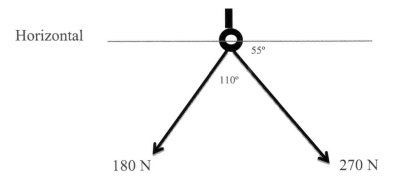

(A) 512.3 N

(B) 401.3 N

(C) 398.3 N

(D) 275.3 N

129) A horizontal curve is defined by its radius of 738 feet, as shown below. The length of the chord AB, in feet, is most nearly:

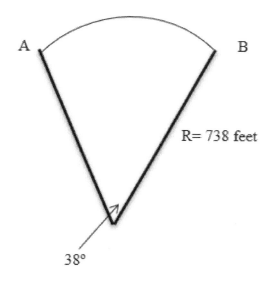

(A) 490 feet

(B) 512 feet

(C) 650 feet

(D) 915 feet

130) A circular shaft .1 m long with a polar moment of inertia, J = 16.7 x 10^{-9} m^4, is manufactured from a metal which has a modulus of rigidity, G = 75 x10^9 Pa. The shaft has a flywheel with moment of inertia, I = 25 kg • m^2 attached to the end. Calculate the undamped circular natural frequency (w_n) of the system:

(A) 19.2

(B) 27.8

(C) 17.3

(D) 22.4

131) The effective overburden pressure (PSF) at the bottom limit of the clay layer in the subsurface section below is most nearly:

Original Ground Surface: 0 feet

Sand (weight = 117 PCF)

Elevation: -10 feet   ▼ Ground water table

Saturated Sand (weight = 128 PCF)

Elevation: -15 feet

Consolidated Clay (weight = 95 PCF)

Elevation: -20 feet

(A) 3457

(B) 3701

(C) 3912

(D) 1,661

132) A construction company obtained 40, 50, 60, 80, and 45 grades in the subjects of Quality Control, Safety, Environmental, Schedule, and Cost. Assuming weights 5, 2, 4, 3, and 1, respectively, for the above-mentioned audit areas. Find Weighted Arithmetic Mean per area:

(A) 55

(B) 65

(C) 55.5

(D) 65.5

133) Find the percent reduction (% RA) in area for a specimen which undergoes a test in which $A_i = 35$ and $A_f = 17$:

(A) 18.3%

(B) 48.2%

(C) 28.9%

(D) 51.4%

134) A 2m diameter pipe (roughness = .016) carries 10 m^3/s of water. What is the slope of the pipe?

(A) .0000652

(B) .00652

(C) .0652

(D) .652

135) The permeability of a soil was evaluated in a falling head permeameter whose head decreased from 45 to 10 in within 7 min. The cross-sectional area of the test specimen is .78in^2 and the cross-sectional area of the reservoir tube is .25 in^2. If the sample length was 3 in, the permeability of the soil is most nearly?

(A) 5.14 x 10^{-5} in/ sec

(B) 3.5 x 10^{-3} in/ sec

(C) 4.12 x 10⁻⁵ in/ sec

(D) 1.04 x 10⁻³ in/ sec

136) A machine is purchased for $1000 and has a useful life of 12 years. At the end of 12 years, the salvage value is $130. By straight-line depreciation, what is the book value of the machine at the end of 8 years?

(A) $580

(B) $290

(C) $450

(D) $420

137) Calculate the force (F) required to hold the 4-meter-wide gate closed:

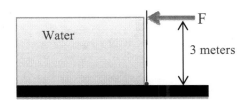

(A) 58,800 N

(B) 48,800 N

(C) 518,800 N

(D) 800 N

138) The truss structure in the figure below is loaded as shown. What is the reaction in the horizontal direction at point A?

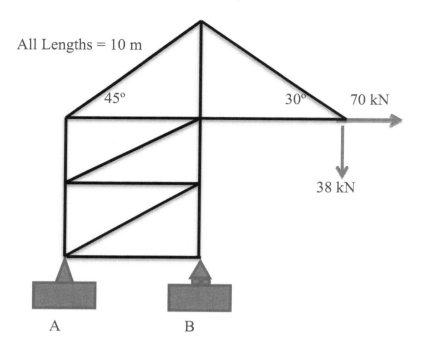

All Lengths = 10 m

45°   30°   70 kN

38 kN

A   B

(A) 50 kN

(B) 60 kN

(C) 70 kN

(D) 80 kN

139) A contractor as part of a levee contract is required to backfill and compact a trench that has a volume of 300 BCY and 540 LCY. The borrow pit is located 38 miles from the construction site. The truck driver makes $45/hr and works 8 hours per day. Assuming the volume of the truck bed and number of trips needed to load and unload, the contractor will need the truck for 15 days. The contractor rents the truck at $550 per day. The cost of soil is $20 per CY bank volume basis. The cost of backfilling the trench is most nearly:

(A) $19,650

(B) $22,780

(C) $24,990

(D) $27,433

140) What is the centroid location for the composite area shown below?

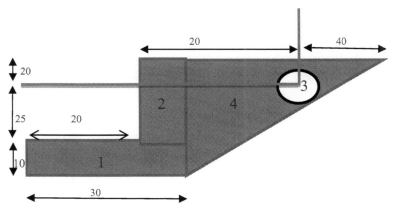

Note: Circle has a diameter of 16.

(A) 37.36, 40.93

(B) 37.36, 30.93

(C) 40.23, 34.21

(D) 30.93, 36.63

141) A Lawn mower engine is started by pulling its cord which is wrapped around a pulley 6 times. The radius of the pulley is 2 ½ inches. If a constant tension of 25 lbf is maintained in the cord at all times, what is the work done?

(A) 76 ft lbs

(B) 143 ft lbs

(C) 196 ft lbs

(D) 376 ft lbs

142) A geotechnical engineer is designing against slope failure for a certain project. If the available shearing resistance along slip surface is 250lb, the factor of safety against slope instability is most nearly:

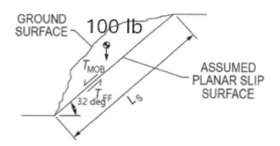

(A) 1.4

(B) 2.9

(C) 3.1

(D) 4.7

143) The graph below shows the probability density function of a population. What is the probability that a sample from this population has a value greater than 7?

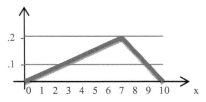

(A) .3

(B) .2

(C) .7

(D) .1

144) You buy one $10 raffle ticket for a new car valued at $15,000. Two thousand tickets are sold. What is the expected value of your gain?

(A) $5.2

(B) -$5.2

(C) -$2.5

(D) $2.5

145) What is the length of a line segment with a slope of 8/6, measured from the y-axis to a point (12,8)?

(A) 10

(B) 14.7

(C) 20

(D) 21.7

146) An engineering firm wants to expand its in-house maintenance program, how much money do they have to save annually to buy a maintenance shop 4 years from now that has an estimated cost of $18,000? The savings account offers 4.0 % yearly interest:

(A) $ 4,309

(B) $ 4,239

(C) $ 5,239

(D) $ 4,209

147) What superelevation rate would you recommend for a roadway with a design speed of 65 mph and a R = 1,250. Assume f = 0.11.

(A) 10%

(B) 10.5%

(C) 11%

(D) 11.5%

148) Consider the following cantilevered concrete beam below: Where should the rebar be designed in the beam?

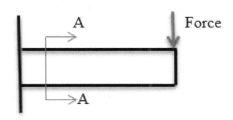

(A)

(B)

(C)

(D)

149) Convert the polar coordinates $(4, -\pi/6)$ to rectangular coordinates.

(A) $(-2\sqrt{3}, -2)$

(B) $(-2\sqrt{3}, 2)$

(C) $(-2, 2\sqrt{3})$

(D) $(2\sqrt{3}, -2)$

150) An exhaust fan is used in an industrial warehouse for ventilation. Calculate the power (HP) supplied by fan which produces a pressure rise of 20 psi and flow rate of 100 ft³/sec? Assume the fan efficiency is 75%. The fan is designed as a typical backward curved fan.

(A) 834 Hp

(B) 550 Hp

(C) 512 Hp

(D) 698 Hp

151) The best estimate for the Hazen Williams resistance coefficient for a new 8 inch diameter ductile iron pipe which is cement lined is most nearly:

(A) 80

(B) 130

(C) 140

(D) 150

152) A continuous footing designed for flood protection is shown in the diagram below. The ultimate bearing capacity is most nearly:

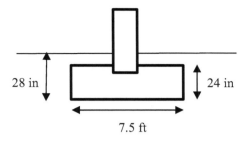

28 in   24 in

7.5 ft

lean clay:

γ= 112 lbf/ft^3

C = 167 lbf/ft^2

N_c = 27, N_q = 22, N_γ = 16

(A) 9,471 psf

(B) 12,987 psf

(C) 14,623 psf

(D) 16,978 psf

153) Which of the following describes the flow through a pipe that has a Reynolds number < 2,100:

(A) Steady State

(B) Laminar

(C) Turbulent

(D) Transitional

154) A load of 150 pounds acts vertically on a block shown in the following diagram. Calculate the stress (psi) in the block:

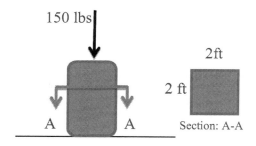

(A) .026 psi

(B) .26 psf

(C) .26 psi

(D) 2.6 psi

155) How many times out of 10,000 attempts would you roll the same numbers using 4 dice?

(A) 0

(B) 64

(C) 46

(D) 5,243

156) Water is flowing through a pipe with an inner diameter of 6 inches. If the velocity of the water is 5 feet per second, what is the volumetric flow rate (ft³/second)?

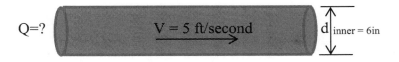

Q=? V = 5 ft/second d inner = 6in

(A) .98 ft³/sec

(B) 54.7 ft³/sec

(C) 43.7 ft³/sec

(D) 32.7 ft³/sec

157) You are a manager and also a licensed engineer at a large supply company that specializes in fasteners. The company you work for has a large government contract supplying fasteners to the city for local bridge projects. As an engineer, you know that the $500,000 purchase order you just received by email for a particular grade bolt for new project - which will be located by the ocean- is not conducive for the salt water environment and will likely corrode. You feel like there must have been a mistake on the purchase order. What should you do?

(A) Fill the purchase order since you are not the engineer of record.

(B) Call the POC of the company to verify the purchase order and express your concerns to them.

(C) Fill the purchase order since $500,000 is a lot of money and it is not your problem.

(D) Just fill the purchase order with the bolts that you think will work.

158) Solve for the determinate for the following 3x3 matrix:

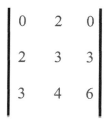

$$\begin{vmatrix} 0 & 2 & 0 \\ 2 & 3 & 3 \\ 3 & 4 & 6 \end{vmatrix}$$

(A) -6

(B) 6

(C) -16

(D) 10

159) In binary phase diagrams, what reaction is defined as two solids coexisting with one liquid?

(A) Eutectic reaction

(B) Eutectoid reaction

(C) Peritectic reaction

(D) Peritectoid reaction

160) Why do engineers need a code of ethics?

(A) To give the public a clear definition of what to expect from a responsible engineer

(B) It keeps management from micromanaging them.

(C) It gives lawyers a stronger case when engineers show they followed the code.

(D) It gets engineers higher pay.

161) A temporary wall structure supports a foundation excavation as shown in the figure below. The total earth force per foot the wall is most nearly:

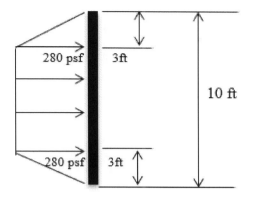

(A) 1000 lb/ft

(B) 1960 lb/ft

(C) 2011 lb/ft

(D) 2801 lb/ft

162) What is the best word to complete the following sentence:

"Engineers are to uphold the health, safety, and public_____ ":

(A) Trust

(B) Confidence

(C) Money

(D) Welfare

163) An environmental engineer is calculating vertical standard deviations of a plume. If the standard deviation (meters) is 10^2 with a Moderately Unstable Coefficient, the distance downwind is most nearly:

(A) 10

(B) 10^2

(C) 10^3

(D) 10^4

164) A composite short column has a steel core (diameter 10 in) surrounded by a snug brass sleeve (inner diameter 10 in, outer diameter 12 in). The column is loaded uniformly (using loading plates) in compression. If the compressive load is 200 kips, what is the stress in the steel? Assume E steel = 29000 ksi and E brass = 17000 ksi.

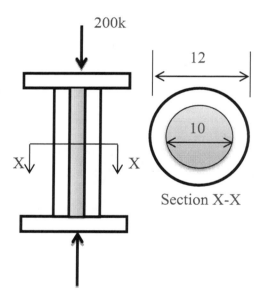

(A) 12 ksi

(B) 2.99 ksi

(C) 1.02 ksi

(D) 2.02 ksi

165) Which of the following statements about metallic corrosion are true?

(A) There must be an anode

(B) There must be a cathode

(C) Presence of an electrolyte

(D) All of the above

166) Which of the following test is used to determine the amount of energy required to cause failure:

(A) Charpy Impact Test

(B) Endurance Test

(C) Tensile Test

(D) Creep Test

167) If the ball in the following picture is released from rest, determine the velocity (in miles per hour) of the ball just immediately before impact:

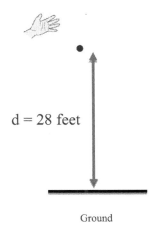

d = 28 feet

Ground

(A) 42.5

(B) 28.9

(C) 23.4

(D) Can not be determined without the weight of the ball.

168) In terms of similitude, in order to use a model to simulate the conditions of the prototype, the model must be all of the following, except:

(A) Geometrically similar

(B) Kinematically similar

(C) Aesthetically similar

(D) Dynamically similar

169) Loose sand is used as fill on a certain project. The time required for 92% consolidation of the clay layer shown is most nearly:

(assume $C_v = 3.8 \times 10^{-5}$ ft^2/sec)

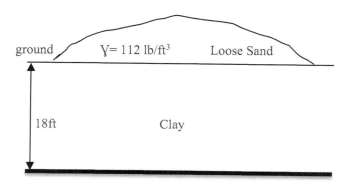

(A) 58 days

(B) 77 days

(C) 93 days

(D) 102 days

170) An Air pollution control device shown below, the number of effective turns the gas makes is most nearly:

CYCLONE DIMENSIONS

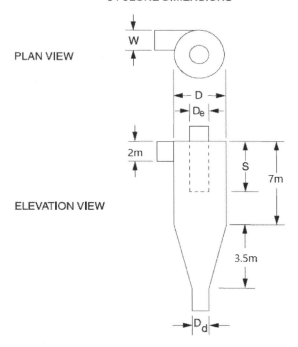

PLAN VIEW

ELEVATION VIEW

W

D

De

2m

S

7m

3.5m

Dd

(A) 4.4

(B) 7.6

(C) 13.2

(D) 22.9

171) Find x for: $\log_3(x+2) - \log_3(x) = 2$

(A) .5

(B) .25

(C) .75

(D) .35

172) A surveyor is calculating the earthwork volume from field data. Assuming $A_1 = 720$ SY, $A_2 = 920$ SY, $A_m = 812$ SY, $L = 1,267$ Y, The volume (CY) is most nearly:

(A) 2,183

(B) 32,183

(C) 1,032,183

(D) 11,032,183

173) A circular footing has a diameter of 10ft and is buried 2 feet below the mudline. If it has a net dead plus live column load of 75 kips and an allowable bearing capacity of 2800 lb/ft², the actual factor safety against bearing capacity failure is most nearly:

(A) 3

(B) 2

(C) 1

(D) .85

174) Which one of the following is true regarding the collision of two bodies as shown
below

(A) Energy is always conserved

(B) Energy is only conserved if the coefficient if restitution is > .8

(C) Momentum is conserved

(D) Momentum is conserved if

175) Which one of the following materials has the lowest representative value of fracture toughness?

(A) Alumina

(B) 4340 Steel

(C) Silicon Carbide

(D) A1 2014-T651

176) An engineer was just hired to design and oversee precast concrete columns that will be used for a bridge supports. The project is behind schedule and there is pressure to start delivering the precast columns to the jobsite. While performing a quality assurance check on the rebar in the layout yard, prior to placing concrete, the engineer discovers that the rebar size is undersized and not to specifications. Performing any corrective measures will delay the delivery date. The engineer's boss says that the rebar is okay and orders him to certify the rebar size and start placing concrete.

What should the engineer do?

(A) Listen to his boss since he is superior. If the columns buckle it will be on him.

(B) Send an anonymous letter to the head of the company.

(C) Discuss with human resources.

(D) Inform the project team of his findings and assure the undersized rebar is replaced with the size specified.

177) An ideal gas is in a holding tank. If the volume of the gas is doubled and its pressure is halved, the temperature is:

(A) Constant

(B) Doubled

(C) Tripled

(D) Quadrupled

178) An architecture firm purchases a high-speed laser printer for $20,000. At the end of its 5-year life its salvage value will be $2000. Using straight line depreciation, find the printer value after 3 years:

(A) $19,000

(B) $9,200

(C) $2,725

(D) $7,750

179) An engineering company will need $25,000 to buy a new part for a piece of machinery in 3 years, how much should they invest now at an interest rate of 10% compounded annually?

(A) $18,782

(B) $18,700

(C) $18,827

(D) $17,882

180) A sand has a maximum void ratio of 0.68 and a minimum void ratio of 0.41. The actual void ratio of the sand is 0.491. The relative density of the sand is most nearly:

(A) 54%

(B) 65%

(C) 70%

(D) 85%

181) A pump is to deliver water through the existing system indicated in the figure below. Which of the following will reduce the tendency for pump cavitation?

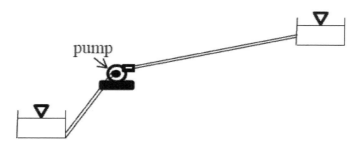

pump

Water Supply Elevation

Not To Scale

I.   Increase the discharge pipe diameter

II.   Lower the pump elevation

III.   Increase the suction diameter.

(A) II only

(B) II and III only

(C) I, II, and III only

(D) I and II only

182) The active resultant (lb/ft) per unit length of the retaining wall show below is most nearly:

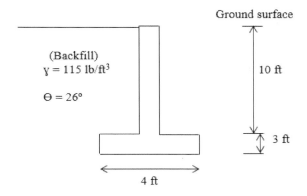

(A) 2,801

(B) 3,297

(C) 3,790

(D) 4,241

183) What is the moment of inertia (I_{xc}) of the following shape?

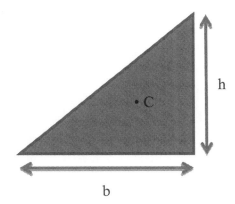

(A) $b^3h/12$

(B) $bh^3/24$

(C) bh³/36

(D) bh⁴/36

184) What is the drag coefficient, C_D, for a sphere when $R_e = 100$:

(A) 1

(B) .1

(C) 10

(D) 100

185) What does the V- diagram look like for the following beam?

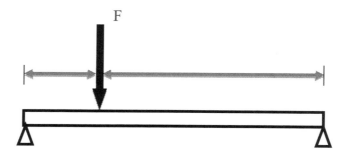

(A)

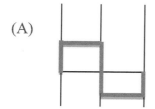

(B)

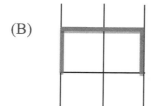

(C)

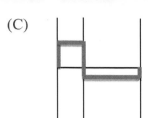

(D)

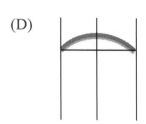

186) Find the resultant moment in the following diagram:

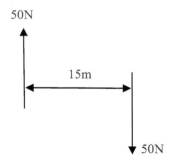

(A) 50 Nm

(B) 100 Nm

(C) 750 Nm

(D) 1,500 Nm

186B) Convert 265° 32' 13" to decimal degrees:

(A) 265.54°

(B) 365.54°

(C) 465.54°

(D) 565.54°

186C) A hydraulic jack is modeled below. If a 100 pound force pushes down on the small reservoir which has a cross sectional area of 1 in², what is the output force that is produced? Assume the large reservoir has a cross sectional area of 2 in².

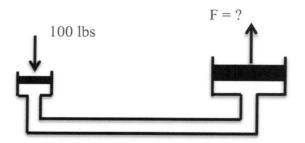

(A) 75 lbs

(B) 100 lbs

(C) 150 lbs

(D) 200 lbs

186D) A manager who is organizing a team for a new project must choose five engineers from a pool of 12 engineers. How many different ways can the manager choose the team?

(A) 279

(B) 972

(C) 792

(D) 297

186E) Integration allows you to determine which of the following?

(A) Inflection points on the curve

(B) Area under the curve

(C) The slope of the curve

(D) The derivative

Solution to Question # 124:

Refer to page 109 of the FE Handbook: Laws of Friction.

Search for key words "laws of friction"

The correct answer is (A).

For movement to occur, the static friction force (which is $F_{static} = u_s N$) must be overcome by the pulling force. Once movement has occurred, if the pulling force equals the friction force (kinetic friction), the block will move at uniform motion since no unbalanced forces will exist on the block (acceleration =0). If the pulling force exceeds the kinetic friction force, the block will accelerate according to $F = ma$.

Solution to Question # 125:

Refer to page 104 of the FE Handbook:

An equation for angular velocity as a function of angular position may be written as: $v^2 = v_o^2 + 2ax$

Use equations of straight-line motion to find the cars distance traveled in terms of acceleration. Apply F=ma to find acceleration in terms of kinetic frictional force. Substitute and solve for distance traveled.

$v^2 = v_o^2 + 2ax$ (this equation is one of the normal equations of motion)

$F = u_k N$
$F = ma$
$W = mg$

Given:

Weight (**W**) of car = 4,000 lb (note: the weight is not mentioned in the problem, but it is shown on the drawing! **Always be mindful of this common trick!** Learn to think an engineer, read the problem AND look at the drawing!

$u_k = 0.03$
$v_o = 10$ mph

Solve:

Apply equation of straight line motion:

$v^2 = v_o^2 + 2ax$

Now, realize that v = 0 (because the car will eventually come to rest), therefore,

$0 = v_o^2 + 2ax$

Now, rearrange this equation on terms of x:

$2ax = -v_o^2$

$x = -v_o^2 / 2a$

(x is the distance the car will travel, however, we still do not know what the value of acceleration is.)

Find friction force :(trying to stop the car from rolling)
$F = u_k N$
[$N = -W = 4000$ lb]
$F = 0.03 (4,000) = 120$ lb

Find acceleration:
$F = ma$

Rearrange to solve for a:
$a = F/m$
$m = W/g = -4000$ lb/(32.2 ft/sec^2) = -124 slugs
$a = -120$ lb/124 slugs
$a = -.96$ ft/sec^2

Now, substitute the value of acceleration back into the original equation:
$x = -v_o^2 / 2a$

Always watch your units! Convert the velocity of 10 mph into feet per second to be consistent with the units in acceleration.

$v_o = 10$ mph (5280ft/mile) (1hr/3600 sec) = 14.7 ft/sec

$x = -(14.7$ ft/sec)^2 / [(2) (-.96 ft/sec^2)]

$x = 112.5$ ft

The answer is (D)

Note: This is good practice to see how all the units cancel out one another. Get into the habit of writing the units and physically crossing them out in the numerator and denominators.

Solution to Question # 126:

You do not need the FE handbook to solve this problem. Think like an engineer.

You know the force, let's find the area.

If the flange is 10 in, the area is:

Area = $\pi D^2 / 4$

$= \pi (10$ in)$^2 / 4$

$= 78.5$ in^2

$P = F/$ Area

P = 150 lbs / 78.5 in^2 = 1.9 psi

However, the solution is in SI units, so let's convert psi into Pascals.

See conversions on FE Handbook. Look towards the bottom of the page, to convert PSI into PA, you need to multiply by 6895.

1.9 psi x 6895 =

= 13,101 Pa

The answer is (A) 13,101 Pa

Solution to Question # 127:

Refer to page 296 of the FE Handbook: Weir Formulas:

Be careful, the question says V-notch. So it's 5/2 not 3/2.

The answer is (D) H$^{5/2}$

Solution to Question # 128:

Refer to page 94 of the FE Handbook: Resolution of a force:

First, let's calculate the x and y components of the 270 N force:

F_x = F cos θ
F_x = 270 N (cos 55°)
F_x = 154.9 N

F_y = F sin θ
F_y = 270 N (sin 55°)
F_y = 221.2 N

Second, let's calculate the x and y components of the 180 N force:

F_x = F cos θ
F_x = 180 N (cos 110°)
F_x = - 61.6 N   (note: F_x is negative because the x component is pointing to the left, which is negative)

F_y = F sin θ
F_y = 180 N (sin 110°)
F_y = 169.1 N

Now, let's add the x components and y components from both forces:

F_x total: 154.9 N + (-61.5 N) = 93.4 N

F_y total: 221.2 N + 169.1 N = 390.3 N

Now, use the Resultant force equation from the handbook:

R = $\sqrt{F_x + F_y}$

$$R = \sqrt{(93.4\text{ N})^2 + (390.3\text{ N})^2}$$

$$R = \sqrt{(8723.56\text{ N}^2) + (152{,}334\text{ N}^2)}$$

$$R = 401.3\text{ N}$$

The answer is (B) 401.3 N.

<u>Solution to Question # 129:</u>

Refer to page 301 of the FE Handbook: Horizonal Curves:

Horizontal Curves:

Don't be scared of horizontal curve problems. Must are usually plug and chug type.

$$D = 5729.578 / R$$

$$D = 5729.578 / (738\text{ ft})$$

$$D = 7.76$$

Now, use the equation:

$$L = 100\,(I) / D$$
$$L = 100\,(38°) / 7.76$$

$$L = 490\text{ feet}$$

The answer is (A) 490 feet

<u>Solution to Question #130:</u>

Refer to page 114 of the FE Handbook: Torsional Vibration:

$$w_n = \sqrt{GJ/IL}$$

<u>Given:</u>

$G = 75 \times 10^9\text{ Pa}$
$J = 16.7 \times 10^{-9}\text{ m}^4$
$I = 25\text{ kg} \cdot \text{m}^2$
$L = .1\text{ m}$

Therefore:

$$w_n = \sqrt{GJ/IL}$$

$$w_n = \sqrt{(75 \times 10^9\text{ Pa})(16.7 \times 10^{-9}\text{ m}^4) / (25\text{ kg} \cdot \text{m}^2)(.1\text{ m})}$$

$$w_n = \sqrt{(1252.5\text{ N} \cdot \text{m}^2) / (2.5\text{ kg} \cdot \text{m})}$$

$$w_n = \sqrt{(501)}$$

$$w_n = 22.4$$

The answer is (D) 22.4.

Solution to Question # 131:

This is a basic geotech problem. You don't need the FE Handbook.

Simply add up the pressure from each layer, don't forget to subtract out the water table! Pay close attention to the elevations of each layer.

117 PCF (10 ft) + 128 PCF (5 ft) + 95 PCF (5 ft) - 62.4 PCF (10 ft)

= 1170 psf + 640 psf +475 psf - 624 psf

= 1,661 psf

(Note: the question wanted the pressure at the bottom of the clay layer. Be careful, it might ask for the pressure at the middle of any layer also. In that case, just be sure you adjust the elevation of each layer.)

The answer is (D) 1,661 psf

Solution to Question # 132:

Refer to page 63 of the FE Handbook: Weighted arithmetic mean:

The formula is:

$X_w = \Sigma\ w_i\ x_i\ /\ \Sigma\ w_i$

Make a simple chart to calculate these variables:

Audit Areas:	Grade: (x)	Weight (w)	(wx)
QC	40	5	200
Safety	50	2	100
Environmental	60	4	240
Schedule	80	3	240
Cost	45	1	45

Total: $\Sigma\ w = 15$ $\Sigma\ wx = 825$

$X_w = \Sigma\ w_i\ x_i\ /\ \Sigma\ w_i$

$X_w = 825\ /\ 15$

$X_w = 55$ grade/audit area

The answer is (A) 55.

Solution to Question # 133:

Refer to page 130 of the FE Handbook: Percent reduction (%RA) in area.

% RA = [(A_i - A_f) / A_i] x 100

Therefore: just plug and chug from here:

% RA = [(35 - 17) / 35] x 100

= 51.4%

The answer is (D) 51.4%

Solution to Question # 134:

Refer to page 185 of the FE Handbook: Manning's Equation:

$v = (k/n) \cdot R^{2/3} \cdot S^{1/2}$

Given:

k = (k = 1 for SI units)
n = 0.016
S = ?
V = Calculate using Q = V •A, 10m³/s = v [(π)(2²)/4], v = 3.18 m/s

$R_h = d/4$, (2)/4 = .5

$v = (k/n) \cdot R^{2/3} \cdot S^{1/2}$

$3.18 = (1/.016) \cdot (.5)^{2/3} \cdot S^{1/2}$

$S^{1/2} = 8.07 \times 10^{-2}$

S = .00652

The answer is (B) .00652.

Solution to Question # 135:

Refer to page 260 in the handbook: Falling head test.

Make sure you are looking at the equation for the falling-head test, not the constant head test. Plug and chug. There are 2 main tests. This problem said the Falling head test.

$K = 2.303[(a\ L) / (At_e)] \log_{10} (h_1/h_2)$ (watch units: inches/sec)

$K = 2.303[(.25)(3) / (.78)(7)(60)] \log_{10} (45/10)$

$K = .0053 \log_{10} (4.5)$

$K = .0035$ in/sec

The answer is (B) 3.5 x 10^{-3} in/sec

Solution to Question # 136:

Refer to page 231 of the FE Handbook: Straight-line depreciation.

The equation is:

$$D_j = \frac{C - S_n}{n}$$

From the question, we can find the givens:

Cost (C) = $1,000
n = 12 year life
S_n = Salvage value = $130

Therefore:

D = ($1000-$130) / 12
D = $72.50 per year (remember that this formula gives you salvage value per year)

Before using the Book Value (BV) equation, the question asks to find book value after 8 years, therefore, we must first calculate the salvage value after 8 years. The salvage value we calculated above is the value per year.

Therefore:

Salvage value after year 8: = 8 ($72.50)

=$580

Now Calculate the Book Value (BV):

BV = initial cost – D_j *(found on page 128)*

BV = $1000 –$580
BV= $420

The answer is (D) $420.

Solution to Question # 137:

Refer to page 180 of the FE Handbook: Forces on submerged Surfaces:

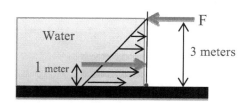

The gate is 4 meters wide and 3 meters high as shown. The submerged gate will have a triangular pressure distribution. Since the shape is a triangle, the net force will act 1/3 up from the hinge, therefore 1 meter up.

To calculate the force due to the pressure of the water,

$F_{water} = \gamma \cdot h_c \cdot Area$

$F_{water} = 9800 \cdot ((3+0)/2)) \cdot (4\times3)$ (The average height is $(3+0)/2 = 1.5$)

$F_{water} = 176,400$ N

Therefore, equate the two Moments:

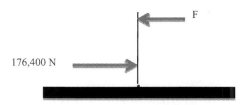

Sum moments about the hinge:

F (3 meters) = 176,400 (1 meter)

F = 58,800 N

The answer is (A) 58,800 N

Solution to Question # 138:

Refer to page 268 of the FE Handbook: Trusses. But you don't need to use formulas.

At first glance, this problem looks to be really involved, however, upon further inspection; the only forces in the horizontal directions are the 70 kN and the A_x. There is no horizontal reaction at point B because of the roller support. Reaction at point B is on the vertical direction only.

Therefore: Draw a free body diagram:

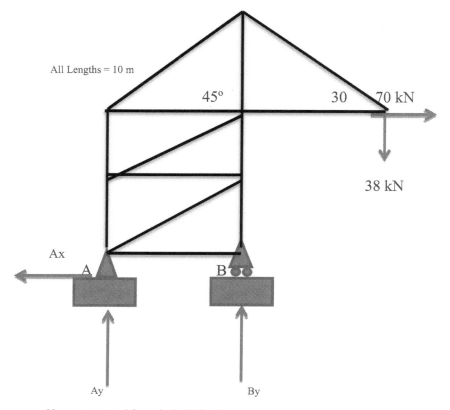

All Lengths = 10 m

45°   30   70 kN

38 kN

Ax

A

B

Ay   By

Now, sum external forces in the X direction:

$\Sigma F_x = 0$: 70 kN – A_x = 0

A_x = 70 kN

The answer is (C) 70 kN.

(Note: Remember that most of the problems on the FE exam do not require a lot of work. The exam is testing your knowledge of basic engineering topics. If a problem seems really difficult, look for a simple easy to solve.)

Solution to Question # 139:

Don't need the Handbook for this.

Calculate Material Costs: in Bank Cubic Yards (BCY). Not Loose Cubic yard (LCY)

$20/BCY x 300 BCY = $6,000

Calculate Equipment Costs: Multiple the equipment cost/day by the number of days required to do the work.

15 days x $550/day = $8,250.

Calculate Personnel Costs:

$45/hr x 120hr (15 days) = $5,400

Sum all the costs = $ 6,000 + $8,250 + $5,400

= $19,650

The answer is (A) $19,650

Solution to Question #140:

Refer to page 95 of the FE Handbook: Statics: The centroid of a volume:

For this type of problem, it is easy to make simple chart for each component shape. If the problem does not split up the section into four component parts, you should do so: Split into well-known shapes: rectangles, triangles, and circles. It is important to select an origin to reference for all distances. For this problem, we selected the bottom left of shape # 1. All distances are referenced from this point.

xi - Horizontal length to the middle of the shape measured from the left side.

yi - Vertical length to the middle of the shape

Shape Area

(A)		xi	yi	xiA	yiA
1	(30)(10) = 300	15	5	300(15) = 4500	300(5) =1500
2	(10)(45) = 450	20+(30-20/2) = 25	10+(25+20/2)= 32.5	11,250	14,625
3	$\pi(8)^2$ = -201.1	30+10= 40	10+25= 35	-8044	-7038.5
4	1/2(50)(55) = 1375	30 + 1/3(50) = 46.67	2/3(55) = 36.67	64171.3	50421.3

(Note: The circle represents a hole in the object and is therefore treated as a negative area, so we must subtract it out)

Now, just sum each one of these up:

ΣA = 1923.9 $\qquad$ ΣxiA = 71877 $\qquad$ ΣyiA = 59508

There, centroid location for the composite area is:

x = $\Sigma x_i A_i / \Sigma A_i$ = 71877/1923.9 = 37.36

y = $\Sigma y_i A_i / \Sigma A_i$ = 59508/1923.9 = 30.93

The answer is (B) 37.36, 30.93.

Solution to Question # 141:

Basic Dynamics.

The Torque on the Engine will be:

T =Fr
T = 25 lbf (2.5 in/12)
T = 5.2 ft lbs

Since the cord rotates the engine 6 (2π) = 37.6 radians,
Work = 5.2 (37.6)
= 196 ft lbs

The answer is (C) 196 ft lbs

Solution to Question # 142:

Refer to page 265 of the FE handbook: Slop Failure Along Planar Surface. See the diagram.

FS = T_{FF} / T_{MOB}

T_{FF} = 250lb (given)

T_{MOB} = W_M sin $Ø_S$
T_{MOB} = 100 lb (sin (32))
= 52.9 lb

FS = 250 / 52.9
FS = 4.7

The Answer is (D) 4.7

Solution to Question # 143:

Refer to page 65 of the FE Handbook: Probability density function:

P(x > 7) = 3 × 0.2/2 = 0.3

There are only 3 numbers greater than 7, therefore, 3 out of 10 = .3, or 30%.

The answer is (A) .3.

Solution to Question # 144:

Refer to page 65 of the FE Handbook: Expected Value:

The formula for expected gain in probability and statistics is E(X) =$\sum$X*P(X). What this is saying "The expected value is the sum of all the gains (positive and negative) multiplied by their individual probabilities."

Therefore:

If you win, your gain will be $15,000 - $10 (cost of the ticket) = $14,990

To win $14,990, there is a 1/2000 chance.

If you lose, the amount that you lose is -$10. There is a 1999/2000 chance that you will lose.

Now, let's sum up amounts multiplied by their individual probabilities:

$14,990 • 1/2000 = $7.495

(-$10) • (1,999/2,000) = -$9.995

Therefore:

= $7.495 - $9.995

= -$2.5   (Note: you should expect to lose $2.5 on average, so this is not a good bet).

The answer is (C) -$2.5.

Solution to Question # 145:

Refer to page 35 of the FE Handbook: Straight Line:

This is a basic type of problem. You just need to know how to do it.

They give us the slope: m = 8/6, and the point (12,8)

Since we know the slope, you use the Point Slope Form Equation:

$M = (y_2 - y_1) / (x_2 - x_1)$ (substitute in what you know)

$8/6 = (y_2 - 8) / (x_2 - 12)$ (ok, let's rearrange the equation)

$8/6 (x_2 - 12) = (y_2 - 8)$ (Rearrange the equation)

$8_{x2}/6 - 8(12)/6 = (y_2 - 8)$ (Now, distribute the 8/6 into (x2 -12))

$8_{x2}/6 - 16 = (y_2 - 8)$ (solve for y2)

$8_{x2}/6 - 16 + 8 = y_2$

$8_{x2}/6 - 8 = y_2$

$y_2 = 8x_2/6 - 8$ (ok, this is the equation of that line)

If you graph what we have, it will look like this:

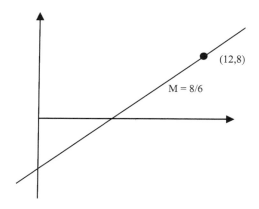

Now, using your equation of the line, let's set $x_2 = 0$, to find out where y_2 crosses the vertical axis.

$y_2 = 8x_2/6 -8$ (set $x_2 = 0$)

$y_2 = 8(0)/6 -8$

$y_2 = 0 - 8$

$y_2 = -8$ (so now we know that the line crosses at $y = -8$)

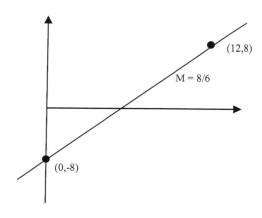

We now have our 2 points. How do we find out the distance?

Use the Distance formula: Distance between two points (page 35)

$D = $ sq root of $((y_2-y_1)^2 + (x_2-x_1)^2)$

$D = \text{sq root of } ((8-(-8))^2 + (12-0)^2)$

$D = \text{sq root of } ((256) + (144))$

$D = \text{sq root of } 400$

$D = 20$

The correct answer is (C) 20

Solution to Question # 146:

You should know how to set this up by now.

Given:

Future value (F) =$18,000
$i = 4\%$
$n = 4$ years.

The question is asking for the annually value, so we need to calculate the annuity (A).

Therefore, since we know that the future value (F) is $18,000, we need to find the value of A given F. (A/F)

Refer to page 235 of the FE Handbook: 4% interest Table:

n= 4 years, find the value of "A/F". Remember, we are trying to find the Annuity (A) value given the Future value (F) of $18,000. So we say "A given P". (A/P)

The value from the chart for A/F is: .2355

Therefore:

$A = F (A/F,i,n)$
$A = (\$18,000) (A/F, 4\%, 4)$
$A = (18,000) (0.2355)$
$A = \$4,239$

The answer is (B) $ 4,239.

Solution to Question # 147:

Refer to page 302 of the Fe Handbook: Horizontal Curves: Table at Bottom.

$0.01e + f = V^2/15R$
$0.01e + .11 = 65^2 / 15 (1250)$
$0.01e + .11 = .23$
$0.01e = .1153$
$e = .1154$
$e = 11.5\%$

The answer is (D) 11.5%

Solution to Question # 148:

Concrete is strong in compression but weak in tension. With the force shown, the cantilevered beam will bend towards the ground. Therefore, the bottom of the beam will be in compression while the top fibers will be in tension (because it is stretching). The rebar should go in the top of the beam where the tension is located.

The answer is (C)

(Note: Remember that many problems most exams only involve 2 to 3 steps -sometimes even 1 step. If the problem seems really involved and complicated, pick it apart and figure out what the question is really asking).

Solution to Question # 149:

Refer to page 36 of the FE Handbook: Polar Coordinate System:

From the given polar coordinates, we know that:

$r = 4$ and $\theta = -\pi/6$

The conversion formulas are:

x = r cos Θ

y = r sin Θ

Substituting:

x = 4 cos (-π/6)
x = 4 (($\sqrt{3}$)/2)
x = 2 ($\sqrt{3}$)

y = 4 sin (-π/6)
y = 4 (-1/2)
y = -2

Therefore, the rectangular coordinates are: (2 ($\sqrt{3}$), -2)

The answer is (D) (2 ($\sqrt{3}$), -2).

Solution to Question # 150:

Refer to page 192 of the FE Handbook: Fan Characteristics: Typical Backward Curved Fans:

Power = Q•ΔP/n$_f$

Given:

Q = 100 ft^3/sec

ΔP = 20 lb/in^2 • (144 in^2/ 1 ft^2) = 2880 lb/ft^2 (convert to lb/ft^2)

$n_f = 75\% = .75$

Therefore:

Power = Q•ΔP/n_f

Power = (100 ft³/sec) • (2880 lb/ft²) / .75

Power = 384,000 ft•lb/sec   (Note: the unit for power is work per unit time, however, the problem statement wants it in Horsepower)

Refer to page 3 of the FE Handbook: Conversion Factors:

= 384,000 ft•lb/sec (1.818×10^{-3})   (Note: the conversion factor 1.818×10^{-3} is just 1/550. It's easy to remember there is 550 ft lb/sec in 1 Hp)

= 698 Hp

The answer is (D) 698 Hp

Solution to Question # 151:

Refer to page 297 of the FE Handbook: Value of Hazen-Williams Coefficient C

The answer is (B) 130

Solution to Question # 152:

Refer to page 264 of the FE Handbook: Ultimate Bearing Capacity.

$$q_{ULT} = cN_c + \gamma' D_f N_q + \tfrac{1}{2}\, \gamma' B N_\gamma$$

Simple plug and chug problem:

$$q_{ULT} = 167\ \text{lbf/ft}^2\,(27) + 112\ \text{lbf/ft}^3\,(28\text{in ft}/12\text{in})\,(22) + \tfrac{1}{2}(112\ \text{lbf/ft}^3)\,(7.5\ \text{ft})(16)$$

Make sure to convert 28 in until feet: 2.33ft. Also, B is the depth below the ground surface. So the height of the footing of 24 in isn't used in this equation.

$$q_{ULT} = 4{,}509\ \text{lbf/ft}^2 + 5{,}749.3\ \text{lbf/ft}^2 + 6{,}720\ \text{lbf/ft}^2$$

$$q_{ULT} = 16{,}978\ \text{lbf/ft}^2$$

The answer is (D) 16,978 psf

Solution to Question # 153:

Refer to page 182 of the FE Handbook: Reynolds number:

Flow through a pipe is generally characterized as laminar for Re < 2,100 and fully turbulent for Re > 10,000, and transitional for 2100 < Re < 10000

The answer is (B) Laminar.

Solution to Question # 154:

Refer to page 131 of the FE Handbook: Uniaxial Loading and Deformation:

You shouldn't need to look this equation up in the handbook, this is a basic concept that you should know.

$\sigma = P/A$

Given:

P = 150 lbs

A = Square, L x W = 2 ft x 2ft = 4 ft^2

Therefore:

$\sigma = P/A$

$\sigma = 150$ lbs / 4 ft^2

$\sigma = 37.5$ lbs / ft^2

Note: The problem statement is asking for the stress to be in psi, not psf, therefore, we need to convert to psi:

$\sigma = 37.5$ lbs / ft^2 • (1 ft / 12 in)^2

$\sigma = 37.5$ lbs / ft^2 • (1 ft^2 / 12^2 in^2)

$\sigma = 37.5$ lbs / ft^2 • (1 ft^2 / 144 in^2)   (Note: the 12 is squared, so be sure to divide by 144, not 12!)

$\sigma = .26$ lbs / in^2, .26 psi

The answer is (c) .26 psi.

Solution to Question # 155:

Refer to page 63 of the FE Handbook: Probability

The key to this question is that the problem asked what are the chances of rolling 4 of the same of **ANY** number. It does not ask for the chances of rolling a particular number.

Therefore, the first dice which is rolled has a probability of 1 of rolling any number. There is a 100% chance that any number will come up. Pretty obvious, but this is important. The second dice which is rolled has a probability of 1/6 of rolling the same number which was rolled by the first dice. The third dice which is rolled has a probability of 1/6 of rolling the same number which was rolled by the first and second dice. Same is true for the fourth dice.

Therefore, to express this mathematically:

P = 1 (first dice) x 1/6 (second dice) x 1/6 (second dice) x 1/6 (third dice)

P = 1/216 (there is a one out of 216 chance of all 4 dice matching after the first round of rolling)

Not finished yet, the question asks for the number of times this would be expected to happen out of 10,000 attempts.

P = 1/(216) x 10,000
P = 46.29

The answer is (C) 46.

(Note: notice how we multiplied the probabilities together, not added them. You add probabilities to find the separate probability that one or the other will happen. Also, if the question asked how about a specific number as opposed to any number, the probability of the first roll will not be 1 anymore, it will be 1/6, and then you would simply just multiply the probabilities of the other rolls as we did)

Solution to Question # 156:

Refer to page 181 of the FE Handbook: The Continuity Equation:

Q = V (A)

Therefore, the velocity is given as 5 feet / second.

Compute the area of the pipe, the diameter is shown in the problem. (d = 6 inches)

$$A = (\pi d^2)/4 \quad \text{(simply the area of a circle)}$$

$$A = (\pi (6 \text{ in})^2)/4$$

$$A = (28.3 \text{ in}^2)$$

Convert in^2 to ft^2, $\quad A = (28.3 \text{ in}^2) * (\text{ft}/12 \text{ in})^2$

$$A = (28.3 \text{ in}^2) * (\text{ft}^2/12^2 \text{ in}^2)$$

$$A = (28.3 \text{ in}^2) * (\text{ft}^2/144 \text{ in}^2)$$

$$A = .19 \text{ ft}^2$$

$$Q = V (A)$$

$$Q = (5 \text{ ft/sec}) (.19 \text{ ft}^2)$$
$$Q = (5 \text{ ft/sec}) (.19 \text{ ft}^2)$$
$$Q = .98 \text{ ft}^3/\text{sec}$$

The correct answer is (A) .98 ft^3/sec.

Solution to Question # 157:

Ethics

Always do the Ethical thing. Since you had a feeling that the order was incorrect, it is YOUR responsibility as the manager to verify the purchase order before filling it.

The answer is (B) Call the POC of the company to verify the purchase order and express your concerns to them.

Solution to Question # 158:

Refer to page 58 of the FE Handbook: Determinates

For a 3rd order determinant,

$$\begin{vmatrix} a1 & a2 & a3 \\ b1 & b2 & b3 \\ c1 & c2 & c3 \end{vmatrix} = a1(b2)(c3) + a2(b3)(c1) + a3(b1)(c2) - a3(b2)(c1) - a2(b1)(c3) - a1(b3)(c2)$$

Therefore,

$= (0)(3)(6) + (2)(3)(3) + (0)(2)(4) - (0)(3)(3) - (2)(2)(6) - (0)(3)(4)$

$= \quad 0 \quad + \quad 18 \quad + \quad 0 \quad - \quad 0 \quad - \quad (24) \quad - \quad 0$

$= 18 - 24$

$= -6$

The answer (A) -6.

Solution to Question # 159:

Refer to page 128 of the FE Handbook: Binary Phase Diagram:

The answer is (A) Eutectic reaction.

Solution to Question # 160:

Ethics

Answer is (A).

Don't need the handbook.   Just calculate the force per foot from each shape:

Total Force = (first triangle) ½(3 ft) 280 lb/ft² + (rectangle)(4 ft) (280 lb/ft²) + (second triangle) ½(3 ft) 280 lb/ft²

= 420 lb /ft + 1,120 lb/ft + 420 lb /ft

= 1,960 lb/ft

(Note: for the rectangle shape, 4ft came from: 10 ft – 3 ft – 3ft = 4 ft)

Work this again until you understand that there are 3 basic shapes. There' nothing special about this problem.
The answer is (B) 1960 lb/ft

Solution to Question # 162: Ethics

Answer is (D) Welfare.

Solution to Question # 163:

Refer to page 314 of the FE Handbook: Table at top.

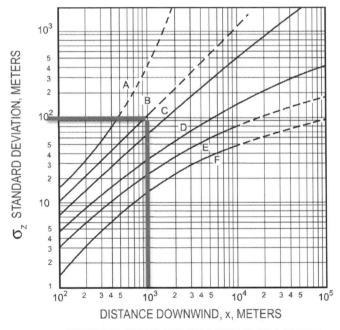

VERTICAL STANDARD DEVIATIONS OF A PLUME

The is answer is (C) 10^3

Solution to Question # 164:

Refer to page 131 of the FE Handbook: Uniaxial Loading and Deformation:

From the problem statement, we can conclude that:

P steel + P brass = 200 kips

However, this is only 1 equation with 2 unknowns so we can't solve it without another equation:

We can relate the

Δ steel = Δ brass

A steel = $\pi/4$ $(10)^2$ = 78.54 in^2, A brass = $\pi/4$ $(12^2 - 10^2)$ = 34.56 in^2

$P_s \, L / A_s \, E_s = P_b \, L / A_b \, E_b$

Therefore:

$P_s = A_s \, E_s / A_b \, E_b \, (P_b)$ (note: lengths cancel out)

    = 78.53 (29,000 ksi)/ 34.56 (17,000 ksi) (P_b) (Note: ksi = 1000 lb/in^2)
    = 3.87 P_b

Therefore: substitute into our original equation:

P steel + P brass = 200 kips

$(3.87 \, P_b)$ + P brass = 200 kips

4.87 P_b = 200 kips

P_b = 200 kips / 4.87

P_b = 41.07 kips, therefore P_s = 200 kips – 41.07 kips = 158.93 kips

The stress in the steel:

$\sigma_{steel} = P_s / A_s$

    = 158.93 kips / 78.54 in^2

    = 2.02 ksi

The answer is (D) 2.02 ksi.

Solution to Question # 165:

Refer to page 92 of the FE Handbook: Corrosion

The answer is (D) All of the above.

Solution to Question # 166:

Refer to page 126 of the FE Handbook: Impact Test: Charpy Impact Test:

The answer is (A) Charpy impact test.

Solution to Question # 167:

Refer to page 104 of the FE Handbook :

An additional equation for velocity as a function of position may be written as:

The equation is: $\quad\quad v^2 = (v_0)^2 + 2a_0(s - s_0)$

Given:

$v_0 = 0$ (since it starts from rest)

$a_0 = 32.2$ ft/s^2 *Refer to page 2 of the FE Handbook:* Fundamental Constants.

$s = 0$

$s_0 = -28$ feet

Therefore: plug values into the equation:

$v^2 = (v_0)^2 + 2a_0(s - s_0)$

$v^2 = (0)^2 + 2(32.2$ ft/s$^2) (0 - (-28$ feet)) $\quad$ (Note: realize that s_0 is a negative number)

$v^2 = 64.4$ ft/s^2 (28 feet)

$v^2 = 1803.2$ ft^2/s^2

$v = \sqrt{1803.2 \text{ ft}^2/\text{s}^2}$

$v = 42.5$ ft/s $\quad$ (Note: Always read the original problem, it is asking for velocity in miles per hour)

So, convert: $\quad\quad$ 42.5 ft/s (3600 s / 1 hr) (1 mile/5280 ft)

$\quad$ Therefore,

V= 28.9 miles/h $\quad\quad$ Watch your units!!!

The correct answer is (B) 28.9.

Answer (D) is not correct because the object's weight is negligible.

Note: Anytime an object is in free-fall, the velocity can easily be determined from the following equation regardless of the weight of the object:

Velocity $= \sqrt{2 \, (g) \, (\text{height})}$

Velocity $= \sqrt{2 \, (32.2 \, \text{ft/s}^2) \, (28 \, \text{ft})}$
Velocity $= \sqrt{1803.2 \, \text{ft}^2/\text{s}^2}$

Velocity $= 42.5$ ft/s

Solution to Question # 168:

Refer to page 197 of the FE Handbook: Similitude:

The answer is (C) Aesthetically similar.

Solution to Question # 169:

Refer to page 262 of the FE Handbook: Time Factor: At the bottom of the page.

$$T_v = C_v \, (t) \, / \, H^2$$

We're looking for little "t", we know H and C_v from the problem but we need to find T_v.

Look at the table above, Variation of time factor, find U(%) of 92 which was given in the problem. At 92%, $T_v = .938$. Since the liner is impervious, this is considered one way drainage.

$.938 = 3.8 \times 10^{-5} \, \text{ft}^2/\text{sec} \, (t) \, / \, (18\text{ft})^2$ (rearrange to find little "t")

$t = .938 \, (18\text{ft})^2 \, / \, 3.8 \times 10^{-5} \, \text{ft}^2/\text{sec}$

$t = 7,997,684.21$ sec $\times$ (day/ 86,400 sec)   (convert to days)

$t = 92.6$ days

The answer is (c) 93 days.

Solution to Question # 170:

Refer to page 316 of the FE Handbook: Cyclone.

$$N_e = 1/H \, [L_b + L_c / 2]$$
$N_e = 1/2 \, [7 + 3.5 / 2]$
$N_e = 1/2 \, [8.75]$
$N_e = 4.4$

The answer is (A) 4.4

Solution to Question # 171:

Refer to page 35 of the FE Handbook: Logarithms: Identities: Very top of the page.

Find the identity equation for quotient: $\log x/y = \log x - \log y$

Therefore,

$\log_3(x+2) - \log_3(x) = 2$

$\log_3((x+2)/x) = 2$

Changing the logarithm form according to the first equation: $\log_b(x) = c$, where $b^c = x$

$(x+2)/x = 3^2$

$x+2 = 9x$

$8x = 2$

$x = 0.25$

The answer is (B) .25.

Solution to Question # 172:

Refer to page 309 of the FE Handbook: Earthwork Formulas. Primoidal Formula:

$V = L(A_1 + 4A_m + A_2)/6$

$V = 1267(720 + 4(812) + 920)/6$

$V = 1,032,183$

The answer is (C) 1,032,183

Solution to Question # 173:

This is one of those conceptual problems that you don't need the handbook to solve. It's basic. If the total load is given, and you already know the area, you can find the actual pressure on the ground. Then just compare it to the allowable. The 2 ft below the surface isn't used.

$P = F/A$

$P = 75,000 \text{ lb} / \pi(10\text{ft})^2/4$

$P = 955 \text{ lb/ft}^2$

Now, to find the factor of safety:

$$FOS = Q_{allowable} / Q_{actual}$$

$= 2800 \text{ lb/ft}^2 / 955 \text{ lb/ft}^2$

= 2.9

The answer is (A) 3

Solution to Question # 174:

Refer to page 108 of the FE Handbook: Impact:

Answer is (C) Momentum is conserved.

Energy is conserved only if the collision is perfectly elastic. Energy may or may not be conserved.

Solution to Question # 175:

Refer to page 123 of the FE Handbook: Representative Values of Fracture Toughness:

The answer is (C) Silicon Carbide.

Solution to Question # 176:

Ethics

Answer is (D) Inform the project team of his findings and ensures the undersized rebar is replaced with the size specified.

(Note: Always play it straight in these types of questions. Remember that YOU are the engineer and public welfare and safety are FIRST! Don't be pressured by clients, bosses, or the schedule.)

Solution to Question # 177:

Refer to page 144 of the FE Handbook: PVT Behavior:

As soon as you read "ideal gas" you should automatically find the ideal gas equation. Just plug in the values.

$PV = mRT$

(1/2P) (2V) = mRT   (Just solve for "T")

T = 1/2P (2V) / mR

T = PV / mR, therefore, $T_2 = (1) T_1$

The answer is (A) Constant.

Solution to Question # 178:

Refer to page 231 of the FE Handbook: Straight-line depreciation.

The equation is:

$$D_j = \frac{C - S_n}{n}$$

From the question, we can find the givens:

Cost (C) = $20,000
n = 5 year life
S_n = Salvage value = $2000

Therefore:

D = ($20,000-$2,000) / 5

D = $3,600 per year (Note: this equation gives you the depreciation value per year)

At the end of the 3rd year, D = $3,600 (3) = $10,800.

Therefore:

The value will be:

$20,000 - $10,800 = $9,200

The answer is (B) $9,200

Solution to Question # 179:

Refer to page 236 of the FE Handbook: 10% Interest Rate Table:

We know: Future value (F) = $25,000, i = 10%, n = 3 years.

Therefore, we need to find the value of P given F. (P/F)

10% interest and n= 3 years, find the value of "P/F". Remember, we are trying to find the Present (P) value given the Future value (F) of $25,000. So we say "P given F".

The value from the chart for P/F is .7513

Therefore:
P = F(P/F,i,n)
P = ($25,000)(0.7513)
P = $18,782
The answer is (A) $18,782.

Solution to Question # 180:

Refer to page 260 of the FE Handbook: Relative Density:

D_r = [(e max – e) / (e max – e min)] x 100

$D_r = [(.68 - .491) / (.68 - .41)] \times 100$

$D_r = [(.189) / (.27)] \times 100$

$= 70\%$

The answer is (C) 70%

Solution to Question # 181:

Cavitation.

This is one of those you just need to know.

The answer is (B) II and III only

Solution to Question # 182:

Refer to page 263 of the FE Handbook: Horizontal Stress Profiles.

$$R_a = \tfrac{1}{2}(K_A)(\gamma)\, H^2$$

Givens:

$\gamma = 115\ lb/ft^3$

$H = 13\ ft$ (note: the base length of 4 ft is not needed. Also, H includes the thickness of the base, don't use 10ft, it's 10 ft + 3ft = 13 ft)

Let's find K_A: Since the backfill is horizontal, the same page towards the top shows an equation:

$K_A = \tan^2(45° - Ø/2)$

$= \tan^2(45° - 26/2)$

$= .39$

$$R_a = \tfrac{1}{2}(K_A)(\gamma)\, H^2$$

$= \tfrac{1}{2}(.39)(\,115\ lb/ft^3)(13\ ft)^2$

$= 3{,}789.8$

$= 3{,}790\ ft^3/s$

The answer is (C) 3,790

Solution to Question # 183:

Refer to page 98 of the FE Handbook: Table

This table has properties of common shapes. This table will come in handy for calculating moment of inertia for bending stress:

If trying to calculate the bending stress in beam, $\sigma = M y / I$ on page 135, I comes from this table:

The answer is (C) $bh^3/36$.

Solution to question # 184:

Refer to page 202 of the FE Handbook: Drag Coefficient for Spheres, Disks, and Cylinders:

Find $R_E = 100$ on the bottom of the table, go upwards until you reach the solid black line which represents a sphere. Go to the left to see that $C_D = 1$.

The answer is (A) 1.

Solution to Question # 185:

You do not need the handbook to solve these types of questions. Don't even have to calculate anything.

Notice that the load, F, is no at the center in the beam. It is offset to the left side. This eliminates answer choice (A) because it is symmetrical. This would be correct if the load, F, was centered in the middle of the beam.

Answer choice (B) is incorrect because the line is horizontal the entire way across and does not take into account the load, F. If the beam has a vertical force acting on it, the V-diagram has to contain a vertical line somewhere on the span.

Answer choice (D) is incorrect because the shape is a parabola. Remember: if the beam is only loaded with a vertical force, the V-diagram will only contain horizontal and vertical lines. The M-diagram would then be diagonal lines. However, if the beam was loaded with a distributed load, the V-diagram would contain diagonal lines, and the M-diagram would contain curved (parabola) lines. That's the easiest way to figure these types of problems.

Answer choice (C) is correct because the left side reaction will be greater than the right side because the load, F is closer to the left side. In addition, it drops vertically at the same location as the load, F is located.

The answer is (C).

Solution to Question # 186:

You don't need the handbook for this question. It's not a trick either, just reason it out.

Whatever this thing is, it wants to rotate counter clockwise by the (2) 50 N forces..
Since a Moment = F x D.   Let's take Moment about the left hand side:

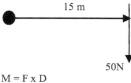

$$M = F \times D$$
$$M = 50N \times 15m$$
$$M = 750 \; Nm$$

(The 50N force acting down is the only force since the 50N acting up doesn't cause a Moment when we take Moments on the left-hand side)

Ok, let's take the moments about the right-hand side:

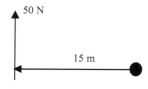

$$M = F \times D$$
$$M = 50N \times 15m$$
$$M = 750 \; Nm$$

(The 50N force acting up is the only force since the 50N acting down doesn't cause a Moment when we take Moments on the right-hand side)

Therefore, the resulting moment is 750 Nm.

The answer is (C) 750 Nm

Solution to 186B:

First convert minutes and seconds to their degree equivalents and add the results.

Decimal degrees = degrees + minutes/60 + seconds/3600

$= 265° + 32/60 + 13/3600$

$= 265° + .533 + .003611$

$= 265.54°$

The answer is (A) 265.54°

Solution to 186C:

You don't need the handbook for this question. Think like an engineer, don't run off looking for equations every time.

The pressure produced by the 100 lbs force is: $P = F/A$

$P = 100 \; lb \, / \, 1 \; in^2$
$P = 100 \; psi$,

The force which is produced at the large reservoir is:

$P = F/A$

$100 \text{ psi} = F/A$

$100 \text{ psi } (2 \text{ in}^2) = F$

$F = 200 \text{ pounds.}$

The answer is (D) 200 lbs.

Solution to 186D:

Refer to page 64 of the FE Handbook: Permutations and Combinations:

Choose 5 starters from a team of 12 players. Order is not important. The number of different *combinations* of n distinct objects *taken r at a time* is:

$$_nC_r = P_{(n, r)} / r! = n! / [r! (n-r)!)]$$

$$_{12}C_5 = P_{(12, 5)} / 5! = 12! / [5! (12-5)!)]$$

$12! / [5! (7)!)]$

$12(11)(10)(9)(8)7! / [5! (7)!)]$ (Note: 7! cancel each other out)

$12(11)(10)(9)(8) / 5(4)(3)(2)(1) = 792$

The answer is (C) 792.

Solution to 186E:

Refer to page 47 of the FE Handbook: Integral Calculus.

The answer to this question is not exactly stated in the handbook, but it is a basic concept that you should know from calculus.

The answer is (B) Area under the curve.

End of Exam 3.

Look, it's normal if you are struggling. Everyone one else is too! Ignore the naysayers. Work like hell. Stick to the plan and vision.

You're chopping down a think vegetative forest, clearing a path, but the path stays open forever... well, not exactly. But it will short term- in order to pass the exam. If you don't do these problems every day, you'll soon forget. But the process is more important because you'll be great at your real engineering job.

187) What is the rolling friction force (in Newtons) of a 3500 kg car moving at constant velocity on a horizontal road?

$u_k = 0.02$

(A) 588 Pounds

(B) 1500 Newtons

(C) 686 Newtons

(D) 500 Newtons

188) A sample from the geotechnical lab is analyzed for its properties. The effective (submerged) unit weight can be determined by which of the following equations?

(A) $\gamma' = \gamma_{sat} - \gamma_w$

(B) $\gamma' = \gamma_w - \gamma_{sat}$

(C) $\gamma' = \gamma_{sat} - \gamma_{\%}$

(D) $\gamma' = \gamma_w - \gamma_{dry}$

189) Find an equation using least squares regression and the below data:

$S_{xy} = 12.4$

$S_{xx} = 14.8$

$\overline{y} = 4$

$\overline{x} = 3$

(A) y = 2.3 + .75x

(B) y = 1.5 + .84x

(C) y = 7.9 + .64x

(D) y = 1.5 + .55x

190) If a construction company's total maintenance budget for the 2nd quarter was $148,000.00, how much more money was allocated to truck repair than forklift repair?

5% Dozers   25% Forklifts

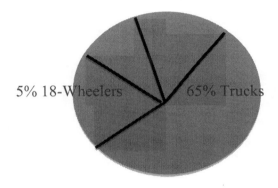

5% 18-Wheelers   65% Trucks

(A) $49,000

(B) $59,200

(C) $69,020

(D) $79,300

191) Find the force in member AB in the frame below.

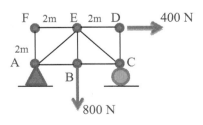

(A) 600 N

(B) 350 N

(C) 1275 N

(D) 0 N

192) A grain size distribution is plotted for a soil as shown below. The coefficient of curvature for this soil is most nearly:

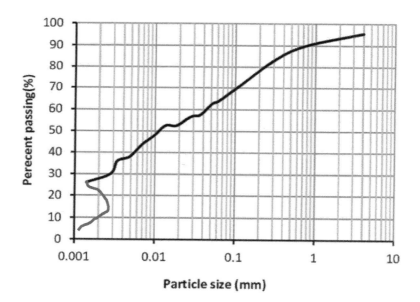

(A) 1.35

(B) .125

(C) .0125

(D) .1125

193) A round flywheel 1 meter in diameter has a mass of 100 kg and is subject to an input torque of 1000 Nm. What is the rate of angular acceleration?

(A) 120 rad / sec^2

(B) 13 rad / sec^2

(C) 138 rad / sec^2

(D) 80 rad / sec^2

194) Find the y-intercepts of $25x^2 + 4y^2 = 9$:

(A) $(^3/_2, 0)$ and $(^{-3}/_2, 0)$

(B) $(0, ^3/_2)$ and $(^{-3}/_2, 0)$

(C) $(0, ^3/_2)$ and $(0, ^{-3}/_2)$

(D) $(^3/_2, 0)$ and $(0, ^{-3}/_2)$

195) Which of the following occurs under load at elevated temperatures?

(A) Elongation

(B) Increased elasticity

(C) Creep

(D) Decreased ductility

196) No code can give immediate and mechanical answers to all ethical and professional problems that an engineer may face. Therefore, which of the following is often called for in ethics, just as in other areas of engineering?

(A) Paid problem solving

(B) Iterative problem solving

(C) Unethical problem solving

(D) Creative problem solving

197) Two coins are tossed; find the probability that two heads are obtained.

(A) 33%

(B) 50%

(C) 25%

(D) 66%

198) What is the dot product of vectors $\mathbf{A} \cdot \mathbf{B}$, if the magnitude of A is 10 units and the magnitude of B is 13 units. The angle between A and B is 59.5°?

(A) 66

(B) 33.3

(C) 99

(D) 77

199) Neglecting velocity head, friction, and minor losses, the motor size (hp) required to lift water from reservoir A to reservoir B is most nearly:

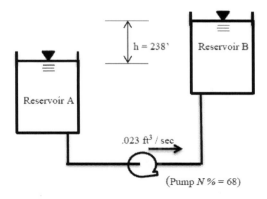

(A) .5

(B) 1

(C) 2

(D) 2.5

200) Which of the following terms has the unit of Pascal second (Pa•s)?

(A) Density

(B) Kinematic viscosity

(C) Absolute dynamic viscosity

(D) Vapor pressure

201) Complex numbers may be designated in rectangular form or in:

(A) Imaginary form

(B) Polar form

(C) Logarithmic form

(D) Root form

202) It costs $75 per year for an engineering company to maintain its online domain name. If the interest rate is 6.0%, how much must be set aside to pay for this yearly fee without touching the principal?

(A) $1,246

(B) $1,264

(C) $1,526

(D) $1,205

203) Calculate the potential energy stored in a spring when it is compressed 1/2 foot. (Assume k = 5 lb/ft)

(A) .525 ft lbs

(B) .319 ft lbs

(C) .899 ft lbs

(D) .625 ft lbs

204) If a rigid 2 force body is in equilibrium, then the two forces holding it must be:

(A) Non-concurrent

(B) Act at a right angle

(C) Similar

(D) Collinear

205) A survey crew is laying out a construction project. They measure out 3,813 feet of supply piping for a new building. The beginning point for the pipe is located at station 9+13. If the piping will be installed in the direction of stationing, the station number of the ending point is most nearly:

(A) 32+18

(B) 47+26

(C) 59+66

(D) 73+41

206) Given the soil profile below, the effective horizontal force is most nearly:

Ground Surface

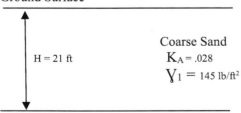

$H = 21$ ft

Coarse Sand
$K_A = .028$
$\gamma_1 = 145$ lb/ft^2

(A) 895 lb

(B) 958 lb

(C) 1274 lb

(D) 1583

207) Convert 235_8 into base 10.

(A) 157_{10}

(B) 213_{10}

(C) 157_8

(D) 175_{10}

208) Two cards are drawn at random from a standard deck of 52 cards, without replacement. What is the probability of drawing a 7 and a king in that order?

(A) 1/4

(B) 4/104

(C) 1/52

(D) 4/663

209) The moment diagram of a simply supported beam with a uniform load over the entire length has the shape of a:

(A) Rectangle

(B) Oval

(C) Diagonal

(D) Parabola

210) A motorist is traveling down a 4% grade at 72 mph and needs to stop because the draw bridge is going up. Assuming a 2.5 sec driver reaction time and a 17 ft/sec^2 deceleration rate, the stopping sight distance (SSD) in feet is most nearly:

(A) 312.89

(B) 475.99

(C) 511.23

(D) 618.70

211) An environmental engineer is designing horizontal standard deviations of a plume. If the distance downstream (meters) is 10^4 with a moderately unstable coefficient, the standard deviation is most nearly:

(A) 10

(B) 10^2

(C) 10^3

(D) 10^4

212) What of the following polymer classifications can be heated to high temperature and then reformed.

(A) Amorphous Materials

(B) Thermosets

(C) Thermoplastics

(D) Plasticizers

213) A survey crew is laying out a new roadway. If a particular section is 2.8 miles in length, the equivalent length in station is most nearly:

(A) 111.99

(B) 132.77

(C) 147.84

(D) 158.23

214) In which case below, Case 1 or Case 2, does the basketball undergo the greatest acceleration?

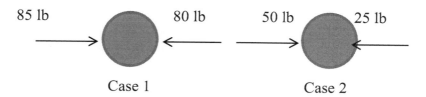

| 85 lb | Case 1 | 80 lb | 50 lb | Case 2 | 25 lb |

(A) Case 1

(B) Case 2

(C) Will be the same

(D) Neither

215) On a stress-strain curve for mild steel, the slope of the linear portion of the curve equals which of the following:

(A) Modulus of Rigidity

(B) Modulus of Elongation

(C) Modulus of Plasticity

(D) Modulus of Elasticity

216) Which of the following theory states that failure occurs when one of the three principal stresses equals the strength of the material?

(A) Coulomb-Mohr Theory

(B) Distortion-Energy Theory

(C) Maximum-Normal-Stress Theory

(D) Maximum-Shear-Stress Theory

217) A high-speed cam shaft costs $10,000 and has an estimated life of 10 years and scrap value of $1,500. Assuming interest rate of 4%, what uniform annual amount must be invested at the end of each of the 10 years in order to be able to afford to replace this component?

(A) $708.05

(B) $1,025.05

(C) $550.05

(D) $289.05

218) If $f(x, y) = y^4 x^3$, calculate $\partial f/\partial x$ (x,y)

(A) $6y^3x^2$

(B) $3y^4x^2$

(C) $3y^4x^3$

(D) $6y^2$

219) The diagram below shows an intersection which is prone to accidents. If the number of reported crashes were 52 and the average daily traffic entering the intersection is as shown, the crash rate per million vehicles is most nearly:

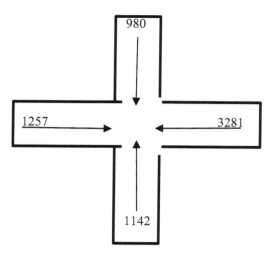

(A) 12.3

(B) 17.8

(C) 19.6

(D) 21.4

220) The critical load for the circular wood (fir) column shown below is most nearly:

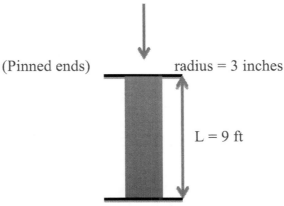

(Pinned ends)   radius = 3 inches

L = 9 ft

(A) 100 kip

(B) 87 kips

(C) 50 kips

(D) 47 kips

221) The manufacture of flying disks uses two different procedures to make their product. Method I utilizes a rigid plastic polymer and method II, a composite plastic. To compare the distance obtained using both types of disks, 12 throwers are allowed to launch the disk of each type, and the length of the throw (in yards) were measured (Assume X = 7, t $_{\sigma/2}$ = 5, s = 3.5) Calculate the confidence interval:

(A) (1.95, 11.12)

(B) (1.95, 11.01)

(C) (1.95, 12.01)

(D) (2.95, 12.01)

222) An engineering company's finance department is considering 2 different models to purchase a new and improved critical timing component for its automation welding process: Using the cost estimates below, what is the annual advantage of selecting Option 1 over Option 2? (Assume i = 6%).

	Option 1:	Option 2:
Initial Cost	$30,000	$47,000
Annual Cost	$1,200	$1,800
Life	3 years	6 years
Salvage Value	$900	$1,500

(A) -$798.61

(B) $995.61

(C) -$995.61

(D) $798.61

223) For corrosion to occur, there must be an anode and a cathode in electrical contact in the presence of an:

(A) Covalent bond

(B) Electrolyte

(C) Diffusion coefficient

(D) Government inspector

224) The continuity equation, $A_1V_1 = A_2V_2$, is only true is based on the following assumption:

(A) Free surface is open to the atmosphere

(B) Velocities < 100 ft/s

(C) Pipe roughness $\leq .05$

(D) Q is continuous

225) Solve the following integral: ∫ tan²x dx

(A) tan x^{2-1} – ax

(B) tan 2x – x

(C) tan x – x²

(D) tan x – x

226) How would you calculate the flow rate for an orifice which discharges freely into the atmosphere?

(A) $Q = C \cdot A_0 \cdot \sqrt{gh}$

(B) $Q = C \cdot A_0 \cdot 2gh$

(C) $Q = C \cdot A_0 \cdot \sqrt{2g(h_1 - h_2)}$

(D) $Q = C \cdot A_0 \cdot \sqrt{2gh}$

227) For a curved roadway with radius 680 feet, the degree of curve is most nearly:

(A) 4°33'67.91"

(B) 6°49'11.63"

(C) 8°25'33.07"

(D) 11°21'34.02"

228) If there are energy losses between (1) and (2), then Bernoulli's equation can be written as:

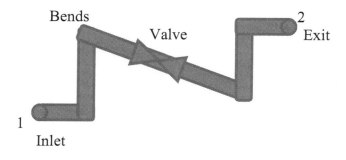

Bends   Valve   2 Exit

1
Inlet

(A) $V_1^2/2 + (g \cdot Z_1) + P_1 / \rho + \text{Energy Loss} = V_2^2/2 + (g \cdot Z_2) + P_2 / \rho$

(B) $V_1^2/2 + (g \cdot Z_1) + P_1 / \rho = V_2^2/2 + (g \cdot Z_2) + P_2 / \rho + \text{Energy Loss}$

(C) $V_1^2/2 + (g \cdot Z_1) = V_2^2/2 + (g \cdot Z_2) + P_2 / \rho + \text{Energy Loss}$

(D) $V_1^2/2 + (g \cdot Z_1) + P_1 / \rho + \text{Energy Loss} = (g \cdot Z_2) + P_2 / \rho$

229) What is the vapor pressure, v_p, (psi) for 50 °F water?

(A) .14

(B) .16

(C).18

(D) .20

230) The length of tangent for a horizontal circular curve with radius equal to 1850 feet and an intersection angle of 45 degrees is most nearly:

(A) 766 ft

(B) 795 ft

(C) 812 ft

(D) 988 ft

231) You are a professional engineer who was licensed 27 years ago. You are asked to evaluate a new and improved method levee armoring considering wave overtopping. You can accept this project if:

(A) You recently read an article pertaining to levee armoring

(B) You are competent in this area of levee armoring

(C) The price is worth your time

(D) You attend regular engineering society meetings

232) A traffic engineer is designing a vertical curve between 2 points shown below in which a -4.5% grade intersects another grade at Station 92+12 at elevation 199 ft. What elevation should the engineer use as the lowest point (x_m) on the curve?

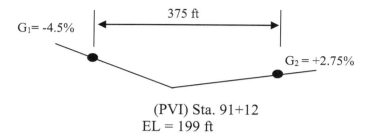

$$G_1 = -4.5\%$$

375 ft

$$G_2 = +2.75\%$$

(PVI) Sta. 91+12
EL = 199 ft

(A) 199.01 ft

(B) 200.99 ft

(C) 201.55 ft

(D) 202.21 ft

233) Calculate the energy (Joules) that is required to lift a 5 pound weight 2 feet high:

(A) 13.56 joules

(B) 10 joules

(C) 2 joules

(D) 20.87 joules

234) An engineer is compiling design criteria for a sedimentation basin for a local municipality's water treatment project. If lime-soda softening is specified for the project, the average surface water overflow rate (gpd/ft^2) for upflow clarifiers is most nearly:

(A) 750 - 1,500

(B) 1,000 - 1,800

(C) 1500 – 2200

(D) 2100 - 3800

235) What is the value of the Hazen Williams Coefficient, C, for 5-year-old cast iron piping?

(A) 150

(B) 120

(C) 130

(D) 140

236) For beams, if the right portion of the beam tends to shear downward with respect to the left, the shear force is said to be:

(A) Positive

(B) Zero

(C) Negative

(D) Insignificant

237) Traffic engineers conducted a study at a certain intersection which was prone to high crash rates. The report findings proposed countermeasures with crash reduction factors of 38%, 27%, and 19%. If all three countermeasures are implemented, the overall crash reduction factor is most nearly:

(A) .63

(B) .35

(C) .81

(D) .10

238) The combination of applied stress and the crack length in a brittle material is referred to as:

(A) Fracture failure

(B) Fracture toughness

(C) Fracture stiffness

(D) Fracture readiness

239) For the "positive bending" beam shown below, the top fibers are said to be in:

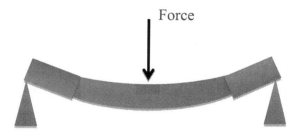

Force

(A) Shear

(B) Tension

(C) Torsion

(D) Compression

240) The mechanical and plasticity test of a soil under consideration as a fill material are shown below:

Mechanical Analysis		Plasticity	
Sieve	% Passing by weight	Liquid Limit	Plastic Limit
10	21	70	30
40	25		
200	66		

(A) CH

(B) GP

(C) SW

(D) CL

241) Licensed engineers should only accept work for clients when:

(A) They need to make money

(B) Only in area where they are technically competent

(C) When their schedule permits

(D) Their bid is the lowest amount

242) A mechanical contractor is preparing to install (8) supply lines (each has a O.D. of 36 inches) at a construction jobsite for a large pumping station. Because of its proximity of a military base and security threat level, the specifications require the lines to be encased in concrete in a duct bank which will be 75ft x 4ft. The total distance of the run is 420 feet. The volume of concrete (yd³) is most nearly:

(A) 3,787

(B) 4,280

(C) 5,611

(D) 9,588

242B) Determine the reaction at point B in the truss shown below:

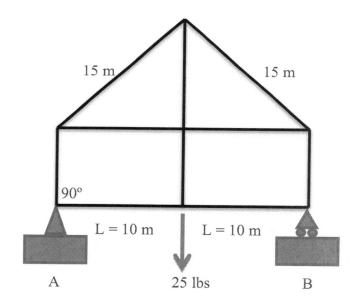

(A) 12.5 lbs

(B) 24 lbs

(C) 8.75 lbs

(D) 22.25 lbs

242C) A canal (wetted perimeter = 75 ft) contains a drainage pipe (inner diameter = 1 foot, roughness factor = .02) which is used to control runoff from the local car dealer parking lot. Assuming a flow rate of 100 ft³/sec through the pipe, find the velocity of the water through the pipe: Assume time of concentration = 15 min.

(A) 50 ft/sec

(B) 127 ft/sec

(C) 75 ft/sec

(D) 211 ft/sec

Exam # 4 (Solutions)

Solution to Question # 187:

Refer to page 109 of the FE Handbook: Laws of Friction.

Apply Newton's law of motion.
Since car is not accelerating, sum forces = 0

To solve for rolling frictional force, you just have to multiply the weight of the car by the coefficient of rolling friction. However, realize that the mass of the car was given in the problem, not the weight of the car. In SI units, mass is usually given in "kg" while force is in Newtons. In English system, mass has units of "lb/ (ft/sec^2)" (commonly referred to as a "slug") while force has units of pounds.

Given:
mass car = 3500 kg
$u_k = 0.02$

By definition:
F = rolling friction force = u_k**N**
W (weight of car) = mg

Solve:
Since the car is on horizontal surface: **N** = -**W**

Since the equation of rolling friction force is **F** = u_k**N,**

You can substitute W for N:
F = -uk(W)

F = $-u_k$mg = -0.02(3500 kg) (9.8 m/sec^2)

(Note: the value of "g" comes the Universal Constants)

F = 686 Newtons, **Answer is (C) 686 Newtons**

Hint: Right off the bat, you could have eliminated answer (A), since the units are in pounds. The question specifically wanted the answer in newtons.

Solution to Question # 188:

Refer to page 259 of the FE Handbook: Phase Relationships.

Effective (submerged) unit weight is:

The answer is (A) $\mathbf{Y}' = \mathbf{Y}_{sat} - \mathbf{Y}_w$

Solution to Question # 189:

Refer to page 69 of the FE Handbook: Least Squares Regression and Goodness of Fit:
y = a + bx

$b = S_{xy} / S_{xx}$, $(12.4)/(14.8) = .84$

$a = \overline{y} - b\overline{x}$, $(4) - (.84)(3) = 1.5$

Therefore:

$y = a + bx$

$y = 1.5 + .84x$

The answer is (B) $y = 1.5 + .84x$

Solution to Question # 190:

Don't need the handbook for basic math type questions:

Let's find out how much money was allocated for trucks and forklift repair:

Trucks: $148,000 (65%) = $96, 200
Forklifts: $148,000 (25%) = $37,000

Therefore:

= $96,200 - $37,000

= $59,200

The answer is (B) $59,200. (Yes, sometimes it's that easy)

Solution to Question # 191:

Statics. Do it.
Draw a free body diagram of the external forces:

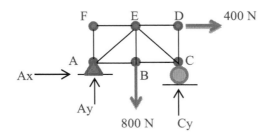

(Note: Point C is a roller support, therefore there is only a force in the y Direction, Cy. Point A is a fixed support, so it has components Ax and Ay.

Let's take moments about Point A:

$+\curvearrowleft \sum M_A = 0$

$+\curvearrowleft \sum M_A$: 800N (2m) – Cy (4m) + 400N (2m) = 0

(Note: 800N force is 2m away from point A.

Cy is 4m away from point A. 400 N is 2m away from point A (vertical direction).

$+\curvearrowleft \sum M_A$: 1600N· m – Cy (4m) + 800N·m = 0

$+\curvearrowleft \sum M_A$: 2400N· m – Cy (4m) = 0

$+\curvearrowleft \sum M_A$: 2400N· m = Cy (4m)

$+\curvearrowleft \sum M_A$: <u>Cy = 600 N</u>

From the diagram, $F_{CD} = 0$, since there is no vertical force at point D. Force F_{ED} and the 400N are horizontal. Sometimes, you can see from the original problem if a member will be zero if it forms a tee like in this problem.

Therefore:

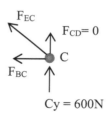

$$Cy = 600N$$

It can be determined that $F_{EC(y)} = 600N$, since it has the only component in the Y-direction. F_{BC} is in the horizontal direction. Also, $F_{EC (x)} = 600N$, since it is a 45° angle.

Therefore,

$F_{EC (x)} = 600N = F_{BC} = F_{AB}$

The answer is (A) 600 N.

Solution to Question # 192:

Refer to page 260 of the FE Handbook: Coefficient of Concavity (or curvature)

If you searched for coefficient of curvature nothing came up. So be careful. Sneaky people aren't they?

$$C_c = (D_{30})^2 / D_{10} \times D_{60}$$

Use the chart to find the 3 values you need. The vertical axis of the diagram says "percent passing" so it's not tricky. Simple find 10, 30, and 60 values. At the end of this problem, I'll show you a potential trick they could ask.

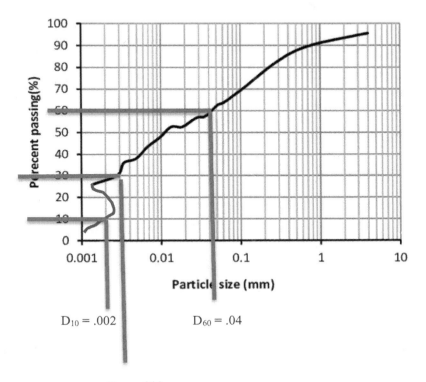

$D_{10} = .002$

$D_{60} = .04$

$D_{30} = .003$

$C_c = (.003)^2 / .002 \times .04$

$C_c = .1125$

Now if the vertical axis was labeled percent "Retained", you would have to choose the value 90 and go across in order to find D_{10}, 70 to find D_{30}, 40 to find D_{60}.

The answer is (D) .1125.

Solution to Question # 193:

Refer to page 111 of the FE Handbook: Rotation about fixed axis:

$T = I \cdot \alpha$, therefore, $\alpha = T / I$

T = 1000 Nm
Diameter = 1m, radius = .5 meter

Flywheel is a circular disk: *page 116 of the FE Handbook*: Mass moment of Inertia:

I = 1/2 (m) r^2 (make sure to use Izz since it's rotating about the z-axis)
I = 1/2 (100 kg) (.5 meter)^2
I = 12.5 kg•m^2

Therefore:

α = T / I
α = (1000 Nm) / (12.5 kg•m^2)
α = 80 rad / sec^2

The answer is (D) 80 rad / sec^2.

Solution to Question # 194:

In order to solve for the *y*-intercept(s), set x =0.

So, substitute 0 for x in the original equation.

$25x^2 + 4y^2$ = 9
$25(0)^2 + 4y^2$ = 9
$0 + 4y^2$ = 9

$y^2 = ^9/_4$
$y = \pm (^3/_2)$ (remember when taking the square root it can be + or -)

Therefore, the *y*-intercepts are the points (0, $^3/_2$) and (0, $^{-3}/_2$).

(Note: If the question asks you to find the x -intercept, you need to set y =0)

The answer is (C) (0, $^3/_2$) and (0, $^{-3}/_2$).

Solution to Question # 195:

Refer to page 122 of the FE Handbook: Creep

The answer is (C) Creep.

Solution to Question # 196:

Ethics.

The answer is (D) Creative problem solving.

Solution to Question # 197:

Refer to page 63 of the FE Handbook; Probability:

Each coin has two possible outcomes H (heads) and T (Tails).

On the first toss, there is a ½ chance that it will land on heads. So, P (1st) = ½

On the second toss, there is a ½ chance that it will land on heads. So, P (2nd) = ½

Therefore:

The problem statement asks for the probability that it will come up heads both times, so we need to multiply the odds together:

P (total) = P (1st) • P (2nd)

P (total) = ½ • ½

= ¼

= 25%

The answer is (c) 25%

Solution to Question # 198:

Refer to page 59 of the FE Handbook: Vectors:

In order to find the dot product, multiply the length of A times the length of B, then multiply by the cosine of the angle between A and B.

$|\mathbf{A}| \times |\mathbf{B}| \times \cos(\theta)$ (Note: |A| means the magnitude (length) of vector A)

Substitute in the values:

$\mathbf{A} \cdot \mathbf{B} = 10 \times 13 \times \cos(59.5°)$
$\mathbf{A} \cdot \mathbf{B} = 10 \times 13 \times 0.5075...$

$\mathbf{A} \cdot \mathbf{B} = 65.98... = 66$ (rounded)

The answer is (A) 66.

(You can only multiply their lengths together when the vectors point in the same direction)

(Note: When two vectors are at right angles to each other the dot product is **zero)**

Solution to Question # 199:

Refer to page 192 of the FE Handbook: Pump Power Equation: Middle pf page.

If the efficiency of the pump is given, by sure to divide by it! It does not have it in the equation so be careful.

From the problem, we know:

hA = 238 ft
Q = .023 ft^3 / sec

Therefore, the equation to use is:

$$Hp = (QY\ h) /\ (\text{pump efficiency})$$

$$= (.023\ \text{ft}^3\ /\text{sec})\ (62.4\ \text{lb/ft}^3)(238\ \text{feet}) /\ (.68))$$

(Note: page 177: specific weight of water is $62.4\ \text{lb/ft}^3$)

$$= 502.32\ \text{ft lb /sec}\quad (\text{page 3: convert ft lb/sec to hp, x } 1.818 \times 10^{-3})$$

$$= .913\ hp$$
$$= 1\ hp$$

The answer is (B) 1

Solution to Question # 200:

Refer to page 199 of the FE Handbook: Properties of Water: Table:

The answer is (C) Absolute dynamic viscosity.

Solution to Question # 201:

Refer to page 36 of the FE Handbook: Algebra of Complex Numbers:

The answer is (B) Polar form.

Solution to Question # 202:

Refer to page 235 of the FE Handbook: 6% Interest Table:

We are trying to calculate the Present worth (P), given the yearly annuity of $75 per year.

Therefore, the value we need to find in the interest rate tables is "P given A", or "P/A" – We want to know "P" and we were given the annuity "A" in the problem.

(Note: an annuity is a reoccurring cost!)

Find the value of P/A (we know i = 6%, and n = 100 years. The number of years was not given in the problem but we are choosing the highest number we can, which is 100 years- assuming the company stays in business the longest possible time)

P/A = 16.6175

Therefore:

$P = (\$75)\ (P/A,6\%,100)$
$P = (\$75)\ (16.6175)$
$P = \$1,246$

The answer is (A) $1,246.

Solution to Question # 203:

Refer to page 107 of the FE Handbook: Potential Energy:

$U = k\, x^2/2$

$U = [(5\ \text{lb/ft})\, (.5\ \text{ft})^2]/2$

$U = .625\ \text{ft lbs}$

The answer is (D) .625 ft lb

Solution to Question # 204:

Refer to page 97 of the FE Handbook: Concurrent Forces:

A *two-force* body in static equilibrium has two applied forces that are equal in magnitude, opposite in direction, and collinear.

The answer is (D) Collinear.

Solution to Question # 205:

$= 913' + 3,813$

$= 4,726\ \text{ft}$

$= 47+26$

The answer is (B) 47+26

Solution to Question # 206:

Refer to page 263 of the Fe Handbook: Horizontal Stress Profiles and Forces:

$= \frac{1}{2}\ Y_1\ K_A H^2$ (use this equation since no groundwater is present)

$= \frac{1}{2}\ 145\ \text{lb/ft}^2\ (.028)\ (21\,\text{ft})^2$

$= 895\ \text{lb}$

The answer is (A) 895 lb.

Solution to Question # 207:

Refer to page 35 of the FE Handbook: Logarithms

Above each of the digits in your number, list the power of the base that the digit represents.

$8^2 \, 8^1 \, 8^0$

2 3 5

It is now a simple process of multiplication and addition to determine your base 10 number. In this example you have

$5 \times 8^0 = 5$
$3 \times 8^1 = 24$
$2 \times 8^2 = 128$

Now simply add these values together.
$5 + 24 + 128 = 157$
Answer: $235_8 = 157_{10}$

(Note: any number to the zero power equals one.)

The answer is (A) 157_{10}.

Solution to Question # 208:

Refer to page 64 of the FE Handbook: Permutations and Combinations:

There are four sevens and four kings in order

$$_4P_1 \quad \cdot \quad _4P_1$$

From a deck of 52 cards $_{52}P_2$ (want 2 cards, r#)

Solution: $\dfrac{4 \cdot 4}{52 \cdot 51} = \dfrac{16}{2652}$

$$= \dfrac{4}{663} \quad \text{(reduced)}$$

The answer is (D) 4/663.

Solution to Question # 209:

Statics

The shear diagram is triangular.

Answer is (D) Parabola.

Solution to question #210:

Refer to page 299 of the FE Handbook: Stopping Sight Distance

$$SSD = 1.47 \, Vt + V^2 / 30((a/32.2) +- G)$$

$SSD = 1.47 \, (72)(2.5) + 72^2 / 30 \, ((17/32.2) - .04)$

$SSD = 264.6 + 5,184/14.64$

$SSD = 264.6 + 354.1$

$SSD = 618.70 \, ft$

The answer is (D) 618.70.

Solution to Question # 211:

Refer to page 314 of the FE Handbook: Table at the bottom:

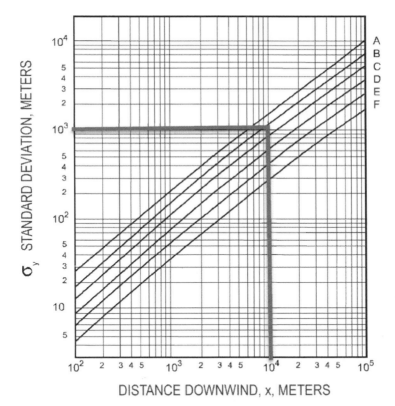

HORIZONTAL STANDARD DEVIATIONS OF A PLUME

The answer is (C) 10^3

Solution to Question # 212:

Refer to page 127 of the FE Handbook: Polymers:

The answer is (C) Thermoplastics.

Solution to Question # 213:

= 2.8 miles * 5280ft/mile

= 14,784 ft * (1 Station/ 100 ft)
= 147.84

The answer is (C) 147.84

Solution to Question # 214:

Not written in the handbook, but you should be familiar with this type of problem.

Case 2 results in the greatest acceleration. Even though the individual forces are greater in Case 1, the net force is greatest in Case 2. Acceleration depends on the net force; it is not dependent on the size of the individual forces.

The answer is (B) Case 2.

Solution to Question # 215:

Refer to page 130 of the FE Handbook: Stress Strain Curve:

The answer is (D) Modulus of Elasticity.

Solution to Question # 216:

Refer to page 448 of the FE Handbook: Static Loading Failure Theories:

The answer is (C) Maximum-Normal-Stress Theory.

Solution to Question # 217:

Refer to page 235 of the FE Handbook: 4% Interest Rate Table:

A = ($10,000-$1,500) (A/F, 4%, 10 years)
A = ($8,500) (.0833)
A = $708.05

The answer is (A) $708.05.

Solution to Question # 218:

Refer to page 45 of the FE Handbook: Partial Derivative:

Partial derivatives are easy to do, in this case since the problem wants to know it with respect to "x" (hence, $\partial f/\partial x$), simply view "y" as being a fixed number and calculate the ordinary derivative with respect to "x". You should treat "y" as though it were number rather than a variable. Basically Ignore "y".

$g(x) = y^4 x^3$

$g(x) = (3)y^4 x^2$ (when taking a derivative, the exponent comes down to the front, and then the new exponent is simply the old exponent minus 1)

Therefore:

$\partial f / \partial x \ (x,y) = 3y^4 x^2$

The answer is (B) $3y^4 x^2$.

Solution to Question # 219:

Refer to page 306 of the FE Handbook: Traffic Safety Equations.

Use the Crash rate at intersections, not Roadway Segments.

RMEV = A x 1,000,000 / V

RMEV = A x 1,000,000 / ADT x 365

RMEV = 52 x 1,000,000 / (980 + 1257+ 3281+ 1142) x 365

RMEV = 52,000,000 / 2,430,900

RMEV = 21.39

The answer is (D) 21.4

Solution to Question # 220:

Refer to page 137 of the FE Handbook: Columns:

$P_{critical} = \pi^2 \cdot E \cdot I / L^2$

Given:

L = 9ft = 108 in

E = 1.6 Mpsi (see page 138 Material Properties: for Wood (fir), E = 1.6 Mpsi)

$I = \pi \cdot r^4 / 4$ (see page 112: Table of different shapes: for a solid circle, $(I = \pi \cdot r^4 / 4)$
$I = \pi \cdot (3 \text{ in})^4 / 4$
$I = 64 \text{in}^4$

Therefore:

$P_{critical} = \pi^2 \cdot E \cdot I / L^2$

$P_{critical} = \pi^2 \cdot (1,600,000 \text{ psi}) \cdot (64 \text{ in}^4) / (108 \text{ in})^2$

$P_{critical} = \pi^2 \cdot (8726.388 \text{ lb})$

$P_{critical} = 86,559 \text{ lb}$

$P_{critical} = 86 \text{ kips}$

The answer is (B) 87 kips.

Solution to Question # 221:

Refer to page 74 of the FE Handbook: Confidence Interval:

Standard deviation is not known, therefore:

$X - t_{\sigma/2} \cdot s / \sqrt{n} \leq \mu \leq X - t_{\sigma/2} \cdot s / \sqrt{n}$

Given:

$t_{\sigma/2} = 5$
$s = 3.5$
$X = 7$
$n = 12$ (stated in the problem, 12 throwers)

Therefore:

$X - t_{\sigma/2} \cdot s / \sqrt{n} \leq \mu \leq X - t_{\sigma/2} \cdot s / \sqrt{n}$

$7 - 5 \cdot 3.5 / \sqrt{12} \leq \mu \leq 7 + 5 \cdot 3.5 / \sqrt{12}$

$7 - 5 \cdot (1.01) \leq \mu \leq 7 + 5 \cdot (1.01)$
$7 - (5.05) \leq \mu \leq 7 + (5.01)$

$(1.95, 12.01)$

The answer is (C) (1.95, 12.01).

Solution to Question # 222:

Refer to page 235 of the FE Handbook: 6% Interest Rate table:

= [-\$30,000 (A/P, 6%, 3 years) - \$1,200 + \$900(A/F, 6%, 3 years)] – [-\$47,000(A/P, 6%, 6 years) - \$1,800 + \$1,500(A/F, 6%, 6 years)]

= [-\$30,000 (.3741) - \$1,200 + \$900(.3141)] – [-\$47,000(.2034) - \$1,800 + \$1,500(.1434)]

= [-\$11,223 - \$1,200 + \$282.69] – [-\$9,559.80 - \$1,800 + \$215.1]

= [-\$12,140.31] – [-\$11,144.70]

= -\$995.61

The answer is (c) -$995.61.

Solution to Question # 223:

Refer to page 117 of the FE Handbook: Corrosion:

The answer is (B) Electrolyte.

Solution to Question #224:

Refer to page 181 of the FE Handbook: The Continuity Equation:

The answer is (D) Q is continuous.

Solution to Question # 225:

Refer to page 48 of the FE Handbook: Derivatives and Indefinite Integrals:

Simply use the table for Integrals to find $\int \tan^2 x \, dx$:

Remember, if you find yourself asking how in the world am I supposed to know this stuff, it's usually a good sign that the answer is stated somewhere in the manual.

Therefore:

The answer is (D) tan x – x.

Solution to Question # 226:

Refer to page 186 of the FE Handbook:

$Q = C \cdot A_0 \cdot \sqrt{2gh}$

The answer is (D) $Q = C \cdot A_0 \cdot \sqrt{2gh}$.

Solution to Question # 227:

Refer to page 301 of the FE Handbook: Horizontal Curves:

$R = 5729.58 / D$

$680 \text{ ft} = 5729.58 / D$

$D = 5729.58 / 680\text{ft}$

= 8.425852
= .425852 x 60 = 25.55112
= .55112 x 60 = 33.07
= 8°25'33.07"

The answer is (C) 8°25'33.07"

Solution to Question # 228:

Refer to page 181 of the FE Handbook: The Energy Equation:

$V_1^2/2 + (g \cdot Z_1) + P_1 / \rho = V_2^2/2 + (g \cdot Z_2) + P_2 / \rho + \text{Energy Loss}$

The answer is (B).

Solution to Question # 229:

Refer to page 199 of the FE Handbook: Properties of Water (English Units):

Just find it on the table:

The answer is (C).18.

Solution to Question # 230:

Refer to page 301 of the FE Handbook: Horizontal Curves:

T = R tan (I/2)
T = 1850 ft x tan (45/2)
= 766.30

The answer is (A) 766 ft

Solution to Question # 231:

Ethics.

The answer is (B) You are competent in this area of levee armoring.

Solution to Question # 232:

Refer to page 300 of the FE Handbook: Vertical Curves:

Let's find the distance of the lowest point from PVC:

Xm = g1 L / g1 – g2
Xm = - .045 (375) / -.045 – .0275
Xm = - 16.875 / (- 0.0725)
Xm = 233 ft

To find the lowest elevation point you use this crazy formula:

Curve elevation: $Y_{PVC} + g1x + [(g2 - g1)/(2L)]x^2$

Be careful, the elevation at PVC isn't given, only PVI is given.

So you need to convert it: Use half of the total curve length and the slope:

PVC elevation = 199 + 375/2 x (.045) = 207.44

Now plug and chug:

$$Y_{PVC} + g1x + [(g2 - g1)/(2L)]x^2$$

207.44 + - .045(233) + [(.0275 - -.045)/ 2(375)] 233²

207.44 - 10.485 + [.0725 / 750]54,289

= 196.955 + 5.25

= 202.21 ft

The answer is (D) 202.21 ft

Solution to Question # 233:

Refer to page 107 of the FE Handbook : Work:

Work = F • D

Given:

F = 5 lb
D = 2 ft

Therefore:

Work = F • D

Work = (5 lb) • (2ft)

Work = 10 ft • lb

The question wants the answer to be in the unit of "joules":

Convert ft lbs to joules:

Refer to page 2 of the FE Handbook: Conversion Factors:

On the left side of the page, multiply ft lb by 1.356 to obtain joules:

10 ft • lbs (1.356) =

13.56 joules

The answer is (A) 13.56 Joules.

Solution to Question # 234:

Refer to page 340 of the FE Handbook. Design Criteria for Sedimentation Basins.

Just read the table

The answer is (B) 1,000 - 1,800

Solution to Question # 235:

Refer to page 297 of the FE Handbook: Values of the Hazen Williams Coefficient, C

The answer is (B) 120.

Solution to Question # 236:

Refer to page 135 of the FE Handbook: Beams:

The answer is (A) Positive.

Solution to Question # 237:

Refer to page 307 of the FE Handbook. Crash Reduction.

To find the overall CR factor for multiple improvements, use this formula:

$CR = CR_1 + (1 - CR_1) CR_2 + (1 - CR_1) (1 - CR_2) CR_3$

$CR = .38 + (1-.38) .27 + (1-.38)(1-.27) .19$

$CR = .38 + .1674 + .085994$

$CR = .633394$

The answer is (A) .63

Solution to Question # 238:

Refer to page 123 of the FE Handbook: Fracture Toughness.

The answer is (B) Fracture toughness.

Solution to Question # 239:

Refer to page 135 of the FE Handbook: Shearing Force and Bending Moment Sign Conventions:

Read # 1 in the parenthesis. Think about it, the top fibers are being "squeezed" (compressed) together while the bottom is being stretched (tension).

The answer is (D) Compression.

Solution to Question # 240:

Refer to page 267 of the FE Handbook: USCS

Less than half of the material is large than No. 200 sieve, therefore the material is a Fine-Grained soil. To figure out the type of soil in this group, calculate the PI.

$PI = LL - PL$

$= 70 - 30$

= 40

Using the graph, this falls above the A-line, in the CH area.

The answer is (A) CH

Solution to Question # 241:

Ethics

Answer is (B) Only in area where they are technically competent.

Solution to Question # 242:

Don't need the FE Handbook. Common sense. Just be careful, the answer must be in yd^3.

Total Volume = volume of duct bank – volume of piping

Volume of duct bank = 75 ft x 4ft x 420 ft = 126,000 ft^3

Volume of piping: 420 ft x (8) π (36 in /12in)^2 / 4 = 23,750 ft^3

Total = 126,000 ft^3 - 23,750 ft^3 = 102,250 ft^3

102,250 ft^3 x (1 yd^3 / 27 ft^3) = 3,787.04 yd^3

The answer is (A) 3,787.

Solution to 242B:

Refer to page 135 of the FE Handbook : Beams:

The first step is to draw a free body diagram of all the <u>External Forces</u>:

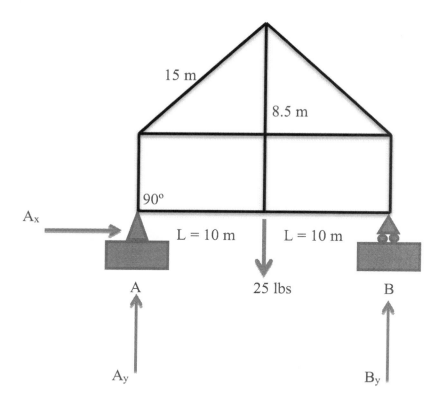

The problem statement wants to know the reaction at point B., Therefore, let's take moments about point A.

$\Sigma M_A = 0$:   (assume clockwise is positive)

25 lb (10 ft) -B_y (20 ft) = 0

(Note: 20 ft came from 10 ft + 10 ft – the distance reaction By is from point A.)

B_y (20 ft) = 250 ft lb

B_y = 12.5 lbs

The answer is (A) 12.5 lbs

(Note: All the other information in the problem was useless to find external forces)

Solution to 242C:

Refer to page 181 (187 of 502) of the FE Handbook: The Continuity Equation:

This is the basic equation: Q = V•A

Note: Most of the information in the problem statement is completely useless. If you know the flowrate, Q, and the Area of the pipe, then you can simply calculate the velocity by using Q = V•A.

Remember, if the problem seems too hard when you first read it, take your time and realize that the solution is probably simple.

Given:

$Q = 100$ ft³/sec

$A = \pi (1\,\text{ft})^2/4 = .785$ ft²

Therefore:

$Q = V•A$

100 ft³/sec = V (.785 ft²)

V = [100 ft³/sec] / (.785 ft²)

V = 127 ft /sec

The answer is (B) 127 ft/sec.

End of Exam 4.

Keeping forging ahead.

243) Find a positive value for x which satisfies the following equation:

$$100 x^2 + 90x - 10 = 0$$

(A) .1

(B) 4.01

(C) .003

(D) .004

244) A structural engineer selected a W18x60 beam for a parking garage project. The available moment is determined to be 367 kips ft. The required bracing (ft) location for the beam is most nearly:

(A) 10

(B) 12

(C) 14

(D) 16

245) A force of 25 pounds acts on a spring which deflects by 1 in. Calculate the spring stiffness, k, (lb/in):

(A) 250

(B) 25

(C) 2

(D) 5

246) A falling head permeability test was carried out on an 8 inch long sample of clay. The diameter of the sample and the standpipe were 4 inches and .75 inch, respectively. The water level in the standpipe was observed to fall from 25 inches to 15 inches in 13 minutes. The hydraulic conductivity (k) of the soil sample in ft/s is most nearly:

(A) .0024368

(B) .0001934

(C) .0000153

(D) .0000393

247) An open channel has a rectangular section of 5 meters wide. The flow rate is 1.2 m^3/s and the depth is 1.4 meters. Calculate the slope of the channel using Manning's Equation for steady flow. (Assume n = .019)

(A) 1.2 x 10^{-5}

(B) 2.2 x 10^{-5}

(C) 1.2 x 10^{-6}

(D) 1.2 x 10^{-7}

248) A contractor is excavating a trench as shown below. He is required to dig the trench 4 ft deep x 2 ft wide. The soil was tested to have an approximate swell factor of 12% and a shrinkage factor of 13%. The contractor is placing a 6" water pipe in the trench and then backfilling with the soil that was removed.

The amount of soil (LCY) that the contractor needs to bring in is most nearly:

(The below dimensions are on centerline).

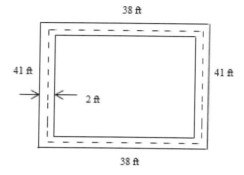

(A) The contractor does not need extra material

(B) 172

(C) 6.4

(D) 10.2

249) How is the bonding produced in a covalently bonded solid?

(A) Sharing of electrons between adjacent atoms

(B) The columbic attraction between oppositely charged molecules

(C) The minimization of potential energy of free electrons

(D) The localization of electrons associated with individual atoms

250) This type of device produces power by extracting energy from a working fluid. The energy loss shows up as a decrease in fluid pressure head.

(A) Pump

(B) Compressor

(C) Turbine

(D) Heat Exchanger

251) An excavator with a 2.5 yd³ bucket is used to remove material at a jobsite. (2) dump trucks with a 16 yd³ capacity are used to haul the material to a different location. This haul takes 16 minutes to dump the material per trip and return to the jobsite. Assuming the excavator can load at a rate of 2 yd³ / minute, the productivity of this hauling operation (yd³/hr) is most nearly:

(A) 39

(B) 51

(C) 67

(D) 87

252) A contractor is developing a storm water drainage plan using NRCS (SCS) Rainfall – Runoff. If the design criteria states to use a precipitation of 8 inches and curve number of 3, the runoff (in) is most nearly:

(A) 4

(B) 8

(C) 12

(D) 16

253) According to Archimedes Principle and Buoyancy, a floating body displaces a weight of fluid equal to:

(A) Its own centroid location

(B) Its own weight

(C) The acceleration due to gravity

(D) Half its own weight.

254) If the Curve Number is 75, using the NRCS (SCS) Rainfall-Runoff equation, the maximum basin retention (inches) is most nearly:

(A) ½

(B) 1

(C) 2

(D) 3

255) A solid steel shaft of circular cross-section, length = 0.5 m, diameter = 20 mm, is twisted about its axis of symmetry by applying a torque of 72Nm. Calculate the maximum shear stress:

(A) 45.83 MPa

(B) 45.83 GPa

(C) 45 N/m²

(D) 4.583 MPa

256) Using the information in problem #255, calculate the angle of twist (degrees):

(A) 64°

(B) 3°

(C) 2.64°

(D) 1.64°

257) 80 pounds of concrete is lifted 30 feet high in 10 seconds. Calculate the horsepower required to complete this task:

(A) 12.5

(B) 1

(C) 5

(D) .44

258) A construction company owns a piece of equipment that has an initial cost of $12,000, a life of 9 years, and a straight-line depreciation value of $850. The salvage value is most nearly:

(A) $4,530

(B) $5,543

(C) $3,530

(D) $4,350

259) Calculate the Mach number for an aircraft which is flying at a speed of 450 mph at an altitude of 30,000 ft. The surrounding temperature is -65 °F. (Gas constant: R = 1716 (ftlb/slug °R))

(A) .67

(B) .77

(C) .87

(D) .97

260) An interstate section of roadway is 8 miles long and has an average daily traffic entering intersection (ADA) of 7,500. If there's been 4 crashes on this section of interstate in the past 2 years, the crash rate is most nearly:

(A) .008

(B) .0913

(C) .1143

(D) .598

261) An engineering company is considering investing $5,000 into a green energy market which is slated to have a 8% annual return. How much will the investment be worth in 25 years?

(A) $34,242.50

(B) $38,242.50

(C) $31,242.50

(D) $21,242.50

262) If $Z_1, Z_2, ..., Z_n$ are independent unit normal random variables, then $X^2 = Z_1{}^2 + Z_2{}^2 + ... + Z_n{}^2$ has a distribution known as:

(A) Unimodule

(B) Chi-square

(C) Central limit

(D) Linear

263) The diagram below shows a contraption built in a lab. If 2cm^3 of water flows into the tube 10 seconds, the hydraulic conductivity (cm/s) is most nearly:

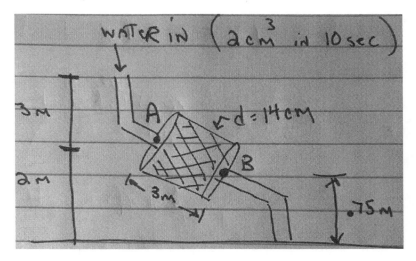

(A) - .0012

(B) - .0085

(C) - .0109

(D) - .0075

264) Find the Laplace Transform for function shown below:

$$f(t) = 6e^{-5t} + e^{3t} + 5t^3 - 9$$

(A) (6/s+3) + (1/(s-5)) + (30/s⁴) – 4/s

(B) (6/s+5) + (1/(s-3)) + (30/s⁴) – 9/s

(C) (6/s-5) + (1/(s-5)) + (30/s⁴) – 9/s

(D) (8/s+1) + (2/(s-3)) + (30/s⁴) – 9/s

265) Determine the head loss for oil flowing through a 10 ft long pipe with a 1 ft diameter and a velocity of .14 ft/s.

(Assume the roughness factor (e) = .002 and Reynolds # = 1 x 10⁴)

(A) 1 x10⁻⁵ ft

(B) 1 x10⁻² ft

(C) 1 x10⁻³ ft

(D) 1 x10⁻⁴ ft

266) Which of the following says that the discharge rate q is optional to the gradient in hydraulic head and the hydraulic conductivity:

(A) Darcy's Law

(B) Dupuit's Law

(C) Thiem's Law

(D) Manning's Law

267) In manufacturing an electric power drill, it was empirically determined that the process yields, on average, 5% defective product. What is the probability that in a sample of ten power drills there are exactly three defective units?

(A) 10%

(B) 3.05%

(C) 5%

(D) 1.05%

268) A simply supported steel beam is loaded with a distributed force as shown in the following diagram. Calculate the maximum beam deflection (inches): Assume $I = 254$ ft^4

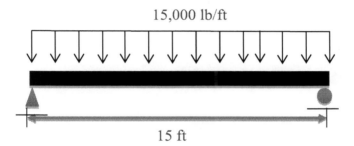

15,000 lb/ft

15 ft

(A) .000001 in

(B) .001 in

(C) .0001 in

(D) 1 in

269) A Cruise Ship 150m long is designed to cruise at 18 knots. It is tested in a tow tank with a model 3 m long. If the model wave drag is 2.2 N, the estimated ship drag is:

(A) 8.7 kN

(B) 38.9 kN

(C) 61.8 kN

(D) 275 kN

270) A geotechnical technician took a soil sample from the field. The weight of the sample was 5.18 lbf. If the moisture content of the soil is 17.3%, the volume of the test hole is .02 ft^3 and the results of the Proctor Test from the lab indicated that the maximum dry density of the soil is 244.8 lbf/ft^3, the percent compaction of the soil is most nearly:

(A) 77.5%

(B) 84.1%

(C) 90.3%

(D) 97.2%

271) 175,000 yd^3 of banked soil from a Corps of Engineers borrow pit is stockpiled before being trucked to the levee project's jobsite. This particular soil has a swell factor of 19% and shrinkage factor of 10%. The final volume of the compacted soil is most nearly:

(A) 148,700 yd^3

(B) 157,500 yd³

(C) 162,900 yd³

(D) 177,712 yd³

272) How are minor losses in piping systems from sudden pipe contractions or expansions usually found?

(A) Equal to the friction factor losses

(B) Head losses that vary parabolically with velocity.

(C) Always ignored when sizing pump requirements

(D) Found by using loss coefficients.

273) Which of the following is produced in a beam by a set of "n" moving loads when the resultant "R" of the load set and an adjacent load are equal distance form the centerline of the beam?

(A) Absolute minimum moment

(B) Absolute beam stiffness

(C) Absolute maximum moment

(D) Absolute moving concentrated load

274) Given: y varies jointly as x and as the cube root of z. Also, y = 12 when x = 3 and z = 8.0. The value of x, when y = 70 and z = 125, is most nearly:

(A) 2.5

(B) 7.0

(C) 12.5

(D) 17.0

275) A 15-pound rectangular block having dimensions 5 ft x 1 ft x 3 ft rests on a horizontal surface. If it takes a force of 7 pounds (applied horizontally) to get the block to move when it is resting on the side with dimensions 5 ft x 1 ft, how much force is required to get the block to move when it is resting on the side with dimensions 1 ft x 3 ft?

(A) 7 pounds

(B) 14 pounds

(C) 3 pounds

(D) 15.33 pounds

276) What is the value of the following limit?

$$\lim_{x \to 0} (\sin(7x)/x)$$

(A) 3

(B) 7

(C) 11

(D) 32

277) A town has a population of 60,000 people. If the average sewer flow is 120 gallons per capita day (gpcd), using Curve B, the peak flow (MGD) is most nearly:

(A) 12

(B) 16

(C) 22

(D) 38

278) Impact tests are repeated over a range of temperatures to determine:

(A) Ductile to brittle transition pressure

(B) Ductile to brittle transition temperature

(C) Ductile to brittle transition stress

(D) Ductile to brittle transition hardness

279) An engineer is using a design wind speed of 125 mph as a design basis. If a structure is located in a Suburban area on flat ground, the velocity pressure (lb/ft²) at the height shown is most nearly:

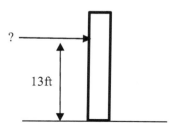

(A) 5

(B) 8

(C) 13

(D) 19

280) What is the general solution to the following differential equation?

$$y'' -4y' +4y = 0$$

(A) $y = (C_1 + C_2X) \, e^{x}$

(B) $y = (C_1 + C_2X) \, e^{9x}$

(C) $y = (C_1 + C_2X) \, e^{2x}$

(D) $y = (C_1 + C_2X) \, e^{4x}$

281) An engineer is designing a vertical curve with the following specifications: g1= -3.8%, g2 = +2%, L = 520 ft, Standard headlight criteria. The expression of the actual stopping distance of the curve is most nearly:

(A) $520 = .058 \ (S)^2 / 400 + 3.5S$

(B) $520 = 1.8 \ (S)^2 / 400 + 3.5S$

(C) $520 = 5.8 \ (S)^2 / 400 + 3.5S$

(D) $520 = 3.5 \ (S)^2 / 400 + 5.8S$

282) Water is flowing through a ½ in diameter pipe at 20 lb/s. Calculate the velocity through the pipe?

(A) 235 ft/s

(B) .235 ft/s

(C) 2.35 ft/s

(D) 23.5 ft/s

283) Which one of the following is <u>incorrect</u>?

(A) Frictional forces act to oppose motion.

(B) Frictional forces are parallel to surfaces.

(C) Frictional forces are dependent on contact area.

(D) Static friction is greater than kinetic friction.

284) A short column shown below using tie reinforcements. ($f_c' = 4500$ psi, $f_y = 70000$psi), The ultimate axial strength, $ØP_N$, is most nearly:

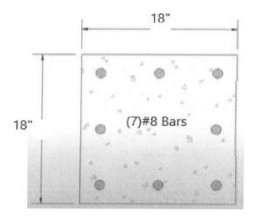

18"

18"

(7)#8 Bars

$Ø = 0.65$

(A) 311

(B) 542

(C) 835

(D) 977

285) A pump which is 80% efficient is used to pump water from +5 meters above sea level to an elevation of +25 meters above sea level. Calculate the power delivered to the pump (W). (Assume the flow rate is 1 m³/min, friction losses are 2.5 m)

(A) 4598 W

(B) 5000 W

(C) 3891 W

(D) 4239 W

286) For the three vectors, what is the value of the following product?

$$A \bullet (B \times C)$$

$A = 2i + 7j + 12k$

$B = i + 4j + 3k$

$C = 3i + 4j + 5k$

(A) 0

(B) -45

(C) -52

(D) 73

287) If the Particle Size Ratio (d_p / d_{pc}) is 1, the cyclone efficiency is most nearly:

(A) 50%

(B) 60%

(C) 85%

(D) 100%

288) A structural engineer is designing a column with a design length of the section between brace points of 40 feet. The column will be fixed at both ends. The lightest W12 section that will support a factored axial load of 130 kips is most nearly:

(A) W12x50

(B) W12x58

(C) W12x45

(D) W12x40

289) A piano has a mass of 82 kg. The piano is lifted from the floor and placed on a stage. If the piano gains 1750 J of Potential Energy, how high is the stage?

(A) 6.2 m

(B) 2.2 m

(C) .75 m

(D) 4.7

290) An A/E firm was hired by a government agency to design a floodwall by developing plans and specifications. Prior to the bid date, several construction companies called the A/E firm to ask specific questions about the plans. The A/E firm:

(A) Cannot reveal information without client's consent unless required by law to do so.

(B) Answer their questions because it will help fast track the bid process later on.

(C) Send them the electronic files via email as long as the information is correct.

(D) Set up a meeting with the company to review their questions.

291) Evaluate the following integral.

$$\int_{1}^{5} (3x^2+4x+1)\, dx$$

(A) 192

(B) 184

(C) 167

(D) 176

292) What is the angle between the two following vectors?

A = 5i + 8j + 9k

B = 12i -7j +6k

(A) 72.9°

(B) 96.2°

(C) 137.2°

(D) 187.7°

293) The differential equation $y + 5x^2y + \sin x = 0$ is:

(A) Linear, homogeneous, constant coefficient

(B) Nonlinear, homogeneous, constant coefficient

(C) Linear, nonhomogeneous, variable coefficient

(D) Nonlinear, nonhomogeneous, variable coefficient

294) Pan evaporation E_p can be expressed by which of the following?

(A) E_L/P_c

(B) $E_L \times P_c$

(C) P_c/E_L

(D) $P_c \times E_L$

295) Which of the following is the primary factor affecting the strength of concrete?

(A) Coarse aggregate

(B) W/C

(C) Fine aggregate

(D) Cement

296) The work done by a force 150 N moving a body 50 m can be calculated as:

(A) 7500 Joules

(B) 7500 N

(C) 7500 M

(D) 7500 Horsepower

297) What does the bolded color mean in each section of the W shapes on the AISI Table 3-2?

(A) The heaviest shape in its row.

(B) The most cost-effective shape in its row.

(C) The lightest shape in its row.

(D) The highest yield stress in its row.

298) From the choices below, what is the lightest wide-flange shape available that can resist a service dead load of 110 kips and a service live load of 125 kips (using LRFD). For this column, assume $K_x = K_y = 1$, and $L = 18$ feet.

(A) W14x74

(B) W14x68

(C) W14x61

(D) W14x53

299) An engineer is receiving royalty payments for a design patent that he is licensing out to a large software company, what is the present value of a series of royalty payments of $50,000 each for 8 years if nominal interest is 8%?

(A) $283,700

(B) $278,300

(C) $387,300

(D) $287,300

300) An archer pulls back 0.75 m on a bow which has a stiffness of 200 N/m. The arrow weighs 50 g. What is the velocity of the arrow immediately after release?

(A) 17.4 m/s

(B) 27.4 m/s

(C) 37.4 m/s

(D) 47.4 m/s

301) Find the roots of the following equation:

$$x^2 - 2x - 2 = 0$$

(A) $1+(3)^{1/2}$, $1-(-3)^{1/2}$

(B) $1-(3^2)$, $1-(3)^2$

(C) $1+(3)^{1/2}$, $1-(3)^{1/2}$

(D) $i+(3)^{1/2}$, $-i-(3)^{1/2}$

302) a 47 cm diameter solid sphere is suspended by a cable as shown below. Half of the sphere is in one fluid and the other half is an another. What is the tension of the cable?

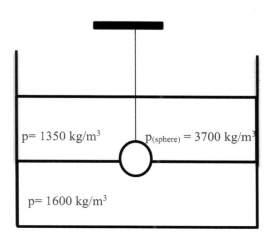

p= 1350 kg/m³ $p_{(sphere)}$ = 3700 kg/m³

p= 1600 kg/m³

(A) 956 N

(B) 1001 N

(C) 1179 N

(D) 1377 N

303) Which of the following are zero-force members?

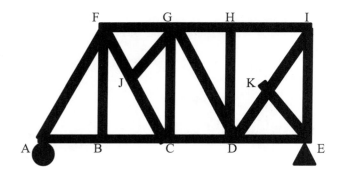

(A) DH, CD, FG, EK

(B) BF, CD, DH, EK

(C) JG, CD, DH, KI

(D) BF, JG, DH, EK

304) A certain fluid with density of 1877 kg/m³ flows at 7 m/s in a 3 cm dimeter pipe. The pipe is connected to a 12 cm diameter section. At what velocity does the flow out of the last section?

(A) .27 m/s

(B) 7.5 m/s

(C) .43 m/s

(D) 3.4 m/s

305) A structural engineer is designing a concrete foundation. The plans call for the following reinforcement bars in the schedule below. The total weight (lb) of the reinforcement bars is most nearly:

Quantity	Bar Size	Length(ft)
16	#3	12
5	#7	6
2	#14	9
11	#18	2

(A) 570

(B) 321

(C) 497

(D) 501

306) Water at 5 °C is flowing in a fire hose with a velocity of 1.0 m/s and a pressure of 200,000 Pa. At the nozzle the pressure decreases to atmospheric pressure of 101,300 Pa, there is no change in height. Calculate the velocity of the water exiting the nozzle.

(A) 24.04 m/s

(B) 14.04 m/s

(C) .5 m/s

(D) 19.07 m/s

307) A W21x57 (Fy= 50ksi) is to be used as a simply supported beam with span length of 15 feet to support a uniformly distributed load. Taking Cb = 1, what is most nearly the maximum design flexural capacity (LRFD) of the beam if only the ends of the beam are laterally supported?

(A) 189 ft kips

(B) 278 ft kips

(C) 311 ft kips

(D) 512 ft kips

308) A productivity rate for placement of rebar in a reinforced concrete retaining wall is 5 hours per ton. A crew consisting of (1) superintendent ($43/hr) and (4) laborers ($27/hr), with a labor burden of 55% is used to install the 31 tons of rebar. The total labor cost to install all 31 tons is most nearly:

(A) $7,56

(B) $1,333

(C) $18,923

(D) $6,184

309) The maximum stress which can be repeated indefinitely without causing failure is known as:

(A) Safe stress

(B) Yield stress

(C) Ultimate stress

(D) Endurance stress

310) Which of the following is a measure of resistance to plastic deformation:

(A) Micrometer

(B) Creep

(C) Hardness

(D) Tensile strength

311) A Plane Frame has 9 members, 3 number of independent reaction components, 7 joints, and 10 condition equations. The classification is most nearly:

(A) Stable

(B) Unstable

(C) Statically determinate

(D) Cannot be determined

312) A traffic study is being conducted to improve safety. Certain improvements will be made. Over the 2-year period before the improvement, the number of crashes occurring per year was 4 and 9. If the CR factor is 25% and the ADT before and after the improvement are 13,000 and 18,500 respectively, the crashes prevented is most nearly:

(A) 1.8

(B) 2.3

(C) 4.7

(D) 9.1

313) Using the boring log show below, what is the dry density (pcf) at a depth of 7 ft?

(A) 127.2

(B) 99.2

(C) 110.0

(D) 96.8

314) Which one of the following labels represent the proper Latitudes and Departures:

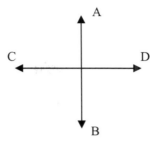

(A) A = - Departure, B = - Latitude, C = + Departure, D = + Latitude,

(B) A = + Latitude, B = + Latitude, C = - Departure, D = +Departure

(C) A = + Departure, B = + Latitude, C = - Departure, D = - Latitude,

(D) A = + Latitude, B = - Latitude, C = - Departure, D = +Departure

315) A W Shape beam is being considered. Assuming the $\emptyset M_{px}$ = 405 kip ft, $\emptyset M_{rx}$ = 256 kip ft, Lp = 10.7ft, and the Lr = 37.4ft, the $\emptyset BF$ is most nearly: Also, what is the beam shape?

(A) 3.59, W12x72

(B) 4.21, W21x55

(C) 5.59, W12x72

(D) 9.01, W18x50

316) Which of the following processes lowers ductility?

(A) Galvanizing

(B) Hot working

(C) Quenching

(D) Cold working

317) Super plasticizers are the most typical way to increase which of the following in concrete?

(A) Workability

(B) Strength

(C) Ductility

(D) Chemical reaction

318) A spring (k = 10 kN/m) supports a block of mass = 5 kg. The block is pulled down 8 mm and released. Calculate the period of vibration:

(A) .24 seconds

(B) .79 seconds

(C) .14 seconds

(D) .091 seconds

319) A beam is loaded as shown below. Determine its proper shear diagram:

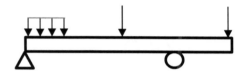

(A)

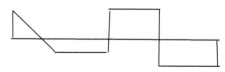

(B)

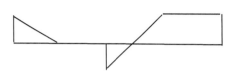

(C)

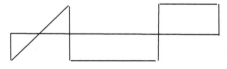

(D)

320) If $(B^2 - 4AC > 0)$ in the conic section equation, which of the following is defined?

(A) Straight line

(B) Ellipse

(C) Parabola

(D) Hyperbola

321) The largest frictional force is called:

(A) Limiting gyration

(B) Limiting friction

(C) Limiting inertia

(D) Limiting acceleration

322) Which of the following is an example of a non-crystalline solid?

(A) Concrete

(B) Steel

(C) Plastic

(D) Glass

323) Given the soil profile shown, the effective vertical stress at the point is most nearly:

Ground Surface

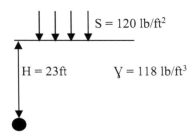

$S = 120 \text{ lb/ft}^2$

$H = 23\text{ft}$ $\gamma = 118 \text{ lb/ft}^3$

(A) 2,834 lb/ft²

(B) 3,834 lb/ft²

(C) 4,834 lb/ft²

(D) 5,834 lb/ft²

324) Convert the azimuth, 235° 28' 53'' to bearing.

(A) S 155° 28' 53''

(B) N 55° 28' 53''

(C) N 155° 28' 53''

(D) S 55° 28' 53''

325) Find the pressure difference between the water and oil if H = 15m in the diagram below:

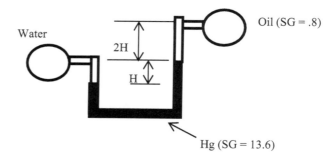

(A) 2,087,400 Pa

(B) 4,087,400 Pa

(C) 1,087,400 Pa

(D) 400 Pa

326) The rate-of-return on an investment is the interest rate that makes:

(A) Benefits and depreciation equal

(B) You the most money

(C) Capital assets and costs equal

(D) Benefits and costs equal

327) The house rolls 10 dice, one die at a time. What are the odds of a player rolling the same numbers in the same order as the house?

(A) 6^{10}

(B) $1/6^{10}$

(C) $1/10^6$

(D) $1/6^9$

328) In the following diagram, what value is shown on the scale?

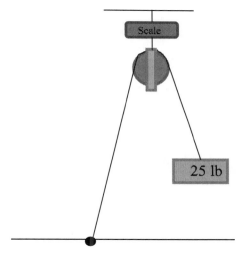

(fixed to the ground)

(A) 50 lb

(B) 25 lb

(C) 12.5 lb

(D) 75 lb

329) Which of the following equations is used to determine head loss due to flow?

(A) Hazen-Williams

(B) Bernoulli

(C) Manning's

(D) Darcy-Weisbach

330) Which of the following set of variables are not included in the Surface Water System Hydraulic Budget Equation?

(A) P, Q_{in}, E_s, I

(B) Q_{out}, ΔS_s, I, T_s

(C) P, Q_{in}, ΔS_s, I

(D) ΔS_s, A, T_s, Q_{in}

331) The depth of a beam is 18 inches and weights 40 pounds per linear foot. The $\emptyset M_{rx}$ is most nearly (kip ft):

(A) 180

(B) 214

(C) 244

(D) 299

332) A simply supported beam with no lateral bracing along the span is loaded as shown below. The Cb value is most nearly:

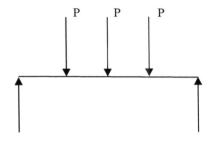

(A) 1.56

(B) 1.32

(C) 1.67

(D) 1.14

333) Refer to the following data:

Dry unit weight of soil in borrow pit	87.0 pcf
Moisture Content in borrow pit	13.0 %
Specific gravity of the soils particles	2.70
Modified Proctor optimum moisture content	17.0%
Modified Proctor maximum dry dentsity	127.0 pcf

Assume that soil from a borrow pit is trasported to a construction site to construct 1,500,000 yd^3 of compacted levee berm embankment. Due to handling and evaporation, the soil arrives at the construction site with the moisture content equal to 11%. The soil is placed and compacted to 90% of the modified Proctor maximum dry density.

The total volume of water (gallons) that must be added to the soil to increase the moisture content to the optimim level is most nearly:

(A) 34 x 10^6 gal

(B) 38 x 10^6 gal

(C) 43 x 10^6 gal

(D) 56 x 10^6 gal

334) A 100 lb block is supported by 2 identical springs as shown below. What is the static deflection?

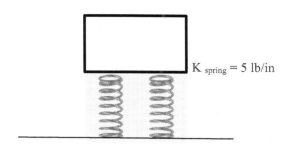

$K_{spring} = 5$ lb/in

(A) 5 in

(B) 10 in

(C) 15 in

(D) 20 in

335) Using the loading diagram below, find the distance from the fulcrum to the 90 lb. load: (Neglect the mass of the beam.)

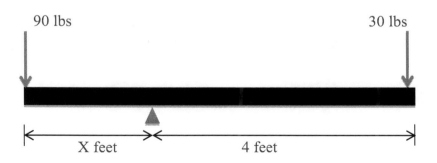

90 lbs

30 lbs

X feet

4 feet

(A) 1.33 ft

(B) 3.33 ft

(C) 7 ft

(D) .33 ft

Solution to Question # 243:

Refer to page 35 of the FE Handbook: Quadratic Equation. Middle of Page.

Realize that page 35 is the actual page number of the document, but it's page 39 (of 498) of the PDF file.

You should know this equation by heart.

The quadratic equation has the form: $Ax^2 + Bx - C = 0$

(Note: As soon as you see this form of an equation, you should automatically think of the quadratic equation formula.)

$x_1, x_2 = [-b +/- (\sqrt{(b^2 - 4 \cdot a \cdot c)}] / 2a)$

$x_1, x_2 = [-90 +/- (\sqrt{(90^2 - 4 \cdot 100 \cdot (-10)}] / 2(100))$

$x_1, x_2 = [-90 +/- (\sqrt{(8100 - (-4000))}] / (200))$

$x_1, x_2 = [-90 +/- (\sqrt{(12,100)}] / (200))$

$x_1, x_2 = [-90 +/- [(110)] / (200)]$

(Note: Since there is a +/- sign, you need to set up two equations separately and solve for x_1 and x_2)

$x_1 = [-90 + 110] / 200$

$x_1 = [20] / 200$

$\underline{x_1 = .1}$

$x_2 = [-90 - 110] / 200$

$x_2 = [-200] / 200$

$\underline{x_2 = -1}$

Therefore, the .1 is the positive value for x which satisfies the equation:

Check answer: Substitute (.1) back into the equation:

$100 x^2 + 90x - 10 = 0$

$100 (.1)^2 + 90(.1) - 10 = 0$

$100 (.01) + (9) - 10 = 0$

$1 + 9 - 10 = 0$

$0 = 0$, okay

The answer is (A) .1.

Solution to Question # 244:

Refer to page 286 of the FE handbook: Table W Shapes.

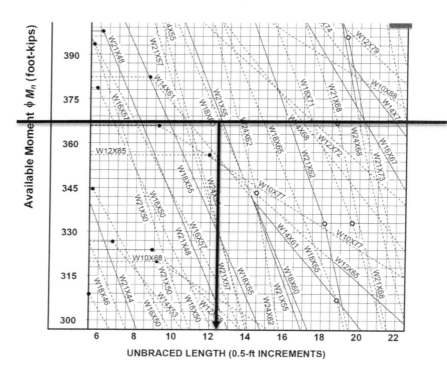

The answer is (B) 12.

Solution to Question # 245:

Refer to page 107 of the FE Handbook: Elastic Potential Energy:

$F = k \cdot x$

Given:

$F = 25$ pounds

$x = 1$ in

Therefore:

$F = k \cdot x$

25 lb = k • (1 in)

k = 25 lb / (1 in)

k = 25 lb / in

The answer is (B) 25.

Solution to Question # 246:

Refer to page 260 of the FE Handbook: Falling head test. Middle of page.

$$K = 2.303 \; [(aL)/(At_e)] \; \log_{10}(h_1/h_2)$$

First, let's find A and a from the given diameters.

$a = \pi \times .75^2/ \, 4 = .4418 \; in^2$

$A = \pi \times 4^2/ \, 4 = 12.6 \; in^2$

$K = 2.303 \; [(.4418 \; in^2 \; (8 \; in)/(\; 12.6 \; in^2 \; 13 \; min)] \; \log_{10}(25/15)$

$K = 2.303 \; [(.0216)] \; (.2218)$

$= .001102 \; in/min$ (but this must be converted to ft/s)

$.001102 \; in/min \times (1 \; min/60 \; sec) \; (\; 1 ft/12 \; in)$

$= .0000153 \; ft/s$

The answer is (C) .0000153.

Solution to Question # 247:

Refer to page 185 of the FE Handbook: Open Channel Flow:

Manning's Equation:

$v = (k/n) \cdot R^{2/3} \cdot S^{1/2}$

Given:

k = 1 (given in handbook) (k = I for SI units)
n = 0.019

R = hydraulic radius

R = Area/Perimeter   (you cannot use R = D/4, because this is a rectangular channel, not a pipe)

Area = 5m • (1.4m) = 7m²
Perimeter = 5m+1.4m+1.4m = 7.8m

R = 7m²/7.8m
R = .8974

Therefore:

v = (k/n) • R²/³ • S¹/²

v = (1/.019) • (.8974)²/³ • (S)¹/²

Now, we have 1 equation with 2 unknowns. But the problem statement gave us the flow rate (Q =1.2 m³/s)

So let's convert to Velocity, using Q= V•A.

Q= V•A *page 181 of the FE Handbook*: The Continuity Equation:

1.2 m³/s = V (7m²)
V = 1.2 m³/s/ (7m²)
V = .17 m/s

Now,

v = (1/.019) • (.8974)²/³ • (S)¹/²
.17 m/s = (1/.019) • (.8974)²/³ • (S)¹/²
(S)¹/² = .17 m/s / [(1/.019) • (.8974)²/³]   (Solve for S in the equation)
(S)¹/² = 3.47 x 10⁻³   (Square each side for solve for S)
((S)¹/²)² = (3.47 x 10⁻³)²   (S¹/² squared equals S)

S = 1.2 x 10⁻⁵

The answer is (A) 1.2 x 10⁻⁵.

Solution to Question # 248:

You should be able to solve this question by basic engineering skills. Do run off searching for formulas, just reason your way through the question.

The length of the trench is: 38' + 41' + 38' + 41' = 158 ft.

The volume of the soil in the trench is: 4' x 2' x 158' = 1,264 ft³

The volume after compaction is:

1,264 ft² (1-.13) =

1264(.87) = 1,099.6 ft³

The volume of soil needed is: Vol of trench – Vol of Pipe

= 1,264 ft³ – π(d²/4)(158 ft)

= 1,264 ft³ – π([6/12]²/4)(158 ft)

= 1,264 ft³ – π([.5]²/4)(158 ft)

$= 1,264 \text{ ft}^3 - 31.02 \text{ ft}^3 = 1,233 \text{ ft}^3$

Does the contractor need to bring in more material?

Volume of compacted soil need – Volume of compacted soil available:

$1,233 \text{ ft}^3 - 1,099.6 \text{ ft}^3 = 133.4 \text{ ft}^3$ (yes)

How much material does the contractor actually need to bring in?

Volume of compacted soil = (1-Shrinkage factor) x BCF

$133.4 \text{ ft}^3 / .87 = 153.33 \text{ ft}^3 \text{ BCF}$

LCF = BCF x 1.12

LCF = 153.33 (1.12) = 172 ft^3

= 172/27   (converting LCF into LCY)

= 6.4 LCY

(Note: The question says that the answer is in LCY = loose cubic yards)

The answer is (C) 6.4

Solution to Question #249:

Refer to page 117 of the FE Handbook: Atomic Bonding:

Covalent bonding is produces by electron sharing between atoms. Hydrogen is an example of an extremely simple covalent compound

The answer is (A) Sharing of electrons between adjacent atoms.

Solution to Question # 250:

Refer to page 194 of the FE Handbook: Turbines:

The answer is (C) Turbine.

Solution to Question # 251:

Don't need the FE handbook:

Find the time required to fill the truck.
Truck capacity / Excavator load rate:

$12 \text{ yd}^3 / 2\text{yd}^3/\text{min} = 6 \text{ min.}$

Total time = time to fill + time to dump/return
= 6 min + 16 min
= 22 min (per cycle)

Total of 2 trucks: 16 yd^3 + 16 yd^3

= 32 yd^3 / 22 min x 60 min/hr

= 87.27 yd^3/hr

The answer is (D) 87.

Solution to Question # 252:

Refer to page 290 of the FE handbook: Rainfall – Runoff

Q = (P - 0.2S)^2 / P +0.8S

P = 8 in

S = use the CN formula:

CN = 1,000 / S + 10

3 = 1,000 / S +10

3(S+10) = 1,000
3S + 30 = 1,000
3S = 970
S = 323.33

Q = (8 - 0.2(323.33)^2 / 8 +0.8(323.33)

= (-56.7)^2 / 266.7

= 12.05

The answer is (C) 12.

Solution to Question # 253:

Refer to page 180 of the FE Handbook: Archimedes Principle and Buoyancy.

The answer is (B) Its own weight.

Solution to Question # 254:

Refer to page 290 of the FE Handbook: NRCS (SCS) Rainfall-Runoff

S = 1,000/CN – 10

S = 1,000/75 – 10

S = 3.33 inches

The answer is (D) 3.

Solution to Question # 255:

Refer to page 134 of the FE Handbook: Torsion.

Torsion stress in circular solid or thick-walled (t > 0.1 *r*) shafts:

t = T• r/ *J*   (*J* = polar moment of inertia (see table page 112).

To Calculate *J* for a solid circular pipe:

$J = \pi \cdot a^4/ 2$

(recognize that "a" is the radius of the pipe, therefore 20 mm/2 = 10 mm, however, let's convert to meters first.)

10 mm • (1 m/1000 mm) = .01 m

t = T• r/ *J*
$J = \pi \cdot (.01m)^4/ 2$
$J = 1.57 \times 10^{-8} m^4$

Therefore,

$t = 72Nm \cdot (.01 \text{ m}) / 1.57 \times 10^{-8} m^4$
$t = 72 \text{ Nm} \cdot (.01 \text{ m}) / 1.57 \times 10^{-8} m^4$

$t = 45{,}837{,}975.4894 \text{ N/m}^2$

$t = 45{,}837{,}975.4894 \text{ Pa}$ (Remember that a N/m^2 is a Pascal (Pa). See conversion factors on page 2)

$t = 45.83 \text{ MPa}$ (Remember that Mega (M) is 1×10^6, See metric prefixes on page 1)

The answer is (A) 45.83 MPa.

Solution to Question # 256:

Refer to page 134 of the FE Handbook: Torsion. Very bottom of the page.

The angle of twist is given by:

$$\theta = \frac{TL}{GJ},$$

All of the values are given except G:

(See Material Properties table on page 138)

G = 80 GPa (the problem statement says "Steel")

$\Theta = T•L/ G•JF$

$\Theta = 72 \text{ Nm} \cdot (.5m)/ (80 \times 10^9 \text{ N/m}^2) \cdot (1.57 \times 10^{-8} m^4)$
$\Theta = 72 \text{ Nm} \cdot (.5m)/ (1256 \text{ N•m}^2)$

Θ = .02866 radians (the answer is in radians, so let's convert to degrees!)

Θ = .02866 radians • (180/Π)

Θ = 1.64°

The answer is (D) 1.64°.

Solution to Question # 257:

Refer to page 107 of the FE Handbook: Work.

Power is defined by energy per time. It has the units of ft • lb /sec (which then can be converted to horsepower, 550 ft lb /sec = 1 horsepower)

Let's calculate the energy (work) first:

Work = F • D

Given:

F = 80 lb
D = 30 ft

Therefore:

Work = F • D

Work = (80 lb) • (30ft)

Work =2,400 ft • lb   (Therefore, it took 2400 ft lbs of energy to life the concrete up 30 feet)

The problem says that it achieved this in 10 seconds, so let's divide by 10 seconds.

Power = Energy (work) / time

Power = 2400 ft lb / 10 seconds

Power = 240 ft lbs / second

Refer to page 3 of the FE Handbook: Conversion Factors:

Convert ft lb / sec to horsepower, multiply by 1.818×10^{-3}

Power (Horsepower) = 240 ft lbs / second (1.818×10^{-3}) =

.44 horsepower

The answer is (D) .44 horsepower.

Solution to Question # 258:

Refer to page 231 of the FE Handbook: Straight-line depreciation.

The equation is:

$D_j = \dfrac{C - S_n}{n}$

From the question, we can find the givens:

Cost (C) = \$12,000
n = 9 year life
D = \$850

Therefore:

\$850 = (\$12,000 – S) / 9

\$850 (9) = (\$12,000 – S)

\$7,650 = \$12,000 –S

S = \$12,000 - \$7,650
S = \$4,350

The answer is (D) \$4,350.

Solution to Question # 259:

Refer to page 189 of the FE Handbook: Compressible Flow: Mach number:

$Ma = V/c$

However, first we have to calculate the speed of sound, c, for this altitude and air temperature:

$c = \sqrt{kRT}$

Given:

k = 1.4 (*refer to page 169 of the FE handbook*: Thermal and Physical Property Tables for Air)

T = -65 °F + 460 °R = 395 °R   (*refer to page 1 of the FE handbook* for temperature conversions)

R = 1716 (ft lb/slug °R) (Given)

Therefore:

$c = \sqrt{kRT}$

$c = \sqrt{(1.4)(1716)(395)}$

c = 974 ft/s

$Ma = V/c$

$V = 450$ mph (given in the problem statement), convert to ft/s:

450 mile/hour (1 hour/ 3600 second)(5280 ft/ mile) = 660 ft/s

Therefore:

Ma = (660 ft/s) / (974 ft/s)

Ma = .67

The answer is (A) .67.

Solution to Question # 260:

Refer to page 306 of the Fe Handbook: Traffic Safety Equations:

Choose the roadway segment equation- not the intersection equation.

RMVM = A x 1,000,000 / VMT

RMVM = 4 x 1,000,000 / ADT x (2 years x 365 days /yr) x 8

RMVM = 4 x 1,000,000 / 7,500 x (2 years x 365 days /yr) x 8

RMVM = .0913

The answer is (B) .0913.

Solution to Question # 261:

Refer to page 236 of the FE Handbook: 8% Interest Rate Table.

F = ($5, 000) (F/P, 8%, 25 years)

A = ($5,000) (6.8485)

A = $34,242.50

The answer is (A) $34,242.50.

Solution to Question # 262

Refer to page 68 of the FE Handbook: Distribution:

The answer is (B) Chi-square.

Solution to Question # 263:

Refer to page 291 of the FE Handbook: Darcy's Law.

Q = -K A dh/dx

Q = Given = 2 cm³/10sec = 0.20 cm³/s

dh/dx = Head at point A and B.

Head at A = z + U$_{water}$(P)/γ $_{water}$

Head at A = 2m + (9.81 x 2)/ 9.81 =

= 2 + 2 = 4m.

Head at B = .5m + (there's not pressure build up, since it's trickling out)

= .75m

dh = 4 - .75 = 3.25 m

dx = 3 m.   (the contraction is is 3m long)

A = π 7²   (Diagram shows the diameter is 10 cm)

Q = -K A dh/dx

.2 = -K (π 7²) 3.25/3

K = -.2 / (π 7²) 3.25/3

= -.0012 cm/s

The answer is (A) - .0012 cm/s

Solution to Question # 264:

Refer to page 56 of the FE Handbook:

$$F(s) = 6\frac{1}{s-(-5)} + \frac{1}{s-3} + 5\frac{3!}{s^{3+1}} - 9\frac{1}{s}$$

$$= \frac{6}{s+5} + \frac{1}{s-3} + \frac{30}{s^4} - \frac{9}{s}$$

The answer is (B) (6/s+5) + (1/(s-3)) + (30/s⁴) – 9/s

Solution to Question # 265:

Refer to page 183 of the FE Handbook: Head Loss due to Flow:

The Darcy-Weisbach equation:

h$_f$ = f (L/d) (V²/2g)

L = 10 ft
V = .14 ft/s
g = 32.2 ft/s²
d = 1 ft
e = .002 ft
Reynolds # = 1 x 10⁴

f= *Refer to page 201 of the FE Handbook*: Moody Diagram:

Locate the Reynolds # 1x10⁴ at the bottom of the chart.
Find the Relative roughness value of e/d which will be used to locate the value of the ride
side the chart. .002 ft/ 1 ft = .002. Now, follow the Relative roughness number through the
curved portion of the line until it intersects the Reynolds number.

To find the friction factor, locate the value .002 on the right side; follow the curve to the
left. When the curve crosses over the value of the Reynolds number at the bottom, draw a
straight line to the left and locate the friction factor. See diagram below.

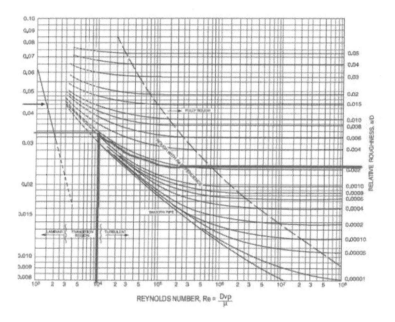

f = .034

Now, solve:

$h_f = f(L/d)(V^2/2g)$

$h_f = .034 (10 \text{ ft}/1 \text{ ft})(.14 \text{ ft/s})^2/2(32.2 \text{ ft/s}^2)$

$h_f = .34 (.0196 \text{ ft}^2/\text{s}^2) / 64.4 \text{ ft/s}^2$

$h_f = .34 (.0196 \text{ ft}^2/\text{s}^2) / 64.4 \text{ ft/s}^2$

$h_f = 1 \times 10^{-4}$ ft

The answer is (D) 1×10^{-4} ft.

Solution to Question # 266:

Refer to page 291 of the FE Handbook: Darcy's Law.

The answer is (A) Darcy's Law.

Solution to Question # 267:

Refer to page 84 of the FE Handbook: Probability and Density Functions:

The binomial probability formula is used when events are classified in two ways such as good/defective, red/green, go/no-go, etc. The binomial probability formula is be used to answer the following question:

What is the probability of x successes in n trials where the probability of a single success is p?

From the table for Binomial (second row form the top), the equation is:

$(_x^n) \, P^x \, (1-P)^{n-x}$

Given:

n = 10, p = .05, x = 3

Therefore:

$= (_3^{10}) \, (.05)^3 \, (1-.05)^{10-3}$

$= 10!/7!3![(.05)^3 \, (.95)^7]$

$= (120) \, [(.000125) \, (.6983)]$

$= .0105$

P (3 defective units) = 1.05%

The answer is (D) 1.05%

Solution to Question # 268:

Refer to page 140 of the FE Handbook: Simply Supported Beam Deflections and Slopes:

Middle column for deflection:

$V_{max} = 5wL^4/ 384EI$ (Great to know where this table is quickly)

Given:

L = 15 ft, so $L^4 = (15ft)^4 = 50,625$ ft^4

w = 15,000 lb/ft

I = 254 ft^4

E = The problem statement says a steel beam, therefore,

Refer to page 138 of the FE Handbook: Material Properties:

For steel, E = 29 Mpsi, or 29,000,000 psi

Therefore:

$V_{max} = 5wL^4/384EI$

$V_{max} = [5(15,000$ lb/ft$)$ $(50,625$ ft$^4)] / [384(29$ Mpsi$)$ $(254$ ft$^4)]$

$V_{max} = [3,796,875,000$ lb ft$^3)] / [2.8$ x 10^{12} (lb/in^2) ft$^4)]$ • $(144$ in^2/ft$^2)$

(note: we needed to convert psi into psf)

$V_{max} = [3,796,875,000$ lb ft$^3)] / [4$ x 10^{14} (lb ft$^2)]$

$V_{max} = 9.3$ x 10^{-6} ft   (note: the problem statements wants the answer to be in inches, not feet)

$V_{max} = 9.3$ x 10^{-6} ft $(12$ in $/ 1$ ft$)$

$V_{max} = .0001$ in

The answer is (C) .0001 in.

Solution to Question # 269:

Refer to page 197 of the FE Handbook, Similitude:

When you see any type of problem dealing with testing models and similarities, the Froude number must be maintained. $(V_p/V_m)^2 = L_p/L_m$. For dynamic similarity, $F_p=F_m(V_p/V_m)^2 (L_p/L_m)^2$, Combining these two equations gives, $F_p=F_m(L_p/L_m)^3$

$F_p=$ prototype drag force, unknown.
$F_m=$ Drag force of the model, 2.2N
$L_p=$ Length of prototype, 150m
$L_m=$ Length of model, 3 m

$F_p=2.2$N$(150$m$/3$m$)^3$
$F_p=2.2$N$(125,000)$
$F_p=275,000$ N, or 275kN

The answer is (D) 275 kN.

Solution to Question # 270:

Refer to page 259 of the FE Handbook: Phase Relationships:

Find the dry weight of the soil sample:

$$W_{dry} = W_{wet} / 1 + w$$

$$W_{dry} = 5.18 \text{ lbf}/ 1 + .173$$

$$W_{dry} = 4.42 \text{ lbf}$$

Find the unit weight of the soil sample:

$$\mathsf{Y}_{sample} = W_{dry} / V_{testhole}$$

$$\mathsf{Y}_{sample} = 4.42 \text{ lbf} / .02 \text{ ft}^3$$

$$\mathsf{Y}_{sample} = 221 \text{ lbf/ft}^3$$

Now, just find the % compaction of the soil:

$$221 \text{ lbf/ft}^3 / 244.8 \text{ lbf/ft}^3 \times 100$$

$$= 90.3\%$$

The answer is (C) 90.3%.

Solution to Question #271:

Refer to page 309 of the FE Handbook.

It doesn't actually give you the equation, but this is fair game.

Since it's already stockpiled, don't worry about the swell factor. You measure shrinkage in terms of the banked condition.

Volume compacted = (100% - 10%)/100% x Volume of bank soil

$Vc = .90 \times 175,000 \text{ yd}^3$

$= 157,500 \text{ yd}^3$

The answer is (B) 157,500 yd³.

Solution to Question # 272:

Refer to page 183/184 of the FE Handbook: Minor Losses in Pipe Fittings, Contractions, and Expansions:

The answer is (D) Found by using loss coefficients.

Solution to Question # 273:

Refer to page 268 of the FE Handbook. Structural Analysis.

The answer is **(C) Absolute maximum moment**

Solution to Question # 274:

This might sound very confusing, but it is very easy. We need to find the k value that makes this true.

Simply set up an equation: since y varies jointly with x and cube root of z:

y = k x (cube root of z)

12 = k (3) (cube root of 8)

k = 2

therefore:

70 = (2) x (cube root of 125)
x = 7
The answer is (B) 7.0

Solution to Question # 275:

Refer to page 109 of the FE Handbook: Laws of Friction.

Friction force is independent of contact area, so it does not matter the orientation of the box.

$F = u_k N$, therefore, only the weight of the box is what matters. Since this is a level surface, weight of the box is equal to the normal force.

The Answer is (A) 7 pounds.

Solution to Question # 276:

You should already know how to do limits at this point. When dealing with a limit, just try to plug and chug first to see if it will work. However, you should see right away that you can't divide by zero!

$$\lim_{x \to 0} (\sin(7x)/x)$$

Just take the derivative. So it becomes:

lim (d/dx (sin(7x)) / (d/dx (x))

lim (cos(7x) d/dx (7x)) / 1)

See page 48 (52 of 498). Table of common Derivatives.
#16. Down on the table says the derivative of sin = cos)

(note: d/d/x of sin 7x = cos (7x) times d/dx (7x), and the d/dx of x = 1) lim (7cos(7x)/1)   (so now you can plug in zero)   (7x became 7 and brought it to the front)

7cox(0) = 7

The answer is (B) 7

<u>Solution to Question # 277:</u>

Refer to page 293 in the FE Handbook: Sewage Flow Raito Curves.

Find 60 on the chart at the bottom, go up until you hit Curve B, then go to the left and hit 2.2.

Or use the Curve B equation on the right side:

= 14 / (4 +Square root P) + 1

= 14 / (4 + Sq rt 60) + 1

= 2.19

Now, find the peak flow:

60,000 x 120 gals = 7,200,000 gal/day

2.19 x 7.2 mgd = 15.8 MGD

The answer is (B) 16.

<u>Solution to Question # 278:</u>

Refer to page 126 of the FE Handbook: Impact Test:

The answer is (B) Ductile to brittle transition temperature.

<u>Solution to Question # 279:</u>

Refer to page 274 of the FE Handbook: Wind Loads:

$$q_z = 0.00256 \ K_z \ K_{zt} \ K_d \ V^2$$

K_z = .57   Use the table for a height of 13 ft shown in the problem. So it's the first row, choose Suburban area, .57

K_{zt} = 1 (flat ground)

$K_d = .85$ (most structures)

$q_z = 0.00256\,(.57)(1)(.85)(125)^2$

$= 19.38$

$= 19$

Solution to Question # 280:

Refer to page 52 of the FE Handbook: 2nd Order Differential Equations:

Don't freak out because it's a Differential Equations problem. It's actually pretty. This is a second order equation because it has the form: $y'' + ay' + by = 0$

Ok, how's our equation:

$y'' - 4y' + 4y = 0$

Let's determine a and b:
a = -4   (The number in front of the y')
$a^2 = 16$ (just square it.
b = 4   (the number in front of y)
4b = 16.   (4(4) = 16)

From the handbook, since $a^2 = b^2$, The solution is in this form:

$$y = (C_1 + C_2X)\,e^{r\,X}$$

So all we need to do is figure out what "r" is:

The equation is:

r = -a +/- square root of $(a^2 – 4b) / 2$ (plug in a and b)
r = - (-4) +/- square root of (16 –16) / 2
r = 4 +/- 0 / 2
r = 4 /2
r = 2

The answer is (C) $y = (C_1 + C_2X)\,e^{2x}$

Solution to Question # 281:

Refer to page 301 of the FE Handbook: Vertical Curve Table.

Sag Vertical Curve based headlight criteria:

L = A S² / 400 + 3.5S

A = absolute value of (g1 – g2) = (-3.8 – 2) = 5.8%

520 = 5.8 (S)² / 400 + 3.5S

(The actual exam might want you to solve this for S – which is a quadratic equation)

The answer is (C) 520 = 5.8 (S)² / 400 + 3.5S

Solution to question # 282:

Refer to page 181 of the FE Handbook: The Continuity Equation

Q = V • A

Given:

D = ½ inch, therefore, calculate the Area
A= π(D)²/4
A= π(.5)²/4
A = .196 in²
A = .196 in² • (1 ft²/ 12² in²)
A = .196 in² • (1 ft²/ 144 in²)
A = .00136 ft²

Mass flow rate = 20 lb/s

m = ρ • Q   (This formula is on the same page)

20 lb/s = (62.4 lb/ft³) • Q

Q = (20 lb/s) / (62.4 lb/ft³)

Q = .32 ft³/s

Therefore:

Q = V A

.32 ft³/s = V (.00136 ft²)

V = 235 ft/s

The answer is (A) 235 ft/s

Solution to Question # 283:

Refer to page 109 of the FE Handbook: Laws of Friction:

See 1st law of friction: The total friction force *F* that can be developed is independent of the magnitude of the area of contact.

The answer is (C) Frictional forces are dependent on contact area.

(Note: (C) is False. Frictional forces are dependent upon the normal force and nature of the surfaces.)

Solution to Question # 284:

Refer to page 278 of the Fe Handbook: Short Columns:Design Column Strength, Tied Columns.

$$\emptyset Pn = 0.80\emptyset[0.85 fc' \ (Ag - Ast) + Ast \ fy]$$

We need to find $Ag - Ast$.

$Ag = 18" \ x \ 18" = 324$ in^2

Ast = See page 277 for the ASTM for Reinform cent Bars.

There are (7) #8 bars, the area of one #8 bar = .79 in^2 (from the table)

7 x .79 in^2 = 5.53 in^2

$\emptyset Pn$ = .8 (.65)[.85(4.5ksi)(324 in^2 - 5.53 in^2) + 5.53 in^2(70 ksi)

= .52 [1218.15 + 387.1]

= 834.73

= 835 kips

The answer is (C) 835 kips.

Solution to Question # 285:

Refer to page 192 of the FE Handbook: Pump Power Equation:

Power = Qγh/n

Given:

Q = 1 m^3/min • (1 min/60 sec) = .0167 m^3/sec   (convert to m^3/sec for this equation :)

h = vertical rise + head losses (don't forget to add in the losses! If losses were not given, you would have to use equation on page 183 The Darcy-Weisbach equation)

h = (25 m – 5 m) + 2.5 m

h = (20 m) + 2.5 m

h = 22.5 m

n = 80% = .80

γ_{water} = 9,810 N/m³ (*Refer to page 177 of the FE Handbook*) Definitions:

Therefore:

Power = Qγh/n

Power = [(.0167 m³/sec) (9,810 N/m³)(22.5 m)] / .8

Power = [(3678.75 kg m²/ s³)] / .8

Power = 4,598 kg m²/ s³ (Note: 1 watt = 1 kg m²/ s³)

Power = 4,598 W

The answer is (A) 4,598 W.

Solution to Question # 286:

Refer to page 59 of the FE Handbook: Dot Product and Cross Product:

Very easy problem, although it's hard to understand the handbook on this one.

Here's the problem statement:

A ● (BxC)

A = 2i + 7j + 12k

B = i + 4j + 3k

C = 3i +4j + 5k

Ok, first you need to take the Cross Product of B x C and then the Dot Product of A and whatever you got for the first answer.   Very very simple, trust me.

To take the Cross Product of B and C:

Draw a table like this and plug in the values in front of the i's, j's, and k's for B and C: Don't ask why just do it. Just list the i,j,k and another i and j at the back. Yes, the first two numbers repeat.

BxC:	i	j	k	i	j
B	1	4	3	1	4
C	3	4	5	3	4

Now, draw 3 diagonal lines down to the right and then to the left, like this:

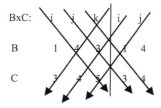

It will be something like this:

$(\quad)i + (\quad\quad)j + (\quad\quad)k$

$(4(5) - 3(4))i + (3(3) - 1(5))j + (1(4) - 4(3))k$

(for the i: multiply the two numbers down to the right and subtract the multiplication of the two numbers down to the left for i)

$(20 - 12)i + (9 - 5)j + (4 - 12)k$

$(8)i + (4)j + (-8)k$

Ok, so that is the Cross Product of BxC, now just substitute it into the A equation to find the Dot Product.

$= 2i + 7j + 12k$

$= 2(8) + 7(4) + 12(-8)$

$= 16 + 28 + -96$

$= -52$

The answer is (C) -52.

Refer to page 317 of the FE Handbook: Cyclone Collection Efficiency.

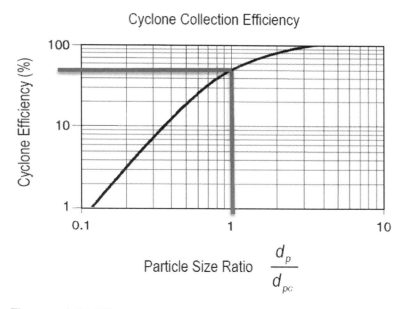

The answer is (A) 50%

Refer to page 287 of the FE Handbook: K-Factor Table:

Since the column is fixed at both ends, the K factor is .65. Choose the correct situation depending on what the problem says. A-F.

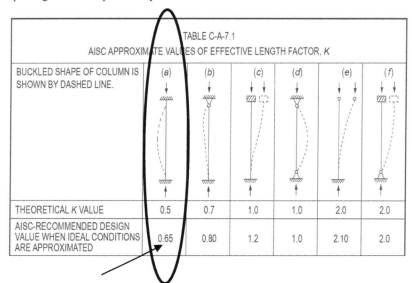

Now, calculate the value of KL: = .65 (40 ft) = 26 feet

Now use the table on page 289 to find the correct section:

		W14				W12					W10	
Shape wt/ft	74	68	61	53	48	58	53	50	45	40	60	54
0	980	899	805	702	635	787	701	657	590	526	794	712
6	922	844	757	633	573	722	659	595	534	475	750	672
7	901	826	740	610	552	707	644	574	516	458	734	658
8	878	804	721	585	529	689	628	551	495	439	717	643
9	853	781	700	557	504	670	610	526	472	419	698	625
10	826	755	677	526	477	649	590	499	448	397	677	607
11	797	728	652	497	449	627	569	471	422	375	655	586
12	766	700	626	465	420	603	547	443	396	351	631	565
13	734	670	599	433	391	578	525	413	370	328	606	543
14	701	639	572	401	361	553	501	384	343	304	581	520
15	667	608	543	369	332	527	477	354	317	280	555	496
16	632	576	515	338	304	500	452	326	291	257	528	472
17	598	544	486	308	276	473	427	297	265	234	501	448
18	563	512	457	278	250	446	402	270	241	212	474	423
19	528	480	428	250	224	420	378	244	217	191	447	399
20	494	448	400	226	202	393	353	220	196	172	420	375
22	428	387	345	186	167	342	306	182	162	142	367	327
24	365	329	293	157	140	293	261	153	136	120	317	282
26	311	281	250	133	120	249	222	130	116	102	270	241
28	268	242	215	115	103	215	192	112	99.8	88.0	233	208
30	234	211	187	100	89.9	187	167	97.7	87.0	76.6	203	181
32	205	185	165	88.1		165	147	82.9	76.4	67.3	179	159
34	182	164	146			146	130				158	141
36	162	146	130			130	116				141	126
38	146	131	117			117	104				127	113
40	131	119	105			105	93.9				114	102

Find 20 feet on the left side, go across to the right until you hit 130 kips. Go up and you hit 50. So the correct W12 section is 50.

= W12x50

The answer is (A) W12x50.

Solution to Question # 289:

Refer to page 107 of the FE Handbook: Potential Energy:

U = mgh

1750 J = (82 kg) • (9.81 m/s^2) • (x)

x = 2.2 m

The answer is (B) 2.2 m.

Solution to Question # 290:

Ethics

Answer is (A) Cannot reveal information without client's consent unless required by law to do so.

Solution to Question # 291:

Refer to page 49 of the FE Handbook: Integrals

Integrate first, $[3x^3/3 + 4x^2/2 + x] \Big|_1^5$

(Note: Remember to add one to exponent and divide by the same number) (Note: Also, any number becomes a variable i.e... the number 1 becomes an x of this example)

Integrate first, $[x^3 + 2x^2 + x] \Big|_1^5$

Now plug in the values,

$$= [(5)^3 + 2(5)^2 + 5] - [(1)^3 + 2(1)^2 + 1]$$

Simplify,

$$= 180 - 4$$

$$= 176$$

The correct answer is (D) 176.

Solution to Question # 292:

Refer to page 59 of the FE Handbook: Vectors

This is one of those things you just need to know. It's simple:

A = 5i + 8j + 9k

B = 12i -7j +6k

Find the Dot Product od A and B:

A . B = 5(12) + 8(-7) + 9(6)

(Just multiply the coefficients of the i's, j's, and k's together from A and B)

$$= \quad 60 - 56 + 54$$
$$= \quad 58$$

Now, square each i,j, and k and take the square root.

A = Square root of: $5^2 + 8^2 + 9^2$
A = Square root of: $25 + 64 + 81$
A = Square root of: 170
A = 13.04

B = Square root of: $12^2 + (-7)^2 + (6)^2$
B = Square root of: $144 + 49 + 36$
B = Square root of: 229
B = 15.1

Now take the $\cos^{-1}$ to find the angle:

$\cos \emptyset = A.B / A \, B$
$\cos \emptyset = 58 / 13.04(15.1)$
$\cos \emptyset = .294559$

$\emptyset = \cos^{-1}(.00149)$
(Make sure you are in degrees, and use the cos -1 function on your calculator)

$\emptyset = 72.9°$

The answer is (A) = 72.9°

Solution to Question # 293:

Refer to page 52 of the FE Handbook: Differential equations:

(Note: The term sin x makes it nonhomogeneous, if it were sin y it would be nonlinear. It has a variable coefficient, x^2. It is linear since the dependent variable y appears to the first power.)

The answer is (C) Linear, nonhomogeneous, variable coefficient.

Solution to Question # 294:

Refer to page 290 of the FE Handbook: Pan Evaporation. At the Bottom.

$$E_L = P_c E_P$$

The answer is (A) E_L/P_c

Solution to Question # 295:

Refer to page 126 of the FE Handbook: Concrete:

The answer is (B) W/C (Water to cement ratio)

Solution to Question # 296:

Refer to page 107 of the FE Handbook: Kinetics

W = Force • distance

Therefore, the work done by a force 150 N moving a body 50 m can be calculated as:

W = (150 N) (50 m)

W = 7500 N• m,

W = 7500 Joules

The correct answer is (A) 7500 Joules.

Solution to Question # 297:

Refer to page 285 of the FE Handbook: AISI Table 3-2.

(C) The lightest shape in its row.

Solution to Question # 298:

Page 289 of the FE Handbook: AISC Table Selected Ws:

But first, see page 272 for basic load combinations using LRFD:

= 1.2D + 1.6L

= 1.2(110 kips) + 2.6(125 kips)

= 132 kips + 325 kips

= 457 kips.

Then, use the table on page 289.

The effective length is (1)(18ft) = 18 ft. follow the chart to the right until you see a number close to 457 kips that you calculated for W14s shapes – that's the shape in the problem. 457 is an actual number, now go up to see the shape is 61.

Selected W14, W12, W10

Shape wt/ft	W14					
	74	68	61	53	48	58
0	980	899	806	702	636	767
6	922	844	757	633	573	722
7	901	826	740	610	552	707
8	878	804	721	585	529	689
9	853	781	700	557	504	670
10	826	755	677	528	477	649
11	797	728	652	497	449	627
12	766	700	626	465	420	603
13	734	670	599	433	391	578
14	701	639	572	401	361	553
15	667	608	543	369	332	527
16	632	576	515	338	304	500
17	598	544	486	308	276	473
18	563	512	457	278	250	446
19	528	480	428	250	224	420
20	494	448	400	226	202	393

KL (ft) with respect to least radius of gyration r_y

The answer is (C) W14x61

Solution to Question # 299:

Given:

Annuity (A) =$50,000 (each year)
i = 8%
n = 8 years.

The question is asking for the Present value (P)

Therefore, since we know that the annuity (A) is $50,000, we need to find the value of P given A. (P/A)

Refer to page 236 of the FE Handbook: 8% interest

n= 8 years, find the value of "P/A". Remember, we are trying to find the Present (P) value given the Annuity (A) of $50,000. So we say "P given A". (P/A)

The value from the chart for P/A is: 5.7466

Therefore:

P = A (P/A,i,n)

P = ($50,000)(P/A,8%,8 years)

P = ($50,000)(5.7466)

P = $287,300

The answer is (D) $287,300.

Solution to Question # 300:

Refer to page 107 of the FE Handbook:

This can be solved using an energy method. We can solve this by equating the potential energy of the bow to the kinetic energy of the arrow. The bow can be treated as a type of spring.

The potential energy of a spring is: $(1/2)kx^2$, where k is the stiffness and x is the amount the spring is stretched, or compressed.

Therefore, the potential energy *PE* of the bow is:

$$PE = (1/2)(200)(0.75)^2 = 56.25 \text{ J}$$

The kinetic energy of a particle is: $(1/2)mv^2$, where m is the mass and v is the velocity. The arrow can be treated as a particle since it is not rotating upon release.

Therefore, the kinetic energy *KE* of the arrow is:

$$KE = (1/2)(0.05)v^2 \quad \text{(convert 50 g to kg)}$$
$$KE = (.025)v^2$$

If we assume energy is conserved, then *PE* = *KE*

$$56.25 = (.025)v^2$$

$$v^2 = 2{,}250$$

$$v = 47.4 \text{ } m/s$$

The answer is (D) 47.4 m/s

Solution to Question # 301:

Refer to page 35 of the FE Handbook: Quadratic Equation

The equation can be rewritten as:

$$x^2 - 2x + 1 - 3 = 0$$

Therefore the equation is equivalent to:

$$(x-1)^2 - 3 = 0$$

Which is the same as:

$$(x-1)^2 = 3$$

Take the square root of each side to solve for x. Since 3 has two square-roots $(3)^{1/2}$, $-(3)^{1/2}$, we get

$$x-1 = (3)^{1/2}, \text{ or } x-1 = -(3)^{1/2}$$

Which give the solutions to the equation:

$$x = 1+(3)^{1/2}, \text{ or } x = 1-(3)^{1/2}$$

The correct answer is (C). $1+(3)^{1/2}$, $1-(3)^{1/2}$.

Solution to Question # 302:

Refer to page 180 of the FE Handbook:

This is a great problem. But very easy.

First, let's calculate the weight of the sphere:

Convert the diameter of the sphere from cm to m.

47 cm (m/100cm) = .47m

See page 40 (46 of 502) for the volume of a sphere:

$$V = \pi \, d^3/6$$

$$= \pi \, (.47m)^3/6$$

$$= .054m^3$$

The Weight of the sphere:

$$W = \Upsilon V \quad (\text{Remember } \Upsilon = pg)$$

$$W = (3700 \text{ kg/m}^3)(9.81 \text{ m/s}^2)(.054m^3) \quad (\text{The picture shows the density of the sphere})$$

$$W = 1960 \text{ N}$$

(Note: The units come out to kg m/s^2 which is a Newton)

Second step, find the buoyancy cause by the 2 fluids – they're raising the sphere up a little bit.

W_{fluid} = ½ Volume ($Y_{fluid\ 1}$) + ½ Volume ($Y_{fluid\ 2}$)

(realize it's ½ volume, because it's only ½ in each fluid!)

W_{fluid} = ½ Volume (pg $_{fluid\ 1}$) + ½ Volume (pg $_{fluid\ 2}$)

(Substitute density times gravity for gamma, Y = pg)

W_{fluid} = ½ (.054) (1350 (9.81) $_{fluid\ 1}$) + ½(.054) (1600(9.81) $_{fluid\ 2}$)

W_{fluid} = 358 N $_{fluid\ 1}$ + 424 N $_{fluid\ 2}$

= 781N. (that's pushing up)

Therefore, the tension in the cable is the Weight of the sphere minus the buoyancy force.

Tension = W $_{sphere}$ – W $_{fluid}$

Tension = $_{1960\ N\ –\ 781N}$

= 1179 N

The correct answer is (C) 1179N

Solution to Question # 303:

Don't need the Handbook. A zero-force member is whenever a member goes into 2 collinear members.

The answer is (D) BF, JG, DH, EK.

Solution to Question # 304:

Refer to page 181 of the FE Handbook: The Continuity Equation:

This is a basic fluids problem we all did in college.

Q never changes.. What goes in must come out.   (The density of the water doesn't matter! it was a trick)

Therefore:

Q in = Q out   (note: Q – AV)

AV in = AV out

π d^2/ 4 (7 m/s) = π d^2/ 4 (V out)   (Note: the area od a pipe = π d^2/ 4)

π (3 cm)^2/ 4 (7 m/s) = π (12cm)^2/ 4 (V out)

$\pi \, (9 \text{ cm}^2) / \, 4 \, (7 \text{ m/s}) = \pi \, (144 \text{cm}^2) / \, 4 \, (V \text{ out})$ (just solve the equation)

V out = .43 m/s   (notice that π, 4, and cm^2 cancel out from both sides)

So, you can rewrite the equation:

V out = (Diameter Pipe1)^2 / (Diameter Pipe1)^2 (V1)

= 9/144 (7)

= .43 m/s

Answer is (C) .43 m/s

Solution to Question # 305:

Refer to page 277 of the FE Handbook: ASTM Standard Re Bars

Find total weight of each bar:

3:   W = (16) .376 lb/ft (12ft) = 72.192 lb

#7:   W = (5) 2.044 lb/ft (6ft) = 61.32lb

#14: W = (2) 7.650 lb/ft (9fT) = 137.7 lb

#18: W = (11) 13.60 lb/ft (2ft) = 299.2 lb

Total W = 570 lb

The answer is (A) 570.

Solution to Question # 306:

Right away you should realize that *answer (C) .5 m/s* can be eliminated because the velocity coming out the nozzle will be greater than 1.0 m/s. If the pressure at the nozzle decreases, then the velocity will have to increase in order to balance the equation. Also, a nozzle decreases the cross-sectional area and therefore increase velocity (Q = V•A)

Refer to page 181 of the FE Handbook: Bernoulli Equation

$P_1 / \gamma + z_1 + (v_1^2 / 2g) = P_2 / \gamma + z_2 + (v_2^2 / 2g)$

Since the problem says that there is no change in height, $z_1 = z_2$, so both terms cancel out.

$P_1 / \gamma + (v_1^2 / 2g) = P_2 / \gamma + (v_2^2 / 2g)$

To find the value of γ:

Page 200 Properties of Water:

At 5 ℃ (given in the problem), specific gravity ($ɣ = 9.807 \text{ kN/m}^3 = 9807 \text{ N/m}^3$)

Now substitute values into the equation and solve for v_2:

$(200,000 \text{ Pa} / 9807 \text{ N/m}^3) + (1 \text{ m/s}^2 / 2(9.81 \text{ m/s}^2) = (101,300 \text{ Pa} / 9807 \text{ N/m}^3) + (v_2^2 / 2(9.81 \text{ m/s}^2))$

$20.3 + .051 = 10.3 + (v_2^2 / 19.62)$

$10.05 = (v_2^2 / 19.62)$

$197.20 = v_2^2$

$v_2 = 14.04 \text{ m/s}$

The answer is (B) 14.04 m/s.

Solution to Question # 307:

Refer to page 285 of the FE handbook: W Shapes Table.

Cb = 1

Lb = 15ft

W21x57

The equation we need is on page 281:

$$M_n = C_b \left[M_p - \left(M_p - 0.7\, F_y S_x \right) \left(\frac{L_b - L_p}{L_r - L_p} \right) \right] \leq$$

You can rewrite this equation as:

= Cb [ØMp – (ØMp – Ø(.7 Fy Sx) / Lr – Lp   x (Lb – Lp)]

= Cb [ØMp – ØBF (Lb – Lp)]

= (1) [484 – 20.1 (15-4.77)

= 278.377 ft kip

The answer is (B) 278 ft kip.

Solution to Question # 308:

Don't need the FE Handbook: Think like a Civil Engineer.

Find the total man-hours:

31-ton x 5 hours/ton – 155 man-hours.

Convert to crew hours:

155 man-hour x 1 crew hour / 5man hour = 31 crew hours

Now find the Crew rate:

Super $43/hr = $43

Laborer: $27/hr x (4) = $108

Total = $151/hr

Labor burden: wage x labor burden.

$151 x 1.55 = $234.05/hr. Therefore: 31 hrs x $234.05/hr = $7,256

The answer is (A) $7,256.

Solution to Question # 309:

Refer to page 450 of the FE Handbook: Endurance Test:

The answer is (D) Endurance stress.

Solution to Question # 310:

Refer to page 124 of the FE Handbook: Hardenability of Steels:

The answer is (C) Hardness.

Solution to Question # 311:

Refer to page 271 of the FE Handbook: Plane Truss.

Statics Analysis:

3m + r   3j + c

3(9) + 3   3(7) + 10
27 + 3   21 + 10

30   <   31

Therefore, it's Unstable.

The answer is (B) Unstable.

Solution to Question # 312:

Refer to page 307 of the FE Handbook: Crash Reduction.

Crashes prevented = N x CR (ADT after improvements) / ADT before

N has to be in per year.

So, 4+9 crashes / 2 year period = 6.5 crashes per year.

= 6.5 x .25 (18,500 / 13,000)

= 2.3125

The answer is (B) 2.3

Solution to Question # 313:

Just read the chart. Sometimes it's not that complicated.

The answer is (D) 96.8

Solution to Question # 314:

Refer to page 309 of the FE Handbook: Latitudes and Departures.

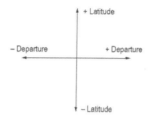

The answer is (D).

Solution to Question # 315:

Refer to page 285 of the FE Handbook: AICI Table 3-2. W Shapes:

You can either find all of the values in the table to find the BF, or you can use the equation for BF at the bottom of the table:

BF = Mpx – Mrx / Lr – Lp

= 405 – 256 / 37.4 – 10.7

= 149 / 26.7

= 5.58 (which matches the BF factor in the table. The beam is a W12x72.

The answer is (C) 5.59, W12x72

Solution to Question # 316:

Refer to page 117 of the FE Handbook: Thermal and Mechanical Processes:

The answer is (D) Cold Working.

Solution to Question # 317:

Refer to page 126 of the FE Handbook: Concrete: Bottom left of page.

The answer is (A).

Solution to Question # 318:

Refer to page 112 of the FE Handbook: Free Vibration:

$2\pi / \sqrt{k/m}$

Given:

m = 5 kg

k = 10 kN/m = 10,000 N/m

Therefore:

$2\pi / \sqrt{k/m}$

$2\pi / \sqrt{(10,000\ N/m) / 5\ kg}$

$2\pi / \sqrt{(2000)}$

$2\pi / (44.72)$

= .14 seconds

The answer is (C) .14 seconds.

Solution to Question # 319:

Engineer it.

The reaction on the left side must point upwards. Eliminates (C). Then a distributed load has a triangular shear diagram coming down. The middle point load makes it go down. Eliminates (A). (C) shows a distributed load that doesn't exist. The circle reaction will point up. And then come back at the right most point load.

The answer is (D).

Solution to Question # 320:

Refer to page 45 of the FE Handbook: Conic Section Equation:

The answer is (D) Hyperbola.

Solution to Question # 321:

Refer to page 97 of the FE Handbook: Friction:

The answer is (B) Limiting friction.

Solution to Question # 322:

Refer to page 127 of the FE Handbook: Amorphous Materials:

The answer is (D) Glass.

Solution to Question # 323:

Refer to page 264 of the FE Handbook: Vertical Stress Profiles with Surcharge.

Since no ground water is present, just use:

$$Stress = S + (\gamma_1 \times H)$$

Stress = 120 lb/ft² + (118 lb/ft³ x 23 ft)

Stress = 2,834 lb/ft²

The answer is (A) 2,834 lb/ft²

Solution to Question # 324:

Don't need the FE Handbook. This would be in the 3rd quadrant.

    235° 28' 53''
   -180° 00' 00''
S 55° 28' 53''

The answer is (D) S 55° 28' 53''

Solution to Question # 325:

Refer to page 179 of the FE Handbook: Manometer:

$P_{water} + (\gamma \cdot H) = P_{oil} + .8\gamma \cdot (2H) + 13.6 (\gamma \cdot H)$

Now, solve for the pressure difference:

$P_{water} - P_{oil} = .8\gamma \cdot (2H) + 13.6 (\gamma \cdot H) - (\gamma \cdot H)$

$P_{water} - P_{oil} = 1.6(\gamma \cdot H) + 13.6 (\gamma \cdot H) - (\gamma \cdot H)$ (combine like terms)

$P_{water} - P_{oil} = 14.2(\gamma \cdot H)$

(H = 15 meters in the problem, γ = 9800 N/m³ -see the table on *page 199* Properties of Water)

$P_{water} - P_{oil} = 14.2(9800$ N/m³$\cdot (15m))$

$P_{water} - P_{oil} = 2,087,400$ N/m²

$P_{water} - P_{oil} = 2,087,400$ Pa   (Remember the unit conversion: 1 Pa = 1 N / m²)

The answer is (A) 2,087,400 Pa.

Solution to Question # 326:

Refer to page 231 of the FE Handbook: Rate-of-Return

The answer is (D) Benefits and costs equal.

Solution to Question # 327:

Refer to page 63 of the FE Handbook: Probability:

Each of the 10 dice could produce 6 different numbers, so there are
6^{10} different arrangements.The probability that a player will get the same numbers in the same
order is:

For the first dice, there is a 1/6 chance of matching. The same is true for each of the following dice rolls.

Therefore:

P = 1/6 x 1/6 x 1/6 x 1/6 x 1/6 x 1/6 x 1/6 x 1/6 x 1/6 x 1/6   (Note: notice how the probabilities are multiplied)

$P = 1/6^{10}$

The answer is (B) $1/6^{10}$

Solution to Question # 328:

You do not need the handbook to solve this type of problem. This is a basic concept in engineering and is very easy to solve using a free body diagram:

Draw a Free Body Diagram.

Since 25 lb acts downward on one side of the pulley, 25 lbs also has to act down on the other side – it's not moving.. right.

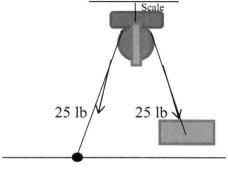

(fixed to the ground)

Since (2) 25 lb forces up downwards, a 50 lb force has to act upwards to balance it out.

F = 25 lb + 25 lb

F = 50 lb

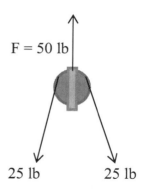

The answer is (A) 50 lb.

(Basically, the weight is doubled as seen by the scale. This old trick was used by fisherman who were paid by the pound for their catch! Pretty slick, right?)

Solution to Question # 329:

Refer to page 183 of the FE Handbook: Head loss due to flow:

The answer is (D) Darcy-Weisbach.

Solution to Question # 330:

Refer to page 290 of the FE Handbook: Surface Water System Hydraulic Budget

A = watershed area (acres) is not part of this equation.

The answer is (D). ΔS_s, A, T_s, Q_{in}

Solution to Question # 331:

Refer to page 285 of the FE handbook: AISC Table 3-2. W Shapes. Just find the W18x40 beam and read the table for the correct value. Next page.

Shape	Z_x in.^{3}	$\phi_b M_{px}$ kip-ft	$\phi_b M_{rx}$ kip-ft
W24 x 55	**134**	**503**	**299**
W18 x 65	133	499	307
W12 x 87	132	495	310
W16 x 67	130	488	307
W10 x 100	130	488	294
W21 x 57	129	484	291
W21 x 55	**126**	**473**	**289**
W14 x 74	126	473	294
W18 x 60	123	461	284
W12 x 79	119	446	281
W14 x 68	115	431	270
W10 x 88	113	424	259
W18 x 55	**112**	**420**	**258**
W21 x 50	**110**	**413**	**248**
W12 x 72	108	405	256
W21 x 48	**107**	**398**	**244**
W16 x 57	105	394	242
W14 x 61	102	383	242
W18 x 50	101	379	233
W10 x 77	97.6	366	225
W12 x 65	96.8	356	231
W21 x 44	**95.4**	**358**	**214**
W16 x 50	92.0	345	213
W18 x 46	90.7	340	207
W14 x 53	87.1	327	204
W12 x 58	86.4	324	205
W10 x 68	85.3	320	199
W16 x 45	82.3	309	191
W18 x 40	78.4	294	**180**

The answer is (A) 180.

Solution to Question # 332:

Refer to page 282 of the FE Handbook: Values of Cb for Simply Supports Beams Table:

Just find the diagram that matches.

The answer is (D) 1.14.

Solution to Question # 333:

Determine the volume of water to be added to the soil from the borrow pit. You should solve this problem based on dry, not moist, unit weights.

First, figure out the weight of the water to be added:

$W_w = (1,500,000 \text{ yd}^3) (27 \text{ ft}^3/ \text{yd}^3)(.9)(127 \text{ pcf})(17\% - 11\%) =$

$W_w = (1,500,000 \text{ yd}^3) (27 \text{ ft}^3/ \text{yd}^3)(.9)(127 \text{ pcf})(6\%) =$

$W_w = (1,500,000 \text{ yd}^3) (27 \text{ ft}^3/ \text{yd}^3)(.9)(127 \text{ pcf})(.06) =$

$= 277,749,000 \text{ lb}$

Now, just solve for the volume of water added:

$V_w = 277,749,000 \text{ lb} / (8.33 \text{ lb/gal})$

$= 33,343, 218 \text{ gal}$

$= 34 \times 10^6 \text{ gal}$

The answer is (A) 34 x 10^6 gal

Solution to Question # 334:

Refer to page 107 of the FE Handbook: Potential Energy: Elastic Potential Energy:

Middle of Page – Spring Constant. $F = k (s)$

The springs are identical, so each has the same stiffness of $k = 5$ lb/in

Let's find the spring equivalent: K total = K1 + k2

K total = 5 + 5 = 10 lb/in   Therefore:

100 lb = 10 lb/in (S)

S = 100 lb/ (10lb/in)

S= 10 in

The answer is (B) 10 in

Solution to Question # 335:

Refer to page 94 of the FE Handbook: Statics

Just sum the moments about the fulcrum of the beam. We will choose clockwise direction to be positive.

$+\curvearrowright \sum M_{\text{fulcrum}} = 0:$ -90 lbs (x feet) + 30 lbs (4 feet) = 0
(now we have one equation, solve for x)

$+\circlearrowleft \sum M_{fulcrum} = 0$: -90 lbs (x feet) + 120 feet (lbs) = 0

$+\circlearrowleft \sum M_{fulcrum} = 0$: 120 feet (lbs) = 90 lbs (x feet)

$+\circlearrowleft \sum M_{fulcrum} = 0$: $\dfrac{120 \text{ feet (lbs)}}{90 \text{ lbs}} = x$

Therefore, x = 1.33 feet

The answer is (A) 1.33 ft.

If you made it this far… that is the Razor's Edge! 97% of the people who purchase this book do not make it to the very end. The road to excellence is lonely. Welcome to the 3%.

If you hung up that blank certificate frame, you will pass.

The inner game is what separates winners from losers.

Please email us at EITFastTrack@gmail.com to tell us when you pass the FE Exam!

We love hearing from all of you each day!

Best of Luck!

"Everything starts with the basic fundamentals and the willingness to work hard and practice good habits".

- Cal Ripken Sr.